I0045199

"*I found the book very interesting and very well thought out. The explanations were very well explained.*"

-Alvin, Business Owner

"*Mr Boucher's book provided me with an opportunity to learn about and put into practice some easy financial investment ideas. Informative and engaging book.*"

-Aileen, 2nd Grade Teacher

"*Corey's book was educational, inspirational and motivated me to want to take a more active role in controlling my plans for my retirement. I could definitely relate to some of the characters and after reading the book reflected on how I could change my spending habits. I for one want to have a long, enjoyable and carefree retirement.*"

-Marian, Licensed Clinical Social Worker

"*A quick yet informative read for both the everyday investor and someone looking to start a portfolio*"

-Dustin, Entrepreneur

EARN MORE

SAVE MORE

INVEST MORE

Corey Boucher

Earn More. Save More. Invest More.
Copyright 2019 by

Printed in the United States
by Piscataqua Press
32 Daniel Street
Portsmouth, NH 03801

ISBN: 978-1-950381-22-7

Table of Contents

For my parents, who made countless sacrifices for my benefit

DISCLAIMER

This book contains statements and statistics that have been obtained from sources believed to be reliable but are not guaranteed as to accuracy or completeness. Neither the author, publisher, or the information providers can guarantee the accuracy, completeness, or timeliness of any of the information in the book. Neither the publisher, author, or information providers shall have any liability, contingent or otherwise, for the accuracy, completeness, or timeliness of the information or for any decision made or action taken by you in reliance upon the information in this book. The information contained in the book and all such information is provided "as is" without warranty of any kind.

Acknowledgements

I rarely paid attention to the "acknowledgements" section of the books I've read. Only now that I've gone through the book writing process myself, do I fully appreciate the collective efforts and support that turn the idea for a book into a finished product. In my case, I'm not a professional writer, so I REALLY needed a lot of assistance. There are a great many people who contributed to the completion of this book and the list of people I now owe favors to is very, very long.

My brother, Joshua, for the initial conversations and feedback on the earliest drafts to really get the ball rolling. Jeff Deck, who also provided some valuable structural feedback on the early drafts. Kate Johnston deserves a ton of credit. Her editing, coaching, and overall guidance through multiple drafts....I cannot say thanks enough. This book would not exist without Kate's help. E.M. Levy, who helped with a copyedit and some final touches that helped to polish what I have.

Tom and Kellsey over at Piscataqua Press, your patience and help with the final editing and formatting are very much appreciated. I freely admit that I am very particular and pestered you non-stop. Tom, your work on the overall project and marketing preparation were crucial.

Tim Landry and Mike Conley, oracles of business wisdom.

My beta readers. Wow. When I gave a rough draft to 15 or so of my friends and family, I was blown away and humbled. Nearly everyone eagerly read the book and provided thoughtful and valuable feedback. Yes, I know how lucky I am.

My parents, family, and friends who supported me all the way through the process. Thank you for the positive energy. For those who were only feigning interest, well, you did a good enough to fool me so you still get credit.

I need to thank the people who helped form the basis of the three "teacher" characters in the book. I need to also thank my mentors over the years within the finance and investment management industry.

PREFACE

"You aren't learning anything when you are talking."

— *Lyndon B. Johnson, former U.S. President*

Because I have been actively involved in finances for a long time, I have often been the target for friends and family seeking information on business, investing, and economics. I've learned a lot just from the questions I've been asked, and from listening to people share their stories: "What should I do with this extra three hundred dollars?" "Got any good stock picks for me?" "Did you hear about [insert random company]'s stock price?" "Can you help me with my 401k?" "How's the stock market doing?" "Is [insert event or election result] going to be good for the economy?" "How do I invest money; how do I even get started?" And then there would always be some wild card financial system conspiracy theory type question like "Do we still need a Federal Reserve?"

Some of these questions were just meant to spark up a conversation, but others were serious and not easy to answer in a few sentences. When I'm at a family barbecue, it's hard to explain what someone should do with their life savings in between Frisbee tosses. But these questions and conversations began to paint a picture for me of the areas in which people needed guidance. They had never been taught and had never found a trusted resource. For them, the prospect of investing in the market was scary and risky.

Even though there is plenty of financial information out there, most of it is overwhelming or difficult to understand. The Internet is crowded with financial gurus writing for various publications or blogs. Banks have their own representatives. There are investment and financial planning offices in just about every town—either from a small local business or a mega-firm with five thousand branches. We all probably know an opinionated loudmouth or two in our personal lives more than willing to give "advice" for free in person. Nowadays you can even get financial advice from robots. I'm not joking, you really can.

I have read many articles and books from great economists or experts in financial planning, but most are about situational events and not the right fit for the types of questions and discussions I have encountered. I have never found any that try to help readers improve their personal financial habits while also explaining in specific terms what they should do with their money once they begin saving it. Being told "invest in the stock market" is meaningless without also being told how.

The idea began to form for putting together a book that would fill this need, one that would focus on the two main aspects of successful investing: 1) making the right lifestyle changes to divert more money to invest, and 2) the actual practice of investing, including the implementation steps and selection of investments.

The following pages are intended to show you how to manage money on your own so that, rather than needing investment advisors, you can flip them off when you see them. Just kidding, that's not very nice. You won't need them. That's the point. And you'll end up saving money on the fees they'd charge you. It's also the best way to make sure your money is managed by someone you trust. You trust yourself, right? Well, at least if you don't, you'll be ripping off yourself.

The purpose of *Earn More. Save More. Invest More.* is to give you the guidance and tools to invest independently. Once you're feeling comfortable and knowledgeable about money management, you may choose to consult an investment advisor. The bonus here is that you'll have learned quite a bit about personal finance, therefore, a conversation won't go over your head. As Uncle Vinny said, "Nobody pulls the wool over the eyes of a Gambino." In other words, you won't be easily swindled.

As you prepare for your own retirement or financial future, you need to be a driver instead of a passenger. You need to invest for yourself if you want to live and retire comfortably.

Take a moment and think about your purpose for reading this book. Are you able to define it? Here are some common purposes this book could fit:

Get a better handle on your personal finances.

Start an Individual Retirement Account (IRA) and start building a retirement.

Start an investment account and grow your assets for whatever purchases you want.

Rearrange your existing retirement account (401k or IRA) or your existing investment accounts into assets that will offer a better return than before.

Become more informed about the economy and investing to better monitor your asset manager or financial advisor.

Assess your purpose for reading this book, whatever it may be, as you continue reading. Get into the frame of mind that you will take actionable steps to improve your financial goals. Make sure you get the most out of the time you spend reading this book and learning how to Earn More, Save More, and Invest More.

INTRODUCTION

"A goal without a plan is just a wish."

— Antoine de Saint-Exupéry, French writer

Three people taught me the most important lessons about money. They were not colleagues in the investment industry, they were not economists or famous investment experts or university professors, and they were not mentors or bosses or supervisors of mine. They were three fairly regular people who were able to show me more than textbooks and expensive educations and work trainings ever could. Their occupations were computer engineer, nursing assistant, and mechanical engineer. None had a background in financial services. They were three people whose paths crossed with mine, and, by observing them, I learned the most useful and practical lessons about money.

My own education and career were spent learning about finance and investing. I attended college, worked on additional certifications within the financial services industry, and spent years in the workforce learning by doing. Yet these three individuals have still had the biggest impact on my personal finances. I intend to share in a simple, straightforward way both the lessons they gave me and my own recommendations about how to invest. You will learn how easy it can be to invest completely on your own, without wasting money on advisors or money managers and without taking much time from your busy life.

Over the last several years, there have been more high schools trying to correct this education oversight by adding personal finance courses to their curriculums. Yours truly has been asked to speak at some of these high schools. That piece of information isn't particularly relevant. I just wanted to brag.

The number of adults in the U.S. who are living paycheck to paycheck is very high. Various surveys and studies usually peg the number in the neighborhood of fifty percent. Having no emergency funds or wiggle room is a stressful way to live. The inability to save up a cushion of money probably also means an inability to invest. People who struggle with saving feel like they are stuck in quicksand—never making any progress.

There were times when it felt like that for me. I'm going to talk about myself for a little bit here. (Don't be so surprised, I'm obviously self-centered—to think I can contribute to society by writing a book, I must be.)

Even though I never took a high school personal finance class, I had enough interest in the topic to pursue an education and then a career in asset management.

I worked various odd jobs all the way up through college and was able to save a little here and there, but never very much. I figured making money and then investing it to make more money would be easy once I learned how in college. That's where I would learn all the answers.

I soon had my college degree (in finance), an overabundance of confidence, and a pretty good work ethic. Around the time of my college graduation, I conservatively estimated I could be a millionaire by age thirty. I really didn't know how or have a plan. College hadn't given me the secret formulas I thought it would, but I was sure all the experts working in the industry would be able to provide them.

My thoughts unrealistically ran something like this: If I saved a thousand dollars, I could make it go up thirty percent in a year, right? Stuff like that has happened before. Maybe even fifty percent in a year. Actually, I could probably just double it. Somehow. After doing that over and over while adding more money—bingo! I'm a millionaire. Pfft, no problem. I had a pretty vivid imagination back then.

Thankfully, I never told anyone my "millionaire by thirty" goal out loud. Had I told my father, for instance, he would have paused briefly before responding, "You watch a lot of TV, huh?" followed by a chuckle and a head shake.

Once I had a steady job and was making an income, I turned my focus to investing money. I had a bank account and transferred some money I had set aside into an investment brokerage account. Some of the more popular companies to do this with are Vanguard, Fidelity Investments, E*Trade, TD Ameritrade, and Charles Schwab.

I chose Fidelity Investments. A brokerage account is like a bank account. You put money into it, but instead of it sitting around and collecting interest, you use the money to buy or sell stocks, bonds, and mutual funds. Brokerage accounts are free to open and maintain. Buying or selling investments is also free in most cases.

In my new brokerage account, I tried many different investment strategies. I bought "hot stocks" that everyone was talking about. Things didn't go quite as well as I hoped, and I soon gave up. There had to be something better.

Researching companies in depth, poring over company financials for hours, and buying the ones I thought were bargains didn't work as well as I had hoped, either. It didn't take long before I gave up again.

I attempted day trading—buying a stock and selling it that same day or the next day if it went up just a little bit, then moving on to another stock. This method didn't work so great for me, either. Next.

Buying stocks that the "experts" said to buy was another letdown. I tried other strategies as well. Nothing was giving me those one hundred percent returns I wanted.

My conclusions:

1. Return expectations need to be realistic. There are no "get rich quick" strategies that magically work.

2. Patience is needed; making money takes time.

3. Like any tool, a brokerage account works only as effectively as the person using it.

By far the most important thing I learned as I got a taste of different investment strategies—and a big premise for this book—is that the old adage is true:

"It takes money to make money."

Sure, it sounds like common sense. It's also a critically important foundational concept for investing. Embracing this realization will shape your expectations and provide a better grasp of what it takes to be a more successful investor. Just keep reading.

Since the end of World War II up to the end of 2017, the U.S. stock market has returned 11.32 percent per year on average. This means it might go up twenty percent one year and down ten percent the next, but the average over time still comes out to 11.32 percent per year. The common way to measure the stock market's return is the Standard & Poor's 500 (S&P 500 for short). This is the representation of the U.S. stock market. It is made up of 500 of the biggest companies in the U.S. Amazon, Apple, Microsoft, Boeing, 3M, and Johnson & Johnson are all in there. The stock prices from these 500 big companies tells us how the U.S. stock market is doing as a whole. A rate of growth of 11.32 percent is pretty good, if you ask me, but having to wait year after year can be painful.

Even at double digit growth rates, investments still need to compound year over year to really get going. It's sort of like building a snowman. You begin with a tiny snowball and it grows as you roll it. As the snowball gets bigger, it grows faster because it can pull more snow than when it was a tiny snowball. (I live in New England. My mind naturally goes to winter comparisons.)

When I was starting out with my own brokerage account in my early twenties, I was able to save up only enough money to put a few hundred dollars into the account. Even that was a challenge. If the stock market went up ten percent, and the stock I had purchased did the same, well, my 300 dollars just increased to 330 dollars.

An entire year might go by and I had thirty dollars to show for it? What could I buy with thirty bucks? Go to lunch two or three times? With such a small return on the money, it's pretty easy to see why people might get frustrated. With so little payoff, how long before you lose interest or give up? It's no wonder why many people have trouble getting into investing and sticking with it.

Now, what if I had more than a few hundred dollars to invest? What if, using the same example, instead of three hundred dollars, we had thirty thousand dollars? We'd end up making three thousand. People care about three thousand dollars; they don't care about thirty dollars. Making three thousand for one year of investing is motivating! It's enough to pay for a home project or get your car fixed. Or make a down payment on a new car. Or pay for all the winter holiday gifts for your undeserving friends and ungrateful kids. Or a prop from the original Star Wars movie. In both scenarios, the investor did the same thing, the same amount of work, and waited the same amount of time. Yet one scenario yields greater results.

For some of us, saving up thirty thousand dollars seems unachievable. It might as well be thirty billion. After seeing my stock strategies go up twenty-five dollars here, down fifteen dollars there, investing soon felt pointless. This is where our three heroes come in. The three people who helped me to revamp and rethink my personal financial situation.

First, Rob will show us the importance of maximizing

income and how we might be able to Earn More. Then, Nathalie's strategies will teach us how to control spending and how we might be able to Save More. And lastly, Mike's successful investing will help us understand that the more you earn and the more you save, the greater your ability to Invest More.

Let's also be clear that you still need the right investment strategy, and you still need to put your money in the right place to grow it effectively. That is something that will be covered in this book. Chances are you have heard of savings accounts and certificates of deposits (CDs). Both of these common savings tools are available at banks everywhere but have pretty much yielded jack squat since late 2008. Back in the 1980s, you could find them yielding 8 to 12 percent, but it's trended down since then and is likely to remain low over the next couple of decades.

We complained earlier about how making thirty dollars after investing three hundred isn't much. Now imagine if you only made thirty cents. Between 2010 and 2015, it was common for a savings account to yield a paltry .10 percent rate. Wow, if you play your cards right, maybe after a few years you could buy one item from a dollar store! Yes, it takes money to make money, but you can't draw water from a stone. Low rates of return make us feel justified to spend money instead of save it.

Part of the problem is many people do not know their options or how to take advantage of them. A scary statistic in a survey by the Federal Reserve, the government agency responsible for overseeing the nation's banking system, revealed that 16 million adults were "unbanked."[1] These people don't have a checking account, savings account, or any other type of bank account.

Opening a bank account is the first step toward smart personal finance, the most basic strategy I can think of (maybe other than learning how to count).

A bank account makes financial transactions easier and cheaper. Applying for a loan typically requires a bank account. Cashing a check is easier and cheaper for people who have a bank account than it is for those who don't. Paying bills through the mail (and having an electronic record) or storing money in a way that is protected from theft are both possible with a bank account. And most importantly, if you want to invest and grow money, it's much easier to move money if you have a bank account.

Another statistic, this time from the U.S. Government Accountability Office, revealed that nearly half of households with people fifty-five and older have no retirement savings.[2] None. Zilch. Think about that for a second . . . How is a fifty-five-year-old supposed to retire in ten years if they have nothing saved for retirement? They can't.

The Government Accountability Office works for the U.S. Congress and monitors how federal money is spent (they must be very busy). You want to be on the right side of their retirement statistics. Use the foundational concepts in this book to get your personal finances and investing in a position for success.

Earn more + Save more = Invest more.

That refrain will be repeated often.

Earn more. Save more. Invest more.

Part of this book is designed to make you think about your own life so that you can enact change and be more successful in your financial and investment endeavors. Throughout this book, I will ask you to reflect on certain things or complete little assignments here and there. Yes, little assignments. Yes, seriously. Don't roll your eyes. It won't be so bad.

The first one is nearly a freebie. Open a bank account. Either a savings or checking account. Chances are you already have one, but if you don't, try to do it this week. Preferably tomorrow. Walk into any bank and tell an employee you'd like to open an account. It's very easy and doesn't cost anything (you might need to keep a minimum account balance of twenty-five dollars). If you don't live near a physical bank, no problem. You can still open an account through online banks like Ally

Bank, EverBank, or Charles Schwab.

The later stages of this book will instruct you on specific investments you can make and why they should outperform the stock market over the next few decades. You may need a bank account as a way to transfer money to an investment account. Plus, bank employees are usually pretty nice. Maybe you'll make a new friend.

Every concept presented in this book will be easy to understand whether you've never had a bank account or you have a PhD in Economics. This book was not written to prove how smart the author is. The only way to make sure people of all ages and levels of financial background will benefit from this book was to avoid being overly technical and to present ideas that can be shared with anyone.

Writing a book isn't fun. It's a lot of work. It takes a long time. And it does not pay very much money unless you can put a name like "Stephen King" or "J. K. Rowling" on the cover. I checked. Supposedly there are laws that don't let me do that. Whatever. I decided to go through the painful process of writing a book anyway. There are many reasons why, but the main one is to offer help and guidance to people. In pursuit of such a noble cause, this book will contain a lot of charts (yay, less reading!), strange analogies, references, and whatever else I can think of to keep it interesting yet informative. Write a book about finance and investing that doesn't put people to sleep? Maybe. Is that even possible? Let's both hope so.

CHAPTER ONE
ROB THE ENGINEER

"Education is not the filling of a pail, but the lighting of a fire."

— William Butler Yeats, Nobel Prize winning poet

I met Rob in the early 2000s. We lived in the same college dorm. He was a confident, carefree guy who enjoyed the "extra-curricular" part of college. He made a ton of friends, joined a fraternity, and always seemed to be out having fun. I never saw him with an open book.

It seemed every time I was on my way to class, I'd see him on his way to the movies, the tennis courts, or cruising around somewhere with friends. He drove this yellow Subaru WRX that was hard to miss. In case you aren't an expert on cars, these are sporty all-wheel-drive sedans modeled after the type of cars used in rally races. They are fast and fun to drive, but new ones aren't cheap.

Rob was majoring in computer engineering. When I heard that, my first reaction was "Really? This guy is studying engineering?" He was charismatic and outgoing rather than studious. I would later realize he was also very smart and mathematically gifted. He had a knack for figuring things out.

His explanation for studying computer engineering was straightforward. He saw it as a clear path to prosperity. He had some no-nonsense talking points about why that was his college major and choice for a career. Computer engineers had high salaries at that time (and he could quote some of the stats and figures), and he believed computers and technology would hold a dominant role in society's future. He insisted that any other field of study would not earn as much. He said it was a "no brainer."

Rob was so confident that his future earnings would be high that he had no qualms about going into debt. He commonly put purchases on credit cards. He assumed when he was making all kinds of money, he would easily pay off his debt, no problem.

While other college students, like me, were eating ramen noodles and wearing clothes our grandmother got for us at garage sales (I'm exaggerating. I declined the clothes. Mostly. Okay, I did accept some old button-up shirts. Thank you, Mémère), Rob dismissed the notion of careful spending.

He would buy brand-name clothing and nice watches on his credit card, eat at restaurants often, all on credit. His plan was to pay for it later, whenever "later" might end up being. Rob was an only child and received a nice allowance from his parents, who acted as a safety net in case he ever needed a bailout. What appeared as reckless to me was normal behavior for Rob. His available line of credit on his credit cards mattered more than the money in his bank account when deciding if he could "afford" something or not.

If something wasn't the best quality or brand name, Rob didn't want it. I observed a pattern developing in Rob's behavior, thought processes, and actions. He was growing accustomed to having expensive material goods, and it was becoming part of his identity.

I picked up on the warning signs based on something an investment professor had once said during a lecture. This professor got paid on the side to counsel people about their personal finances. One of his clients was making over 120,000 dollars per year. This was back in the early 2000s, I might add. This individual had confided to my professor that he had recently been trying to cut back on expenses and simply been unable to do so, no matter how hard he tried. He concluded that he could not possibly live on less than 100,000 dollars per year.

As a broke college student with only a few hundred dollars to my name, this story bugged me. I was eating a lot of spaghetti and oatmeal while wearing soccer T-shirts from middle school that were two sizes too small for me. I was buying thirty-packs of Natural Ice beer for ten bucks. (I'd splurge on Miller High Life for special occasions.) I was drinking awful beer and eating Ramen noodles and this out-of-touch tool bag couldn't live on less than 100,000 dollars a year?

I remember this professor's story because of how stupid it sounded to me. As if a person needed so much money to survive. Yeah, right. How can they not change their lifestyle?

I began to think there might be some connections between Rob and Mr. 120k. Rob was accustomed to certain spending habits. Changing these habits can be difficult. Anyone who has ever gone from a flip phone to a smart phone will know what I'm talking about. After you've used a smart phone, try going back to a flip phone without data/Internet capability. It'll feel like cruel and unusual punishment.

Besides spending money he didn't have on material goods, Rob also had no trouble spending money he didn't have for his education. It's not breaking news that college is expensive and most people have to borrow money to pay for it. If you are someone who enjoys partying, college can be a fun place. If you are naturally smart and the "school" part is a piece of cake for you, it's even better. That is why Rob decided to embark on the "five-year plan" in college for what is typically a four-year program.

As a student from outside of the state, he was already paying the more expensive tuition rate, a good chunk higher than the "in-state" tuition rate locals paid. The school had a great computer engineering program and we've established Rob was more than willing to pay extra for quality.

To get a sense of cost difference between in-state and out-of-state tuition, the University of Massachusetts in-state rate total for fall 2017 was 27,669 dollars versus an out-of-state total of 45,735 dollars – a difference of nearly 20,000 dollars per year!

Even though some of the decisions Rob was making were more about the here and now, the career he was gearing up for proved to be a smart long-term decision. Now over ten years later, we know the growing role technology has in our lives.

CareerBuilder conducted a poll of nearly 2,400 hiring managers and HR professionals in early 2017, asking what were the most sought-after college majors.[3] The survey revealed that engineering, computer sciences, and communication technologies were among the most in demand. After reading these results, I became curious about whether college students were studying the types of trades employers wanted. The Institute of Education Sciences (IES), part of the U.S. Department of Education, publishes data showing the bachelor's degrees conferred to college seniors in each field of study. In May of 2016, they reported, almost two million degrees were conferred.[4]

As you might have guessed, the results didn't match up. Employers will see shortages of graduates in the fields they are seeking. Not enough students are following Rob's footsteps. I was able to graph the percentage of employers looking for a specific college major compared to the percentage of college seniors in that major (see figure 1 to the right).

As you can see, many of the majors in demand are the STEM (science, technology, engineering, math) oriented fields.

Rob the college student may have built some habits of reckless spending, but he was also brilliant. Rob the Engineer

Figure 1. Employees' preferred majors versus college seniors' actual majors

College Majors Employers Want

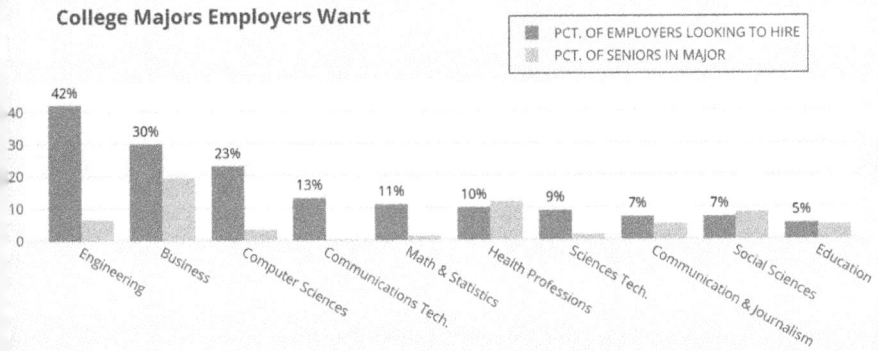

Legend: PCT. OF EMPLOYERS LOOKING TO HIRE / PCT. OF SENIORS IN MAJOR

Bars: Engineering 42%, Business 30%, Computer Sciences 23%, Communications Tech. 13%, Math & Statistics 11%, Health Professions 10%, Sciences Tech. 9%, Communication & Journalism 7%, Social Sciences 7%, Education 5%

turned out to be right about his career earnings power.

But Rob isn't representative of many people in that respect. What if you're not mathematically gifted and can't major in something like business or engineering? Are you stuck?

No. As you'll see in the next chapter, there are options that may surprise you.

CHAPTER TWO
IMPROVE YOUR SKILLS TO
EARN MORE

"Experience is a hard teacher because she gives
the test first, the lesson afterwards."

— *Vernon Law, former Pittsburgh Pirates pitcher*

The goal I want to underscore in this section is Earn More. Earning more will give you extra money that can be used for investing. This is the first major piece of the investing plan to Earn More. Save More. Invest More.

Whether you are fifteen and thinking about starting a career or fifty-five and looking to retool your career for one last push before retirement, you can develop skills needed to Earn More. We'll review some data and trends going on in America's job market that you can relate to your current job. (For the vast majority of people, day jobs are where we make the most coin.) It might help you think of ways to increase your future earnings.

All too often, the image of what it takes to Earn More is a college or advanced degree, but that's not always true. A college degree might have worked for Rob, but it's not the only option for a well-paying job. No employer will pay a lot of money for a job that anyone off the street can do. This means you need some level of skill or experience that matters to employers. However, the qualifications for skilled jobs come in many forms. Some require a four-year college degree or two-year associate degree – others, a six-month apprenticeship program, specific certification or license, or some other form of training or accreditation. But basically, improving your skills will earn you more money. These days, that means earning beyond a high-school diploma.

Plenty of opportunities exist to earn a higher income without spending the time and money on the ever-growing cost of college. The National Association of Manufacturers (NAM) has predicted that U.S. companies will be facing two million job vacancies in the manufacturing space by 2025 (typical pay today in that sector is 40 to 50k per year). The American Welding Society has said that 300,000 more welders and welding instructors will be needed by 2020[5] (average over 40,000 dollars per year salary).

One reason jobs like manufacturing and welding, traditionally known as "blue collar," will have so many openings is the large number of workers in those areas who will be retiring in coming years. Back in 2012, Emsi Analytics (part of CareerBuilder) reported that about 53 percent of all workers in the skilled trades were older than forty-five[6] (here is where the baby boomers are!). It's also true that very few people in the skilled trades are able to work beyond age sixty-five due to the physically demanding nature of the jobs. In many other areas, it's common to work past age sixty-five, because people enjoy their work and want or need to continue earning.

Let's look at some unemployment and wage data to learn more about the jobs market. The Bureau of Labor Statistics is a U.S. government organization that tracks unemployment rates. Whenever you hear people say something like "the unemployment rate is 5 percent," they are probably referring to a number released by the Bureau of Labor Statistics (BLS).

Figure 2 is a snapshot of data released by the BLS at the end of 2017 that relates a person's education level to ballpark weekly earnings.[7] Despite its being based on 2017 data, the relationships it shows between education, unemployment rate, and wages tend to be similar no matter what year the data is examined.

Figure 2. Unemployment and salary rates by educational level for 2017

Unemployment rates and earnings by educational attainment, 2017

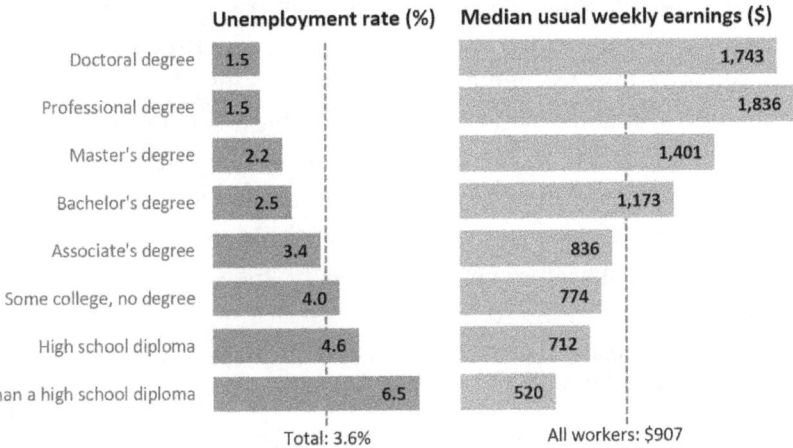

Education level	Unemployment rate (%)	Median usual weekly earnings ($)
Doctoral degree	1.5	1,743
Professional degree	1.5	1,836
Master's degree	2.2	1,401
Bachelor's degree	2.5	1,173
Associate's degree	3.4	836
Some college, no degree	4.0	774
High school diploma	4.6	712
Less than a high school diploma	6.5	520
	Total: 3.6%	All workers: $907

Note: Data are for persons age 25 and over. Earnings are for full-time wage and salary workers.
Source: U.S. Bureau of Labor Statistics, Current Population Survey.

The left side of the chart ties the unemployment rate to the level of education attained, and the right side shows an estimated weekly salary for each level of education. Overall, the chart might not come as a surprise to anyone, but some aspects of it are worth pointing out. Remember, the goal is to maximize the amount of money each of us can make. I'll say it over and over. Like a parrot. Like a parrot. Jobs are the starting point. This chart shows that having only a high-school diploma (or not finishing high school) will probably result in lower earnings.

That's because employers see you as not having unique skills.

The next tiers up on the chart are having some college or having an associate degree. An equivalent for those categories could be types of jobs requiring certifications, training programs, or some sort of further qualification beyond high school—for example, appliance repairmen, bus drivers, subway operators, installation technicians. The cost of technical certifications is much less than the price of a four-year college degree. Using the pay scale from the BLS chart, learning skills will result in better pay than being unskilled. Bigger paychecks mean you'll wake up and go to work with a bit more skip in your step, and more money to invest, which is our ultimate goal.

Your job is safer, as well, if it requires more skills and education. As the figure shows, among those with a bachelor's degree in 2017, the unemployment rate was just 2.5 percent. It was almost double that (4.6 percent) for high-school graduates and 6.5 percent for those without a high-school diploma. The case for higher skills is crystal clear: higher earnings and a better chance of having a job (lower unemployment). The chart probably corroborates what you already knew. We don't need Albert Einstein to weigh in.

The Bureau of Labor Statistics has another monthly data release that breaks down the current job market. It's called the Job Opening and Labor Turnover Survey (JOLTS). The JOLTS reports on the number of full- and part-time job openings in the U.S. economy and what fields they are in.

There were a *thunderous* 6.1 million job openings in the United States according to the July 2017 JOLTS report. Some 232,000 open jobs in construction and 625,000 in retail, for example. There were over a million openings in health care and social assistance. The economy was doing pretty nicely in 2017, so this information might not *shock* you.

The JOLTS survey has been around since 2000. Here is a chart from the BLS website that shows job openings from early 2000 to early 2019:

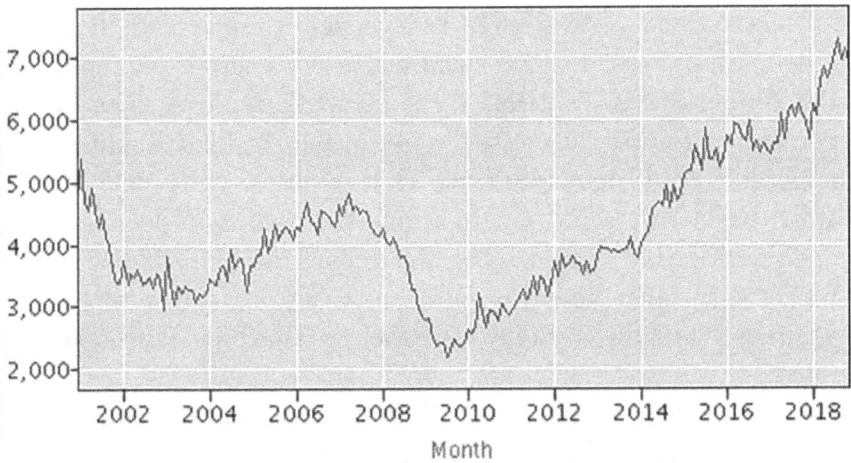

Figure 3. Job openings from early 2000 to 2019

It should hit you like a *bolt of lightning* (I can make electricity puns all day) that job openings correspond to how the U.S. economy is doing. The higher the line, the more job openings. After the tech bubble burst in the early 2000s, and the economy went into recession, job openings declined. After the Great Recession of 2008, there is another noticeable decline as the economy plummeted.

Back in 2010, there were about half as many job openings as there were in 2017. Information technology, finance and insurance, professional and business services, health care, and social assistance were all high-paying sectors of the economy that had hundreds of thousands of job openings even during the recession. Most of those jobs require skills or education that go beyond a high-school diploma.

The JOLTS data also dispels the myth that for the last decade there have "just been no jobs out there." The more accurate assessment would be "there were just no jobs for unskilled workers out there." Even in the depths of the Great Recession,

35

there were millions of job openings. But scan the report and you'll see there weren't many openings in areas where a high-school diploma was all you needed.

The National Federation of Independent Business (NFIB) is a network of over 325,000 small business owners throughout the United States. In early 2017, the NFIB reported that 45 percent of small businesses were unable to find qualified applicants to fill job openings.[8] That is nearly half! Half of small businesses could not find qualified applicants for their open positions. And remember, this report from January 2017 was shortly after the November 2016 presidential election, where jobs and the economy were the top issue on most voters' minds.

You might be wondering, "What does any of this have to do with investing? Job information? Unemployment numbers? Huh?" Your job is likely where you make most of your income. You need to make sure you are maximizing that income if you are going to have money to put toward investing. I have learned if you are not investing very much money, the payoff is so small it won't seem worth it. Finding ways to increase your income is crucial.

You could be thinking, "My job is fine. I don't need to change jobs." That's awesome. You can still connect some of the dots in this chapter. Skills translate into earnings. Try to think about ways you can improve your earnings within your existing career.

You might also be thinking, "I'm too old to change careers," or "Changing careers is too much work for me." Neither is true if you find the right opportunity. Let me use an example.

Bloomberg News published an article in March of 2017 about a program called KentuckianaWorks—a *free* program that offers education and training programs. At the time of the article, the program had trained almost a thousand individuals varying in ages from 18 to 60 years old to work for companies like Ford and Kellogg. The article specifically detailed how a fifty-nine-year-old who hadn't been in a classroom for decades took a five-week training program through Kentuckian Works and is now working on a manufacturing production line.[9]

If you want job security and a good paycheck, you need to push yourself. Increasing the main source of earnings is a core piece to successful investing and building wealth.

The Bureau of Labor statistics compiles a list of jobs and their average salaries. The list is long as all heck (1000+ jobs), so the full version is in Appendix A. Here is a chart of job categories and their 2016 median hourly wage from highest to lowest.

Figure 4. Job Categories and Median Hourly Wage from Highest to Lowest

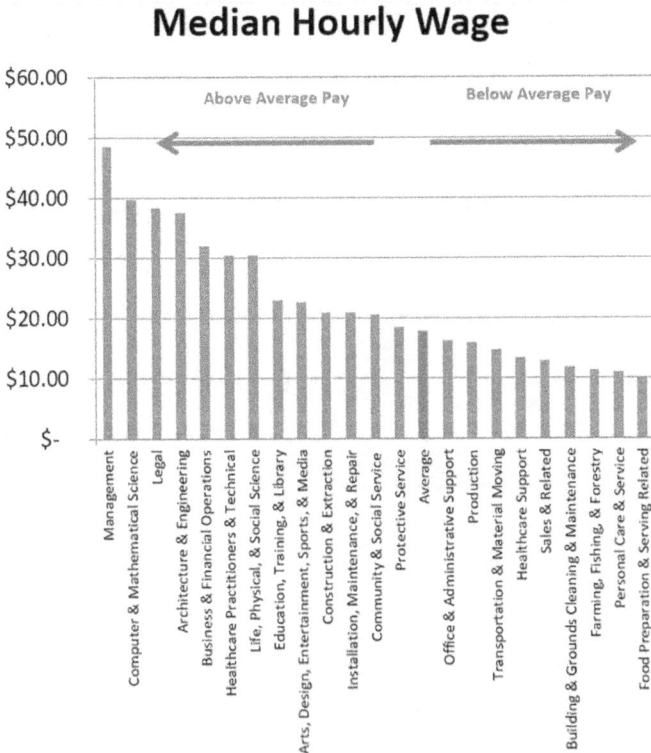

Median Hourly Wage

While we aren't all capable of becoming attorneys, many of the job shortages available on the JOLTS report are in above-average paying jobs. And, as I've mentioned, career change isn't the only path. Perhaps getting additional certifications within your field or taking safety courses would help. Take a course on Excel or finish your GED—do whatever it might be to make you more valuable or enable you to get a slightly better job or promotion.

The data in this section shows that Rob's confidence was warranted: Highly skilled jobs do in fact pay more. Highly skilled jobs also have lower rates of unemployment. This is especially true in technological jobs. It was true when Rob was in college and as the data showed us, it remains true today. He turned out to be right. Perhaps he wasn't such a blowhard after all. After his five-year college experiment, he got a high-paying job at a tech company. It seemed as though he was in the perfect position to start paying off his debt.

CHAPTER THREE
THE JOB MARKET OF THE FUTURE

"One finds limits by pushing them."

—Herbert Simon, American economist,
psychologist, and computer scientist

Rob envisioned future trends and took them into account for his job decisions. Since it worked for Rob, let's look at major themes in the economy and how they might affect future jobs.

Two of the big trends are globalization and technological advances. Global competition can mean a job loss risk for all workers but particularly for the unskilled. If you don't have a high-school diploma, what separates you from someone in India, China, or certain other Southeast Asian countries? They can do what you do. Will you do it for a dollar an hour as they will?

Is it possible for a robot to do what you do? Robots keep getting more sophisticated, well beyond electric toothbrushes. CBS aired a *60 Minutes* segment where a small robot on wheels in a barn went from stall to stall milking cows. Udderly stunning.

Yes, it is true that machines and robots are taking over a lot of jobs humans do. This transition will continue and probably intensify. Technological improvements keep increasing the capability of machines.

Existing industries will be disrupted. Humans require higher salaries, medical and retirement benefits, and someone to complain to, while machine costs are decreasing, and efficiency is improving. For comparison, think about how much the cost of TVs, music players, and personal computers has decreased and how much their capabilities have increased. Robotics is following the same trend, making it easier for employers to replace human workers. As I've been preaching, the skills you develop, and the career moves you make will determine your vulnerability for job disruption. That little robotic dog you saw on TV isn't so cute now, is it?

That was the bad news. There is good news, though . . . right? Well, I think so, yes. Japan is one of the most automated countries in the world, with many robots. Yet as of December 2018, their unemployment rate was the lowest in the developed world, at 2.5 percent.

The International Federation of Robotics (IFR) consist of companies in the robotics industry and various robotics associations, and robotic research institutes. The IFR publishes information showing robot density in various countries. See figure 5 (right) for a chart they produced showing which countries use the most robots.

The chart displays the number of multi-purpose robots per 10,000 people in the manufacturing industries of developed nations. The average is seventy-four robots per 10,000 workers. As you can see, Japan ranks fourth and Germany is third. In December 2018, Germany had its lowest unemployment rate in decades. Japan and Germany are proving that increased robotics does not create a population of unemployed people.

Machines don't always replace humans; in many cases, they complement the work being done. Or make it faster—like using an electric drill instead of a screwdriver! I'm sure our servicemen and women appreciate bomb-squad robots. The fear

Figure 5. Number of Robots per 10,000 Employees

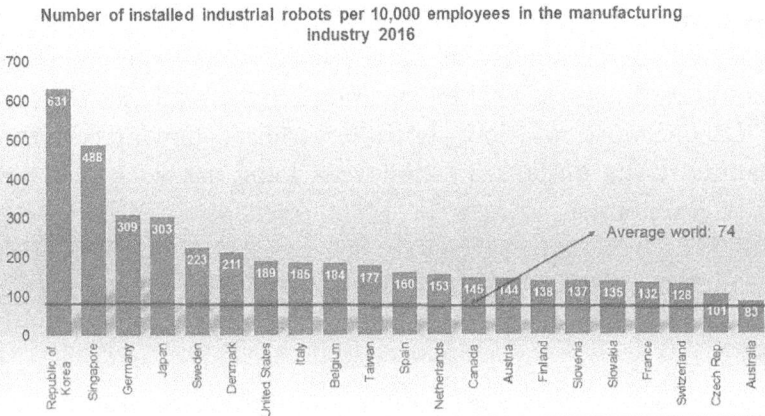

IFR
International
Federation of
Robotics

Number of installed industrial robots per 10,000 employees in the manufacturing industry 2016

Average world: 74

Source: World Robotics 2017

of automation leaving millions unemployed is perhaps overdone.

And don't forget Old MacDonald. He had a farm—*had* being the operative word. Back in 1850, farm workers in the United States made up about sixty-four percent of the working population. Fast forward a little to the 1920 U.S. census and that figure goes down to about thirty percent of the labor force.[10] Decade after decade, agricultural technology and automation increased and the proportion of workers who were farmers decreased. By 1960, there were about 15.6 million farmers, but they made up only 8.3 percent of the U.S. workforce.[11] See the trend? Nowadays farmers are about 1 to 2 percent of the workforce.

What happened to everyone who lost a job due to increased technology in farming? Well, we know they found other jobs. If jobs hadn't been created to replace farming jobs, the nation's unemployment rate would be over fifty percent. Despite only two percent of the workforce being agricultural workers, the

U.S. produces more food than ever. A Purdue University study showed that a farmer got about twenty-five bushels of corn on an acre of land in 1925. In 2012, that same acre was providing 162 bushels.[12] That's a lotta corndogs.

Something similar has happened in the U.S. with manufacturing jobs. We can view manufacturing output over time and compare it to the number of workers with manufacturing jobs. That information is released by the Bureau of Labor Statistics. Below (figure 6) is a chart showing both the manufacturing output and employees doing the work over the forty years or so:

Figure 6. Manufacturing Output Versus Number of Employees

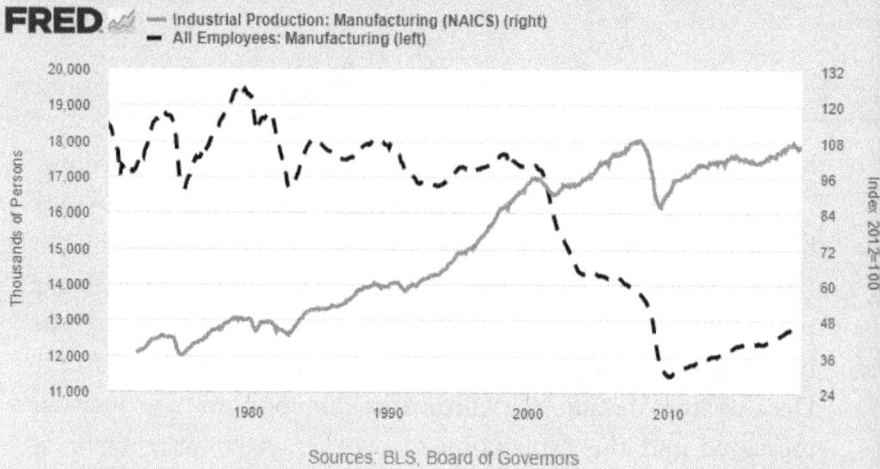

FRED

— Industrial Production: Manufacturing (NAICS) (right)
— All Employees: Manufacturing (left)

Sources: BLS, Board of Governors

The dotted line shows the total number of jobs in manufacturing at any point in the sixty-year period, indicated in the left column. The solid line shows total production during the same period, indexed in the right column. From the early 1970s to 2018, the U.S. lost one-third of its manufacturing workers— but at the same time, output almost tripled. Like farming, the U.S. manufacturing output was higher than ever. How was this possible with fewer workers? Automation and robotics.

Good paying manufacturing jobs are disappearing. The data shows this to be true, and it looks like the main culprits are productivity and automation. If that were not the case, the lines would have moved in the same directions. Jobs lost from manufacturing were replaced by other jobs. If they weren't, the unemployment rate would be through the roof. Take a moment and think about your grandfathers and what they did for work. Does it scare you if whatever job they had is no longer around? You probably haven't given it a lot of thought. One of my grandfathers worked in a potato house, a building where farmers could store potatoes at a certain temperature to prevent them from rotting. Nowadays, this job is uncommon. In modern times, due to decades of technology improvements, farmers and potato distributors tend to need only seasonal workers.

My other grandfather worked for the U.S. Postal Service. This job is still around but has been drastically altered by technology. Back in his day (1950s), there were about 375,000 employees moving about 55 billion pieces of mail per year. Skip forward to today, where the postal service moves 154 billion pieces of mail. Nearly three times as much mail, but do they have three times as many employees? Nope. Technological efficiencies have allowed them to accomplish this with 500,000 employees, rather than the million or so you might have expected.

Let's not forget the millions of women who joined the workforce in the 20th century. My grandmothers spent most of their working age at home. Millions of women joined the workforce while millions of jobs were disrupted by technology—yet people were still able to find jobs. Progress in the job market has been occurring for decades in one form or another. Better to acknowledge and prepare than to fear it.

Trying to preserve existing jobs by slowing the pace of change will never work economically. It's like trying to prevent cell phones from being used in the United States in order to protect the electrical workers installing telephone landlines. Or prohibiting tractor usage to keep the horse-and-plow industry going.

Despite all the robotics, remember the JOLTS (job openings)? We have millions of job openings despite the self-checkout counters, thousands of warehouse robots, and ATM machines.

The University of Oxford researchers put together a list of those jobs with a high probability of being disrupted by technology and those less likely to be. Let's run through some of the most at-risk jobs first. Cashiers, waiters, food preparers, freight and stock labor, and retail sales round out the top of the list. Each of these jobs currently employs more than 2.5 million Americans and does not require high levels of skill or education.

Some other jobs requiring at minimum a high-school diploma likely to be replaced are administrative assistants, bookkeepers, telemarketers (aw, gee, that's too bad), accountants and auditors, and clerks. I want to emphasize: These are jobs with an increased *likelihood* of replacement. I'm not saying every accounting job will be replaced. But as with farm workers or postal workers, these job roles will make up a smaller part of the workforce in the future.

Oxford researchers believe teaching, childcare, cosmetology, nursing, fitness training, and law enforcement are some of the jobs that will be less affected.

Electricians, chefs, lawyers (phew, there will still be plenty of personal-injury attorney ads), and many supervisory or managerial positions across most industries are also less at risk. I've just noted some of the highlights here—I've thrown the whole list of nearly seven hundred jobs into Appendix B. One thing you may have noticed (and I'll sound like a broken record for pointing it out again), is that all the safer jobs require skills and education.

You may already have had confidence in your future job prospects prior to reading this section. Hopefully, you are beginning to think about and relate some of this data to your own situation. By this point, we've established *ad nauseum* that to maximize your job-related income, to Earn More, you need to have a good job. If you or someone you care about needs to improve their job skills or education level, age or current job situation doesn't matter. It's never too late to get to work on this.

CHAPTER FOUR
SALARY DOES NOT EQUAL WEALTH

"Education costs money, but then so does ignorance."

— *Claus Moser, British statistician*

Some things change. Others, not so much. It was a few years after college that I began interacting with Rob the Engineer again. He was working for a prominent tech company and doing pretty well for himself. His life had changed. He was working a nine-to-five job, living on the West Coast, and had a new circle of friends. But his personality and attitude were the same as they had always been. He was still supremely confident, loud, and entertaining, but brainy enough to know what he was talking about.

Before we continue, you might be wondering how I knew certain details about Rob's finances—details such as how he was earning a good salary. The quick answer is that websites like Glassdoor and other resources online provide salary information for various jobs. Some of it is common sense—we know doctors and lawyers tend to earn quite a bit of money.

For the record, I never did Rob's taxes (or the other individuals I'll discuss later). Never saw W-2s or credit card statements. Much of the information comes from observation and from countless conversations spanning years. In many cases, due to my background, people would share financial details that they might not have shared so casually with other people.

I've known Rob for roughly fifteen years. I've met his parents and visited the house he grew up in. I don't have data or documentation to say that when he was twenty-three years old he made 53,854.00 dollars, but I can positively say that because of his job title he was making more than most people his age. I can also say I knew him well enough to know he wasn't sitting on a trust fund or some big inheritance.

A friend and I decided to head to the West Coast to visit with Rob and also do some touristy-type things. One of the rumors I had heard and wanted to check out for myself was that Rob had started working part-time as a server at Applebee's.

After getting off the plane, we three amigos were soon catching up. It didn't take long for us to ask Rob why he had this part-time job. He said he originally took the job to make friends since he was new to the area. That's reasonable, right? Then he said he also wanted to make a little extra money. He admitted his lifestyle was "a little expensive" and extra money would help out.

Working a second job is obviously a way to supplement your earnings (hint hint, if you are considering options to increase your earnings), but I was a little confused. Rob was making more money than my other friend and me combined, yet I had never thought about getting a part-time job. I wondered what his lifestyle was that he needed the money. After being in town with Rob for several days, I no longer wondered. The catch phrase for Applebee's used to be "Eating good in the neighborhood." Well, metaphorically speaking, Rob's lifestyle was the definition of eating good. In this neighborhood. That neighborhood. In every neighborhood.

Rob's lifestyle involved 200+ dollar nights out a couple of times every weekend. That is how much he'd spend at his favorite restaurants, clubs, and bars with his friends. Every single weekend. Overpriced drinks, late night food—it adds up. Another twenty bucks on a cab (this was pre-Uber) each way. Taking the subway or a bus? No, I don't think so.

His big salary also allowed expensive hobbies. He had not only taken up golf, he'd really gone all out. He had purchased an expensive golf club membership for a few thousand, and golf equipment for hundreds to thousands of dollars. Then add on fifty to a hundred dollars each day of golfing for food, drinks, cart rentals, and miscellaneous expenses. One or two trips per year to places like Arizona, Oregon, Hawaii, Europe—all to play golf. Oh, and just because you have a membership at one course doesn't mean you can't go play another course with friends (for a charge of course). Massive golf budget.

Rob also still had his prized yellow Subaru WRX. The way he drove, I'm sure he was frequently replacing his worn-out tires. He liked to refresh the look of the car by getting new rims, adding different accessories to the interior, or after-market parts for one thing or another.

These expensive hobbies were in addition to things that most twenty-somethings were already doing. Taking vacations with friends (non-golf-related), going to concerts, eating at restaurants, after-work drinks, and sporting events were factored into the equation, in addition to traveling home a few weekends per year to visit with friends and family.

We had kept up with each other on Facebook, but sometimes the real-life get-togethers and detailed stories hit home for me more than Facebook photos. After a few days visiting with Rob, I began thinking he might need a second part-time job.

When Rob spoke about his future, he had the same level of confidence as he did back in college. He anticipated promotions or moving on to other companies at more advanced positions.

I noticed that he seemed to equate salary with wealth. He thought *only* high earnings determined his wealth. Those are distinctly different things. Salary is how much you get paid from your day job, but wealth is the total amount of money you have built up. If your earnings come in one hand and it all goes out the other, what do you really have left? For example, someone who makes a million dollars per year but spends a million dollars per year is not a millionaire.

I perceived Rob the Engineer's mindset to be awfully similar to when he was back in college. If salary instead of wealth was his barometer for financial well-being, debt wouldn't matter to him. At this point in his life, he was in the same trap he had fallen into in college—taking on debt as a means to buy goods and services.

Rob anticipated annual raises and even higher future earnings. Debt was fine as long as he could make the interest payments. He had gotten into the habit of bingeing on credit because it was easily available. Rob was not alone. In June 2017, total household debt was at a record peak of 12.73 trillion dollars.[13] American dollars, not Monopoly money.

Rob was spending his money as he made it rather than building savings or making investments. Like half of the American population, he was living paycheck to paycheck.

Despite his high earnings, his finances were derailed by excessive spending and borrowing. If he ever ran into a financial emergency, he would be forced to borrow money from sources like friends and family, retirement accounts, credit cards, or a payday lender.

Borrowing money comes with its own set of problems, however. Friends and family who lend money to each other usually don't include detailed payment terms as a bank would. This can lead to repayment issues and tension between both parties. Those who lent money may run into their own financial emergencies and come looking for repayment sooner than expected. It's also more complicated to enforce repayment when the loan is from a friend or family member. We've all seen enough episodes of *Judge Judy* to know those situations can get hairy.

Both credit cards and payday lenders usually charge

high interest rates, making them poor choices for long-term borrowing. They are probably one tier better than a loan shark. Carrying a balance on a credit card is just bad math. The minimum payments on a credit card barely move the needle in paying it off. A credit card balance of $3,000 with a fairly reasonable rate of 12.99% usually would have a minimum payment of around 2% of the balance per month (first payment would be $60). Paying the minimum would take fourteen years to pay the balance off! For the $3,000 balance, over $2,628 is paid in additional interest! It's also very likely that it will never be paid off because before the fourteen years are up, more credit card spending will take place. It's a very bad and expensive idea to carry credit card balances.

Borrowing from a retirement account is rarely a smart strategy. It could cost a lot of upside potential, and you hinder the growth of your investments. That is money that could have grown into more money. Sure, you pay yourself back, but you are using after-tax dollars rather than pre-tax dollars, as you do when you fund it. A typical rate for paying yourself back might be 4.25% but you should be averaging higher returns on investments.

If tapping into investment funds becomes a habit, you risk stunting the growth of your retirement account significantly. Those investments need time to grow big enough to fund your retirement. Earlier in the book we used the example of building a snowman, noting that more snow is collected as each snowball gets bigger. If you take too many breaks from rolling snowballs, you won't end up with a very big snowman.

Put another way: If all your earnings go toward paying debt, you have nothing left over. You can't invest if you have no money to invest.

Avoid the temptation of spending money in correlation to your earnings. A dangerous outcome of pay raises is to increase spending by the amount of the earnings increase. This could potentially lead to borrowing more, because you've told yourself you're making enough to pay off more debt.

Rob the Engineer illustrated his desire to spend more and borrow more because he was making more. Unspent excess money was "burning a hole in his pocket." Don't get caught in this cycle where any income increases are exactly offset by spending or borrowing increases. In that situation, anticipated job promotions or pay increases will not build actual wealth. Those income boosts will go only toward paying off your debt or paying for new, exciting things. More/better/newer golf trips, cars, Amazon shopping sprees, or rounds of drinks with friends are all fantastic in the short term, but directing the money toward saving and investing will have a bigger payoff in the long term.

Once you get trapped in the spend and borrow mindset, living more or less paycheck to paycheck is unavoidable.

The New York Federal Reserve branch has tracked consumer debt. Since 2012, much of the additional debt has been avoidable (story of Rob's life). It is in student loans (are you choosing a school that is a good value?), auto loans (are you buying too much car?), and credit cards (are you carrying debt at high rates?).

Coming off the five-year college plan at out-of-state tuition rates, Rob checks all the boxes for contributing to this nearly 13 trillion in debt. Student loans? Check. Auto loans? Check. Credit card debt? Check. Translation? Not enough money to invest and build wealth. Of course, investing and building wealth are probably not at the forefront of the minds of most twenty-somethings.

Most interest rates to borrow money (for cars and houses, for example, or just credit cards) have been pretty low the last few years by historical standards. But over time (usually as the economy does better), the rates to borrow money normally go up. When Rob wants to buy his next car, his new car payment might be higher (due to a higher interest rate). Or his monthly minimum credit card payments might get bumped higher. With so much debt, even small increases in interest rates can be a rude awakening for Rob's borrow, borrow, borrow lifestyle.

Certain debt comes with what is called a "floating rate," which can cause monthly payments to change over time. You might also hear the term "variable rate loan," which is the same thing. Other types of debt are "fixed rate," which means the interest rate is locked in when the borrower enters into the loan. Remember, almost half of adults in America are living paycheck to paycheck and just making things work by the skin of their teeth, like Rob. Higher interest rates (and monthly debt payments) can cause major cash flow problems. Floating rate mortgage loans were a big contributor to the recession of 2008. Many people could only marginally afford their mortgage payments to begin with, so that when their payments went up, that little extra proved too much and they lost their homes in foreclosure.

Rob was juggling a mix of floating and fixed rate loans. Credit cards, auto loans, mortgage loans, student loans, or business loans can all be either fixed or floating, depending on what the lender offers on each specific loan.

As a quick aside, my view is *not* that all debt is bad. Getting a loan for financial security makes sense—if you can finance a home that builds equity. Or a car, so that you can make it to work every day (and make money). Or if you are paying for education or training that will result in earning more. Especially if this debt is at a low rate, and the payments are not a large portion of your income. Not everyone can live in a tent and walk to work.

There isn't a formula or magic number for the right amount of debt. Getting into debt to go on a vacation, buy nice clothes, dine at too many expensive restaurants, or purchase a lot of expensive equipment for your hobbies is not helping your overall financial security.

Choose what fits your lifestyle the best, but here is one consideration: The more "debt drag" you have, the more your income will have to go toward paying debt off instead of toward investing.

CHAPTER FIVE
LOOKING AT ROB'S DAY TO DAY

"The courage to imagine the otherwise is our greatest resource, adding color and suspense to our life."

— *Daniel Boorstin, historian and twelfth Librarian of Congress*

A few years would pass before I saw Rob again. I was relocating and looking for temporary housing in a new area. Rob had since moved back to the Northeast and was looking for a new roommate at precisely the same time. In precisely the same area. Of course, I was a bit hesitant. You would have been, too. There was concern about his spending habits. If history was any indicator, it would be stupidly expensive for me to keep up with his spending. Going out or partaking in the same hobbies and resuming a close friendship with Rob could break the bank.

But the alternative was Craigslist and finding a random person to live with. Since I didn't feel like getting stabbed, I rolled the dice. Living with Rob is what gave me the firsthand view of how he handles everyday spending.

First was the cable-TV setup. Rob's idea of "necessity" was to have a good cable and Internet package. Okay, fine. Add HBO—they have the best shows. Oh, and add on Showtime, too. Might as well get Netflix. Can't forget about Hulu, need that too. Amazon Prime. Free shipping on Amazon orders after all. We paid the bargain price of approximately two hundred bucks a month and barely watched any television.

Since we had so few television options (sarcasm), Rob decided he wanted an extensive Blu-ray collection of movies. He had about a hundred on a shelf in the living room. He'd order one or two from Amazon every week. Only so many could be displayed, so older ones were boxed up and put into storage... right beside his extensive but now obsolete collection of DVDs.

Just wait—it gets stranger. Rob had trouble keeping track of which movies he did and did not own. Some he might have had on DVD, some he had on Blu-ray, some in storage, some he had only seen in theaters. He was always lending out Blu-rays; it was like he ran a free movie library to friends. There were times a friend would return a stack of Blu-rays and Rob and I would look at each other and chuckle.

By now, between the confusion about which Blu-rays were owned and how many TV services we had, it should be pretty clear that Rob didn't let twenty bucks here or there slow him down. Most cable TV subscriptions allow customers to rent movies "On Demand." It's usually five or six bucks automatically added onto your monthly bill. Why do I mention this? Oh, because Rob liked to rent a movie from time to time . . . including movies that he already owned . . . including movies that were sitting on the kitchen table.

I'm not joking or exaggerating. I noticed on multiple occasions a movie would be purchased "On Demand" that was in our apartment already. Was it from confusion? Perhaps. Laziness? Perhaps. A waste of money? Absolutely.

Housecleaning can be another contention between roommates. Not in this case. As the new guy moving in, I had two choices: Do all the cleaning or split the cost of the cleaning service he used. He didn't "waste his time" cleaning. Cleaning a small 800-square-foot apartment is such a Herculean effort, right?

The same rules applied to his personal vehicle. He had

traded the yellow Subaru WRX for a Mercedes-Benz sedan. Why clean it yourself when you can pay someone to do it? So, a couple of times a year, he would get the car cleaned and detailed professionally.

Let's take a moment to talk about cars. Cars cost a lot of money, and they are usually worth something, but you shouldn't think of a car as an asset. An asset is something you own that is worth money, but once you begin to think like an investor, it should also be something that either provides you income or increases in value. Cars *lose* value over time. Unless the car is collectible or somehow used to earn money, it won't fit the description of being an asset. Don't think of your car as an asset.

Rob taught me a few lessons about cars. The first has to do with the cost of a car. An expensive car comes with high maintenance costs. For the sake of simplicity, we'll compare Rob's Mercedes-Benz CLA 250 sedan to a Ford Focus sedan manufactured in the same year. I'm not debating the quality or the options of the two vehicles, just the money involved. We know the sticker price for a new Mercedes is significantly higher than it is for a new Ford.

The Mercedes-Benz will also cost more for oil changes, tire rotations, tune-ups, and any other routine maintenance. If the dealer does these for "free," don't be fooled—you paid for it as part of the sticker price. Fuel might be more expensive (premium versus regular). Insurance will be more expensive. Registering the vehicle will be more expensive. You get the picture.

But the biggest cost of a new vehicle is actually the depreciation. According to *Edmunds*, the average car will depreciate about nineteen percent of its value in the first year. Then another twelve percent in the second year. After five years, the average car has depreciated by over sixty percent.[14] So I say again, cars are not assets. It's true that some cars hold their value more than others, but more expensive cars will always experience higher depreciation costs.

In addition to the costs he was incurring for owning an expensive vehicle, Rob was heavily indebted, which meant he didn't always have the best car loans. When I first moved in with him, he was in the process of refinancing his Mercedes car loan. He had been making monthly payments of over 700 dollars. Refinancing is when you roll over a loan into a new loan. The old loan is paid off and the new loan is usually at a lower rate, resulting in lower monthly payments. If you have a five-year loan for a car and you refinance it, you usually have to start a new five-year loan. Rob was refinancing to get his payments down to about 500 dollars but would begin a new five-year loan. Stop and think about this for a second. Rob was two years into his car loan. He began a new car loan with lower payments, but he had to start the five years over again. It would take him seven years to pay off his car instead of the original five.

Refinancing at a lower rate can be a good idea, because you will have lower monthly payments. Of course, it depends what you do with the saved money. In Rob's case, the 200 dollars per month in reduced car payments all got spent. We've talked about "debt drag" on cash flow in the last chapter, but if you reduce this drag only to spend the money, the savings doesn't make any difference. You need to put it toward investing.

If you refinance into a new loan, it will take longer to pay off the car. Your car will depreciate in value faster than you can pay it off. Remember, cars depreciate quickly. If you extend your car loan to seven or eight years, you might reach a point where you owe more on the loan than the car is worth. Once you are in that position, it's obviously tough to switch vehicles. You gotta come up with the difference (the shortage between the loan and car value) out of pocket or find a dealership that will add the difference to a new loan as they sell you a new car. But that really worsens an existing problem instead of fixing it. You get a new car but keep your old car loan! The new car loan is combined with the remaining loan from your old car.

Rooming with Rob, I observed a continuation of the same indulgent lifestyle I first witnessed in college. It's not about what you *should* buy, but what you *could* buy.

Living with this type of person can be difficult if you are trying to save money (which I was). I was startled by curious habits he had—like "grocery shopping" at a corner convenience store instead of an actual grocery store. Milk, bread, eggs, and snacks—all overpriced—from a convenience store were Rob's go-to because it was quicker. Not once in a while but every few days. He was their best customer. He'd walk out with two to three bags at a time.

Going out of the way to save money was stupid to Rob. We'd get coupon booklets in the mail for places that we frequented, like nearby restaurants. He'd scoff when he saw me saving some of them. "Coupons?" he'd chuckle condescendingly. He shook his head at my coupons, while at the same time setting aside the newest magazine subscription offer that came in the mail. He had subscriptions (which he'd never read) to golf, snowmobiling, sports, and entertainment magazines. The only ones he read were the *Good Housekeeping* magazines. Yeah, I wish.

I figured the restaurant coupons were all mine to use. The more, the merrier. Rob did spend quite a bit of time dining at restaurants and bars. His regular hangout was an Italian restaurant/sports bar/brick-oven pizza place. You know how they say mullet haircuts are business in the front and a party in the back? This place was a fancy Italian restaurant in the front and a raucous sports bar in the back. He'd hang out in the back two to three times a week for dinner, have a few drinks, and chat up the bartenders and wait staff while watching baseball and hockey games. Each night was probably a thirty- or forty-dollar endeavor.

I soon got used to Rob's high regard for status. He'd crack jokes here and there about the brands I wore. "You still wear those Adidas sneakers?" "Think it's time to get a new shirt yet?" Yes, I would sometimes wear a ten-year-old T-shirt from my high-school tennis team while I hung around the apartment. What's the big deal? If I were having dinner with the queen or Al Roker, I'd stop at Burberry for a shirt.

While sitting on the couch in my TJ Maxx ten-dollar shirts (maybe I'm a Maxxinista), I'd observe Rob come through the door with whatever new thing he had purchased.

Rob was a computer engineer. Unsurprisingly, he was into electronic toys. It was a relatively small apartment. That didn't stop Rob. He had some big-rig computer with multiple monitors—for "work." Then there was the iPad—more convenient than the big computer. Then an expensive speaker system—which wasn't even hooked up to anything half the time. A GoPro and an Oculus VR—because those always get heavy usage, right? Throw in a smart watch, an Xbox, and a pair or two of Beats headphones. There were weird boxes and remotes with wires coming out of them. Half the stuff I didn't recognize. There were USB drives all over the place.

Our apartment had electronics of one sort or another in every nook. Most collected dust. I'm glad he didn't cook or I'm sure the kitchen would have been cluttered with stuff too. The one gadget we could have used, a Roomba, he never bought. Strangely, he never bought a new TV. No. Of course, I'm kidding. He bought two. After a while, I just stopped asking questions.

Accessories, clothing, sporting goods equipment (mainly for golf). Saturday with nothing to do? Spend money. Perhaps buy a mountain bike. Or join a kickboxing gym. Maybe buy a new tennis racquet. The fact that he already owned five didn't matter. Spending money was a leisure hobby. It didn't matter if he used the stuff he bought or not.

Rob was able to make frequent, expensive purchases because of how much money he earned. He no longer had a second job, but he hadn't been idle. He had completed various engineering certifications and received an MBA. He had become a supervisor at his place of work and was candid about making a six-figure salary. A simple Google search of his job title would have given me the same information. We were nearing thirty years of age, but he was earning significantly more than any of our other friends. He just also happened to be spending way more too.

Rob considered buying a house every now and again. He always ended up convincing himself to wait a little longer. You could guess that with his tastes, his preference was for a nice, expensive house. Part of his reluctance was due to the extra work involved with owning a home and part was the effort of saving for a down payment. Unless he changed his spending habits, he couldn't save up the money. In May 2017, the *Wall Street Journal* published an article titled "Millennials Want to Buy Homes but Aren't Saving for Down Payments," reporting that seventy percent of 18- to 34-year-olds had less than 1,000 dollars saved for a down payment.[15]

Before you instinctively shrug it off as a "millennials" problem, you should know that this issue affects all age groups. The homeownership rate among all Americans declined after the housing crisis and the Great Recession of 2008–09. The U.S. Census Bureau's data shows while over sixty-nine percent of Americans owned a home in the mid-2000s, that number had declined to 62.9 percent by mid-2016. 55- to 64-year-olds were affected just as much as millennials. The homeownership rate hasn't been that low since 1965.[16] Several years after the housing crisis, the homeownership rate was still bottoming out.

In the earlier sections of the book, we covered the prevalence and growth of student debt. Rob's lack of a down payment and his existing debt were like a ball and chain, prohibiting him from buying a house.

Other financing options for a house purchase could be to use money from a retirement account. We mentioned earlier that this is a bad idea. It gives up the growth potential you will need for retirement, and you may have to pay some sort of penalty, depending on what sort of retirement account you have. Retirement accounts work most effectively when the gains are able to compound on one another over time.

A 401k retirement is offered by many employers. It is a retirement account that receives money before being reduced by income taxes. With some of his first jobs out of college, Rob didn't take advantage of the 401k programs offered because he had wanted to spend the money. During the time we lived together as roommates, Rob contributed to a 401k plan, but he was playing catch up for the lost years. Rob never made the mistake of borrowing from his 401k because he didn't want to slow its growth.

If your employer matches the money you put into your 401k account, take advantage. You should always get the maximum employer match available, otherwise you are giving up free money. For example, an employee might have the opportunity to put a percentage of their paycheck into their 401k. The employer might match three percent for employees who participate. If you choose not to participate in the 401k program your employer is offering, that is three percent of your paycheck out the window.

Student loan debt is another factor affecting home ownership. The New York Federal Reserve tracked a huge increase in the amount of outstanding college debt over a fifteen-year period (figure 7).[17]

In 2004, student-loan debt was under 400 billion dollars. By 2016, it had more than tripled. The graphic also breaks down debt by age. Debt increased across the board for all age groups, but there was a big increase for the 30-to-39 age group and older. This means people are carrying debt later into their lives and the potential debt drag lasts longer. I bring all this up because Rob chose to add a year of college—he thus added a year of debt.

Always consider the value you get when choosing an associate degree, a bachelor's degree, or any kind of skill building course.

Figure 7. New York Federal Reserve Chart Showing Increase in College Debt

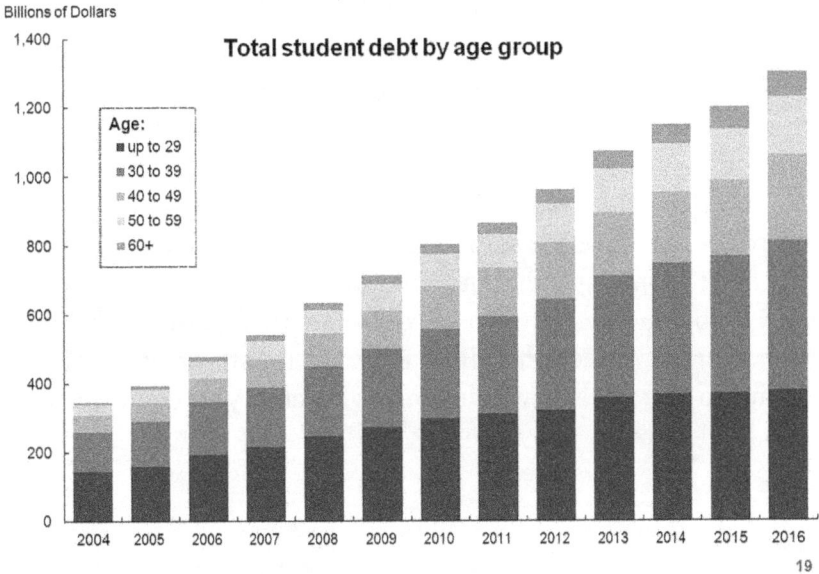

Student Debt Totaled $1.3 Trillion in 2016, Up 170% from 2006

Source: New York Fed Consumer Credit Panel/Equifax

Colleges point to data linking college degrees to higher wages, but they can also provide prohibitively expensive educations.

Many colleges have enhanced amenities, like fancier dormitories, workout facilities, and newer stadiums. Some even provide "free" laptops, movie theaters, and campus landscaping comparable to botanical gardens. Non-teaching staff on campus has doubled in the last twenty-five years.

If you want a luxury resort college experience, you'll be paying for it the rest of your life.

The Consumer Price Index (CPI) is a common calculation for inflation in the United States, showing how the cost of living changes over time. The CPI shows that the cost of tuition has gone up a lot faster than the cost of everything else.

It is calculated by the Bureau of Labor Statistics. The average tuition cost at a university was 9,438 dollars in 1980 versus 23,872 dollars in 2014.[18] Let's compare some of these numbers to overall inflation.

1980 Tuition Price: $9,438.00

2014 Actual Tuition Price: $23,872.00

2014 Tuition Price at normal inflation of CPI: $11,325.60

The costs are more than double today than what they were in 1980 and have gone up at a rate much faster than the cost of other things.

Was Rob's five-year college plan wise in this regard? You've heard the expression "rat race." Rob was trapped in the rat race, like most people, spending his life working to repay money he'd already borrowed. Between his out-of-control spending habits and poor debt decisions, Rob was never getting ahead. His ability to buy a house was hindered; his ability to build wealth was hindered.

CHAPTER SIX
RECAP OF ROB

A year after Rob and I were no longer roommates, we got together with friends at a bar to catch up. Rob was doing well, he had changed roles within his company, positioning himself for some future promotion. He also told us about his new luxury SUV we saw pictures of on Facebook. As the night wore on, I noticed he was generous with his money—the first to buy rounds of drinks and he wasn't the type to keep track of whose turn was next. To be honest, he probably would have bought every round if nobody else volunteered. He ordered drinks for people who asked him not to or other friends who still had unfinished drinks in front of them.

I began to wonder where the line was between generosity and wastefulness. The free drinks were accepted appreciatively and I'm sure the recipients viewed the gesture as unselfish. After a while, I perceived his spending as wasteful. Rob was spending money on drinks that weren't wanted and would be left behind.

Rob updated me on all the home décor changes (he had redone everything, including all new furniture) to our previously shared apartment. My old room was being used for storage—

this was in addition to a self-storage unit he was renting on a monthly basis. Part of that was for his motorcycle, but the rest? I guess the museum of electronic gadgets must have expanded.

If his high earnings were not derailed by his high spending, he could have had a lot of money to put toward investing. Think of how wealthy he could have been.

Let's do a quick exercise to prove how much money Rob the Engineer could have had. Take a moment and imagine one of those thought bubbles as we think about this alternative reality. Anybody can invest directly in the stock market. Anyone can buy an index fund, which mirrors the stock market. The index fund will probably charge a tiny fee, but it's less than a tenth of one percent of the money invested. Consider it negligible.

The most common barometer for the U.S. stock market is the Standard & Poor's 500 (S&P 500). We mentioned it earlier, but I'll remind you: It is a collection of the 500 biggest companies in the U.S. When we measure the stock market, we measure the stock prices of these 500 companies.

Rob had the Earn More part down, but he derailed it by spending. It's fair to say he could easily have saved 5,000 dollars per year by cutting back on travel or expensive hobbies. Easily. We will imagine that Rob put 5,000 dollars per year into the S&P 500 index fund. Rob entered the workforce mid-2007, not long before the Great Recession. For easy math, let's pretend he began investing on January 1, 2008. We'll calculate to the end of 2015, which was when he wished to purchase a house.

Date	Value	Yearly Return	End Value
1/1/2008	$5,000.00	-37.00%	$3,150.00
1/1/2009	$8,150.00	26.46%	$10,306.49
1/1/2010	$15,306.49	15.06%	$17,611.65
1/1/2011	$22,611.65	2.11%	$23,088.76
1/1/2012	$28,088.76	16.00%	$32,582.96
1/1/2013	$37,582.96	32.39%	$49,756.08
1/1/2014	$54,756.08	13.69%	$62,252.19
1/1/2015	$67,252.19	1.38%	$68,180.27

This rough example shows Rob could have had nearly 70,000 dollars to put toward a house. Instead, he had zero. Sure, 40,000 dollars was his own money. He really made "only" a little over 28,000 dollars. If you go back and look at the numbers, it wasn't clean. The values didn't go up like an escalator, it was choppy and sometimes barely moved over the course of a whole year. The first year was like getting punched in the gut, losing almost two thousand dollars right away. Most people probably wouldn't have had the *cajones* to add another five grand the following year.

This example shows us that when you spend money buying different things, you also give up the money you *could* be making if you knew how to invest that same money. Remember, this scenario used real-world numbers and real-world returns. This wasn't some crazy theoretical example. In actuality, saving 5,000 dollars per year wasn't asking too much of Rob. Imagine if it were more.

Let's recap some of the things we learned about Rob.

Lifestyle habits that require spending more money can be difficult to break.

Find ways to earn more. Explore adding certifications, additional education, a part-time job, or even consider a career change.

Consider your hobbies. Expensive hobbies will make it difficult to save money.

Cars are not assets. Luxury vehicles usually have high depreciation costs as well as higher ownership costs.

Refinance loans for lower interest rates, not solely to extend the life of the loan. Use any monthly savings wisely.

Borrowing from retirement accounts is usually not a good idea. Money needs to be allowed to grow and compound.

Excessive debt can trap you in the "rat race." Your money suffers from "debt drag." It goes toward debt repayment instead of toward building wealth.

Here is a visual snapshot of Rob's financial situation:

	EARNINGS	SAVINGS	DEBT	INVESTMENT RETURNS
Rob	High	Low	High	Uninvested

We've learned from Rob the Engineer that it doesn't matter how much money you earn if your instincts are to spend. High earnings were thwarted by excessive spending. We saw it from college, through his twenties, and then even at the start of his thirties. He was unable to break this cycle.

In some ways, Rob is like most people. He didn't know how to invest his own money and he never even thought about it. He made money and then he spent it. As you read about Rob, it may have looked like he was heading for disaster. The power of high and growing earnings successfully kept him ahead of his spending. An earnings juggernaut covered up any financial missteps he might have been making. High earnings also provide flexibility. Rob would need to make only minor adjustments if he eventually decided buying a house was a priority. Despite getting a slow start on his 401k, with his high earnings, he'll have a comfortable retirement as long as he continues to add money consistently.

You may know someone who spends like Rob, or maybe you are a version of Rob. If you've had to take a 401k loan, needed your tax return to pay monthly bills, or don't have money set aside to cover something like unexpected car repairs, you might be living beyond your means.

If you are always waiting on the next bank loan or the next credit card balance transfer, you are overextended and living outside of your means. Do you decide when to buy your next car, or do you wait until you get permission to borrow more? In my years observing people and my years in the investment industry managing money, I've yet to meet a single person who lived that way and built wealth or became rich.

That takes us to your next homework assignment. You thought I forgot about those, I bet.

Compare your lifestyle to that of Rob the computer engineer. Try to come up with one thing you can do to increase the amount of money you earn. Write it down. Anywhere. Get up and grab a pen and paper if you need to.

Next, think about anything excessive in your budget. Think about your hobbies, how much you spend at bars or restaurants, and what your typical mentality is when it comes to spending money. Are you generous? Or wasteful? Do you spend too much on nonessentials like gadgets, coffee, or weed? Do any of your habits mimic Rob the Engineer? Jot it down on paper next to the one way to earn more money.

It can be hard to change habits. You might have to change some of your personal relationships. Or make changes to your daily routine.

Rob the Engineer also showed us the power that the right skills can command in the workplace. Despite some of his reckless spending habits—he had the money to spend because of his high salary. Try to emulate that part of his life—Earn More. Try to think about the example a few pages back and how Rob could have built a financial fortress if he had invested some of his cash flow. As we cover topics in the book, we'll come back to Rob from time to time. But for now, we'll move on to our next teacher. She'll help re-examine your saving habits and generate ideas to cut spending. Read on to learn about Nathalie the Single Mom for lessons to Save More.

CHAPTER SEVEN
NATHALIE THE SINGLE MOM'S
MONEY-SAVING HABITS

"With self-discipline, most anything is possible."

— *Theodore Roosevelt, former U.S. president*

I met Nathalie in my mid-twenties when saving money had begun to be a priority for me. Right away, I determined her to be some kind of superhero. Oops, I mean supersaver.

Nathalie was tiny, only a little over five feet and barely weighed a hundred pounds. Like me, she was in her mid-twenties. She was shy and generally kept personal stuff to herself. She had a quiet ferocity and a determination that reminded me of qualities found in world-class athletes, not suburban soccer moms.

She was one of the strongest people I'd ever met. She was also terribly stubborn. For example, she willed herself to spend as little money as possible. I liked her immediately. She was the teacher who showed me ways to Save More, the second rule of personal finance and investing. If you reduce your spending and save, it will give you money to Invest More.

When I first met her, she was the single mother of twin

six-year-old boys. The father was not in the picture and not providing support of any kind. Everyone knows how difficult being a single mom can be. Nathalie didn't let that stop her, not for a second. She was able to provide for her sons and showed me tons of money-saving moves. She was like a savings ninja.

At the time, Nathalie worked as a nursing assistant, doing in-home care for elderly or disabled people. It's a thankless, underpaid job that can be both mentally and physically difficult. I think Nathalie was making around thirteen to fourteen dollars an hour. I never saw Nathalie's W-2s, just as I'd never seen Rob's. Much of what I know about her was through observation and many conversations spread over the years once we became close friends.

One of the biggest problems with her job was that she wasn't always able to get forty hours a week of work. Being paid hourly, if she worked less than forty hours, she was paid for less than forty hours. Her total number of work hours depended on the health of her patients or their ability to pay for home nursing. If a patient she was seeing eight hours a week no longer needed her, her paycheck was reduced until she was assigned new patients, which could take several weeks.

Since demand for her services was unpredictable, and so was her paycheck amount, she had to become an expert at saving money. Extra money was a financial cushion to cover the weeks here and there where she temporarily worked only twenty-five hours. Her schedule also created some problems. She could only work from roughly eight in the morning to five in the afternoon, while her sons were in school and in after-school programs. Paying for evening or weekend care didn't make sense with her budget, so she took advantage of the "free babysitting" the school provided. Her sons went to an after-school program that was subsidized for low-income families.

Nathalie had a lot of hobbies that didn't cost anything. She loved to go hiking and on nature walks. She was also an avid jogger. She'd jog while her kids rode bikes. Nathalie was also a frequent visitor to public parks and public beaches. She was like an encyclopedia of public parks. If you wanted to find a local park with a fire pit and picnic tables, she'd list the options in a heartbeat. Public beach with free parking that isn't busy mid-July? She'd know. Once she was wrong. Just once. We traveled to a state park to BBQ in late April and they weren't yet open for the season. She was so embarrassed. In disbelief. Like Wonder Woman letting a common thief get away.

And the planning. Oh, the planning. I'm ashamed to say that I was not used to planning day trips very well. I had good habits for saving on major expenses like housing and hobbies, but Nathalie was showing me I still had a ways to go. My "planning" usually consisted of making sure I had my wallet, phone, and keys. Then I'd make like a rocket and take off. If I was going somewhere, say to the beach, I'd buy lunch at a store or restaurant around the beach. If I forgot sunblock, I'd buy it at a convenience store or kiosk. Need something to drink? Buy it wherever.

Nathalie took a different approach. For a trip to the beach, she would always bring a cooler full of stuff. She'd make lunches, bring snacks, drinks, sun block, beach toys, everything that was needed. She never had to buy anything. I could tell she would get annoyed if I or one of our other friends would buy something while we were out. She saw it as a waste of money. Although, maybe it was the nurse in her getting annoyed at our eating mega slices of greasy pizza or giant slabs of fried dough drenched in butter and sugar. Fried dough is good, though. So good.

She did the same level of planning for parks or picnics. In some ways, she was the opposite of Rob. She would always do the inconvenient thing and spend the time and effort and planning to *not spend* money. He'd drop ten dollars at a convenience store on snacks on a whim. Nathalie would never need to stop at a convenience store for an impulse buy.

The same went for her grocery shopping and meal

preparation. She would check out what food was on sale in the grocery store flyers and plan every meal for the week based on what was on sale. Unlike Rob, she used coupons. She always had a good inventory in her head of what food she had in her apartment and how long it would last. She would probably get by on fifty dollars per week of groceries for her sons and herself. This was a shock to me. My experience with Rob taught me that some people drop fifty dollars for one meal multiple times a week.

She never ate out. Never. I mean literally never. Even after a long day on the road or at the beach, when others were exhausted and wanted to hit a restaurant or grab a pizza—not Nathalie. She would respectfully decline and prepare her own dinner at home. Even when she had what appeared to be no food in the apartment. My cousin and I once saw her turn leftover cabbage and half a pita bread into a meal. She made egg rolls, a pita pizza, and nachos, I think. And it was all really good. It was pretty impressive, actually. Sure, it helps to know how to cook. Beyond that, though, this example shows how disciplined she was about saving money rather than do the easy thing and go out to a restaurant.

She never threw leftovers away because she "didn't feel like" eating them. This was the opposite of Rob, who never ate leftovers. He'd put leftover food in Tupperware with the intention of eating it, but he never followed through. After several days he would throw it away.

Besides saving money, Nathalie's couponing and planning doubled as a hobby. Her all-time favorite was Rite Aid, because they accepted manufacturers' coupons in addition to their own for the same products. Using the coupons in tandem with Rite Aid's "up rewards" program resulted in a discount extravaganza.

I remember that she would get giddy about the deals she was getting. She somehow always found ways to pay nothing for her hygiene or toiletry products. Rite Aid eventually changed to a different program. "Plenti Points" was a term Nathalie spoke with disdain (she was NOT a fan of the changes). The point is that coupons were another weapon she used to save money—I'd estimate about fifty dollars a month.

Nathalie and her sons lived in a one-bedroom apartment. The bedroom was large enough to allow her to put up a makeshift wall separating her "bedroom" from the boys.' I knew she spent most of her time enjoying what the outside world had to offer, but man, the Spartans had more amenities than she did. There were plenty of toys lying around, but the furniture was pretty simple and there weren't many electronic gadgets or weird kitchen appliances. It was spotless, and all the decorations around the apartment were either plants or her boys' artwork.

They had only basic Internet at the lowest rate of bandwidth. No cable. They were "cord cutters," but you couldn't really stream shows with the Internet connection she had. They had one TV, a thirty-inch tube TV with a built-in VCR/DVD player. Much of the apartment was open space to do activities.

The apartment was in a great location, within walking distance of a lot of playgrounds, parks, and bike paths. There was a small porch where Nathalie would grow tomatoes and cucumbers as a hobby. Since she loved being outdoors, gardening (even with just a few plants) was fun. Not only did she save a few bucks not having to buy tomatoes, but more importantly, gardening was a pleasant hobby that didn't require spending very much money.

Another trick Nathalie used to save money was to listen to the radio and call in to win free tickets to various things. Or show up at radio station functions that were offering giveaways for events she could take her boys to. She won free tickets to museums, water parks, and concerts. Nathalie was fairly shy, so this level of action took a lot of courage for her. She did it because she wanted to make sure her kids had the experiences other kids were having.

Nathalie knew she wasn't living like most other twenty-seven-year-olds. She wasn't watching the "hit" TV shows other adults were talking about. She didn't do much traveling. She wasn't plugged in on Facebook or Instagram. While most people had iPhones, she was using a prepaid phone that could make phone calls or text, but that was it. No data plan, no Internet, no fancy ring tones, games, or high-resolution camera.

All the time Nathalie was saving money, she was driven by her own goals. She understood she was competing only against herself—not her friends, not other parents, not other people. It's easy to think an upgrade to a smartphone isn't *really* that much money. Why shouldn't Nathalie just spend an extra thirty bucks a month on a smartphone? She certainly felt the pressure to. It's hard to explain to someone why you don't want to spend extra money. It takes a strong person to follow their own compass and not be influenced by other people.

Nathalie had no magazine subscriptions or subscriptions of any kind. Nothing with automatic renewal payments. No gym membership. Besides jogging and biking with her kids, she did yoga by herself in her apartment. She'd always have her coffee thermos when I met her—filled with coffee she brewed herself every morning. No Starbucks ever. Save money. Don't waste money. Be organized. This was what I was learning from Nathalie.

The habits of savers like Nathalie can be tough to break once they become a part of your lifestyle. Author, finance professor at Santa Clara University, and contributor to the *Wall Street Journal* Meir Statman agrees. People who have more than they need find it hard to break the habits that made them such successful savers in the first place.[19] Just like the habits of a spender who can't stop, good savings habits can be tough to break.

That is the right mentality to be able to build wealth and put aside money for investing. Nathalie was saving as a survival strategy, but she was developing good habits that would be tough to break.

CHAPTER EIGHT
THE CONCEPT OF UTILITY VALUE

"Price is what you pay. Value is what you get."

— *Warren Buffet, CEO and renowned investor*

You might be thinking, "Okay, so Nathalie was good at saving money. I get it." But there was more to it than that. Try to see the thought process behind the financial decisions she was making. There was a certain self-discipline, yes, but there was also a way she chose to value one thing over another. It was more than simply "she was frugal."

One of the concepts I'll talk about in this book is "utility value," the amount of incremental benefit you get out of one thing when you compare it to something else. Think of it as the level of enjoyment you get out of something that you have to pay for.

Let's say there was a movie coming out that you wanted to see called *Fast and Furious 17: Speedboats and Canals.* One movie venue was charging ten dollars per ticket for a showing in a standard theater. Another venue was charging twenty dollars per ticket, but the movie was in a 3D IMAX theater. It also had nicer seats—they reclined! And the more expensive theater was always super clean.

Some people would be fine with the standard movie experience. They understand that the 3D IMAX is better quality, but for double the price, they wouldn't get double the enjoyment. That is utility value. Everyone might see the value differently, so you have to ask yourself what it means for you. Some people find the experience at a 3D IMAX theater so amazing that they would be willing to spend fifty dollars on a movie they're excited about. Twenty dollars to them is a bargain in that scenario. The standard theater would be so underwhelming as to ruin their experience.

One way Nathalie demonstrated utility value was with the alcohol she drank. She preferred your good ol' wine in a box! One box of wine equals more than five bottles of wine—for only twenty dollars. Any wine connoisseurs reading this might see it as blasphemous (boxed wine? seriously? no thanks), but that is why determining utility value is specific to personal tastes.

Nathalie viewed it as a value proposition. That twenty-dollar box of wine might last her a month or two. If, instead, she had bought a bottle of wine for twenty dollars, it would last her only a couple of weeks. She certainly felt the bottled wine tasted better, but it would have had to give her five times as much enjoyment as the boxed wine to be worth it. She was satisfied with how boxed wine tasted so she chose to drink that and save a ton of money.

These examples illustrate how you can examine where you spend money and cut back on things that don't provide you enough enjoyment, or utility value, for the price.

Nathalie told me that she used to be an avid skier, taking weekend trips to Vermont throughout the winter. She also enjoyed ice skating, hiking, and biking, but not quite the way she liked skiing. Then, before the boys were born, she quit skiing. The excess enjoyment of skiing compared to her other hobbies was not worth the exorbitant cost.

Making good financial decisions based on utility value

allows you to get enjoyment out of life while saving money. As we continue reading about Nathalie, try to think more about her mindset. Focus less on mimicking her literally and more about her way of thinking. Similar to Rob's career choice not being a reasonable expectation for everyone, Nathalie's money-saving strategies will also not be a good fit for everyone. Rather than focusing on specific actions Nathalie took, step back and consider her overall way of thinking and how the concept of utility value might play out in different aspects of your life.

CHAPTER NINE
THE OPPOSITE OF EASY

"If you do not change direction, you may
end up where you are heading."

— *often attributed to Lao Tzu,*
Chinese philosopher and
founder of Taoism

Fast forward a few years, and what was Nathalie the Single Mom up to? For starters, she was struggling with the constraints of her in-home nursing assistant job. In addition to dealing with inconsistent hours, she was confronted with the company's strong desire (which was also industry-wide) that she work nights and weekends. That kind of schedule was not an option for Nathalie. She didn't have relatives or friends to regularly babysit who would be both dependable and free.

Compounding all of that was the simple fact that the pay was no longer enough to support Nathalie and her boys. As kids grow, so do their costs. (I'm sorry, Mom and Dad.) And her kids were growing bigger and smarter every day. They were just hitting their eighth birthday. Now that her nursing assistant job wasn't enough to pay her bills, she knew she had to make changes.

Meanwhile, Nathalie was attempting to move to a partially

subsidized apartment complex where she could live in a two-bedroom apartment. She had applied and been waiting for several months before the federal government approved her. Two bedrooms! No more homemade partition splitting one bedroom. Moving on up!

So, Nathalie quit her job to work for a big box retailer because it offered a guaranteed forty hours per week. Even at the lower hourly pay, her weekly salary would be higher because she was working full-time. I'm the last person to judge someone for doing what they have to do to pay their bills. It's not easy to make a job change that many people might see as a "downgrade." And to work alongside high school kids as an adult really tests your mettle. Nathalie swallowed her pride and took the job because it was her best option available.

Nathalie didn't plan to work at Target long term. She understood the vulnerability of low-skilled jobs in the ever-changing economy. She liked helping people, and other than the workweek limitations, she liked her previous nursing job. She knew she wanted to return to the medical field. She had direction at least.

Nathalie also desired a better paying job and knew that it might require further training or going back to school. She had enough work experience to see that lower paying jobs tend to stay that way.

I analyzed data put out by the U.S. Census Bureau for the period 2010 to 2017 that shows a big divide between annual pay raises in various salary ranges. Imagine every job and its salary was put on a list. The bottom twenty percent would be minimum wage jobs or low paying jobs. The top twenty percent would be jobs like doctors, lawyers, and executives. It might not surprise you, but the jobs in the top twenty percent get bigger pay raises each year than the bottom twenty percent.

The chart below shows the annual income changes for the lowest twenty percent of earners, the twentieth to fortieth percentile of earners, and then the fortieth to sixtieth percentile of earners. This shows that the gap between specialized and low-skilled jobs, noted earlier, continues to increase. Nathalie wasn't thinking of becoming a doctor, but she knew that even moving up to an average paying job would mean bigger annual raises.

Figure 8. Annual Income Change Among All Levels of Earners

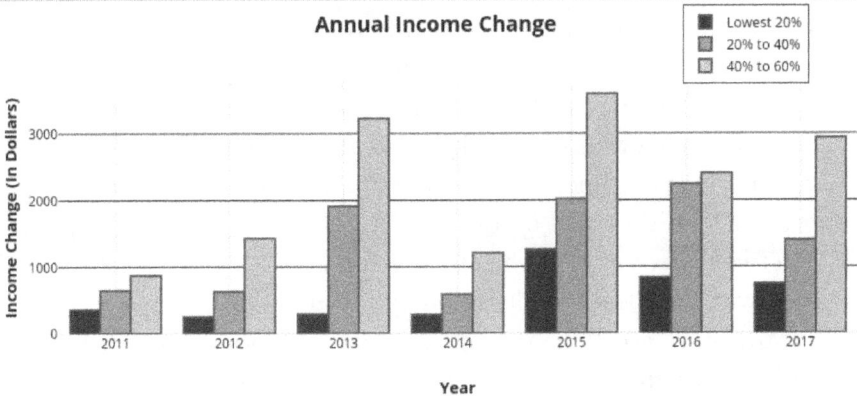

A four-year college degree was not an option for Nathalie. Too much money. Too much time. Even a two-year associate degree probably wouldn't work, for the same reasons. Quitting work to go to school full-time would mean no income at all. Dragging out school as a part-time student while working at Target for years was not appealing, either. It would take too long and still be a financial struggle. It seemed like a short vocational program that could build on her existing background made the most sense. She began looking into different training programs and short-term college programs that might enable her to find a better paying job within the medical industry.

Another aspect of Nathalie's planning for her career change was the question of what to do with her savings. She had managed to save up here and there by living within her means and it summed up to a few thousand dollars. With the steady paycheck from Target, she wasn't sure if she needed such a large emergency cash cushion.

It was during a bike ride through a state park that she casually asked if I'd help her invest the money into the stock market, though she wasn't sure she had enough money to make it worthwhile.

I explained that some savings for emergencies is a very good idea. I also explained she didn't need a lot of money to try out investing; even a portion of her savings was enough to get started. The real issue was whether or not she would need the money soon. If the money was going to pay for her education or to supplement her living within a few months, it would not be a good idea to invest in the stock market. Over long, multi-year periods of time, stocks have done well, but it is difficult to predict how they will do over short periods. If it's money you can't lose, investing in the stock market for only a few months is unwise. She was disappointed by my answer.

You may recall in the opening of this book I mentioned that money in a savings account or a CD did not yield much in the years following the '08 housing collapse. So, while she kept hoping the returns would get better, Nathalie's savings hadn't been growing very fast. She didn't have experience with investing, and had been naturally reluctant to do anything with her money other than add to her savings account. And now that she had a free resource (me) to help her get her foot in the door to investing, the timing wasn't right.

Nathalie put her attention back on what kind of training to get. She eventually settled on cardiographic technician school. Cardiographic technicians work with doctors to monitor a patient's heart on EKG machines. Beep . . . beep . . . beep. Because of her existing background, the training program was going to be four months and was defined as "full time." It was going to be difficult for her to swing financially. She used some of her excess savings, but liked keeping some for emergencies. She decided it was worth getting a small loan from a bank to cover the school costs. Despite her full-time status, she was able to keep working part-time and use the extra money to supplement where needed. Throughout her training, she did about fifteen to twenty hours a week at Target. She'd work day shifts around her class schedules and then do schoolwork in the evenings, usually after her boys went to bed.

Without living such a thrifty lifestyle, Nathalie would never have had the money to do this. Her savings gave her the flexibility and opportunity. Whatever your financial goals might be, living within your means and Saving More is a huge part of meeting your goals.

Leading up to these big decisions, Nathalie wanted to make sure she ended up with a good job. What constitutes a "good job" exactly? In 2015, Georgetown University's Center on Education and the Workforce defined a job paying 35,000 dollars per year as "good" for workers under forty-five. For workers over forty-five, the figure was 45,000 dollars.[20] The values were based on national averages. In New York City or San Francisco, 35,000 dollars isn't as good a job because of the higher cost of living. In San Francisco, thirty-five thousand bucks a year wouldn't cover the rent you pay to live in somebody's tool shed.

Georgetown also studied U.S. jobs from 1991–2015 and found that the availability of "good jobs" decreased for those

Figure 9. "Good Jobs" in 1991 Versus 2015

Change In "Good Jobs"

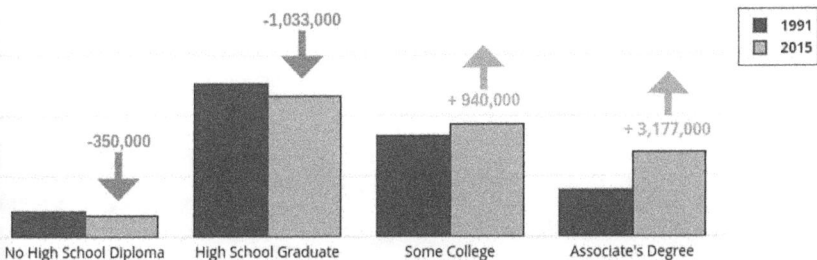

-350,000	-1,033,000	+ 940,000	+ 3,177,000
No High School Diploma	High School Graduate	Some College	Associate's Degree

Legend: ■ 1991 ▫ 2015

whose highest level of education was a high school degree or who didn't finish high school. Those with associate or four-year college degrees fared better. Figure 8 shows the data from the analysis.

Compared to 1991, there were about 2.7 million more good jobs in 2015. They required a bit more education or training but not a bachelor's degree. The number of "good jobs" for individuals with a high school diploma has gone down by over a million. For high-school dropouts, the number of good jobs has gone down by three hundred fifty thousand. All the gains in good jobs have come from people developing their skills beyond high school. Nathalie never saw this study, never talked to economists, job coaches, or high school counselors, never took a test that advised her to increase her education. She figured it out on her own. She chose to increase her skills to both make more money and increase her job security.

CHAPTER TEN
GOVERNMENT PROGRAMS
EXIST TO BE USED

"To avoid criticism, say nothing, do nothing, be nothing."

— *Elbert Hubbard, American writer and philosopher*

Besides housing support, Nathalie had also been getting assistance in the form of the SNAP program, aka food stamps, administered by the United States Department of Agriculture. She received a few hundred dollars per month. This safety net, along with more affordable housing, helped her pursue the cardiographic-tech school certification. Without this federal government aid, it's unlikely it would have been possible.

Our culture has an unfair habit of looking down on anyone who participates in the SNAP program, lives in subsidized housing, or is on welfare. There are some individuals who illegally trade their SNAP benefits for cash. There are some welfare recipients that are just plain lazy. While some people have abused the system, the fact remains that these programs do a lot of good for honest hardworking folks, too. These programs provide a safety net when people fall on hard times and they allow people in difficult situations like Nathalie's to better their lives.

You are only against yourself in this life. I'll say that again for emphasis: *You are only against yourself.* If your life is a football game, you are the only team on the scoreboard. You need to do what is in your own best interest and take care of yourself with every option and opportunity available. Don't let what other people think or the negative connotation associated with these programs prevent you from taking advantage of them. Don't let pride prevent you from saving money. Get out of your own way.

Frankly, I feel there is some misguided disdain toward people who use these programs. When homeowners use the mortgage interest tax deduction when filing their taxes, they are taking money from the federal government. Plain and simple. The same goes for people who use the child tax credit when filing their taxes. If a Fortune 500 company uses an army of accountants and finds tax loopholes and deductions to save millions of dollars, they are considered smart businessmen. If an agricultural company uses subsidies from the government, no one cares. A business that takes advantage of government subsidies or tax deductions is seen as being operated wisely, but a person on welfare is a lazy bum?

According to the U.S. Department of Agriculture's website, the total food stamp program cost 71 billion dollars for the year 2016. And about 36 billion was spent on subsidized housing in 2016 per the U.S. government budget. That compares to a cost of 70 billion for the mortgage interest tax deduction (according to the Joint Committee on Taxation).

The U.S. budget is around 3.8 trillion dollars (that's $3,800,000,000,000). What portions are food stamps, the mortgage deduction, or housing subsidies?

SNAP (Food Stamps):	1.868%
Mortgage Deduction:	1.842%
Housing Subsidies:	.94736%

Due to the scale of the country and how much money flies around, the portions of government spending which get deemed as "handouts" and rub people the wrong way are tiny slivers of the pie. Housing subsidies are less than one percent of the government's spending. If you want to increase your wealth, you need to Save More. That includes using any tax breaks, government subsidies, or government programs you qualify for.

Getting back to Nathalie the Single Mom's specific situation, she was also preparing for her sons' eighth birthday. And this year, she decided to have the party in a public park (OMG what a shock!). Her apartment was too small and messy from her recent move. Reserving or renting a venue would have cost money. Nathalie knew the perfect place in her mental Rolodex of local parks.

She chose a park with picnic tables and enormous trees that she was able to decorate with streamers. The weather was perfect, and all the kids had a wonderful time. Nathalie even lucked out when a charitable organization set up their own event nearby with ponies. They invited all the kids to come over and pet the animals, to much excitement and glee.

The simultaneous charity event at the park was dumb luck that time, but it was the kind of thing Nathalie typically kept an eye out for. She carefully checked the city websites to see what free events were being offered by parks, schools, churches, or civic organizations. She went to local libraries for readings and other library-sponsored events. Local libraries also tend to have pretty good movie rental sections—all free of charge. Parks and libraries are government funded, but they exist to be used.

Nathalie's boys were getting old enough to start figuring out they didn't always have the same privileges as other kids. They didn't have a smartphone (some eight-year-old friends had smartphones . . . yeah, I know). They weren't taking the same vacations other kids were or living in a big house with an outdoor trampoline or swimming pool.

They were also at the age where kids start to do more costly activities. Nathalie had to be careful when selecting music programs, sports leagues, and summer camps. She was able to find after-school programs and a week-long summer camp that were either cheap, free, or discounted based on family incomes (they frequented the YMCA down the street). Local recreation and parks programs for kids are commonly reduced for lower income families.

Every parent wishes they could give their child everything, and Nathalie was no different. Saying "no" was difficult for her, but she knew she couldn't compete with the level of spending of other parents. Her decisions always came back to utility value. She couldn't spend several thousand dollars on a trip to Disney World, but she could find deals on local amusement park tickets.

CHAPTER ELEVEN
NATHALIE'S SUCCESS

"Diligence is the mother of good fortune."

— *Miguel de Cervantes, Spanish writer*

Nathalie completed the vocational program to become an EKG tech, yet surprisingly, she didn't end up with an EKG tech position. She accepted a position in a medical office that not only fit her schedule of working eight to five, but it paid more than what she would have made as a technician. It might appear she wasted her time on the vocational training, but in fact it was the skills she gained from that training—and her desire to learn new skills—that made her desirable to her future employer.

Eventually, she accepted an opportunity to transfer. Having continued her voracious money-saving habits, she was able to buy a small house in Arizona. Her vocational training from years earlier cost less money than she had anticipated and it didn't take long before she was back to saving. Since her credit was good and her debt to income ratio was very good, a bank was comfortable giving her a loan for a house. Her home loan didn't require a twenty percent down payment, but she still needed thousands of dollars saved up for the down payment (which she had). Her years of hard work and savings had paid off now that she met her goal of owning a house with a low-interest rate loan and manageable monthly payments.

She got out of subsidized housing and off the SNAP food stamp program. All of her money-saving habits were vindicated by the changes she was able to make for her family. Getting all those cheap haircuts at the Paul Mitchell School by cosmetologist trainees or nights of staying in with a box of wine paid off. And now, instead of growing tomato plants on her balcony, she had room for an entire garden at her new home.

I saw the home for myself. It was probably 1,300 square feet and a couple of decades old, but it had a good sized yard and was in good condition. Everything from the kitchen to the wiring to the plumbing was fully functioning. It was perfectly livable, with plenty of potential for projects for an ambitious homeowner.

One of the reasons I've talked about Nathalie was obviously to show how powerful savings habits can be. But saving is also a very hard thing to do, especially for someone who is not making a ton of money to begin with and is saddled with the heavy responsibility of raising children. It takes a really strong person to save money when they don't have very much. Compare Nathalie to Rob, a very intelligent and bright guy who was unable to develop money-saving habits despite his high salary. If you were to judge thirty-year-old Rob the Computer Engineer and thirty-year-old Nathalie the Single Mom based on their education, salary, and responsibilities, you wouldn't guess that it was Rob who couldn't afford to purchase his own house.

The ability to save money goes against the grain of how most Americans live today. The Federal Reserve's branch in St. Louis, Missouri produced a graph (figure 10) of the U.S. savings rate over time.

The graph shows some trends. Throughout the 1960s and 1970s, Americans tended to save at least ten percent of their

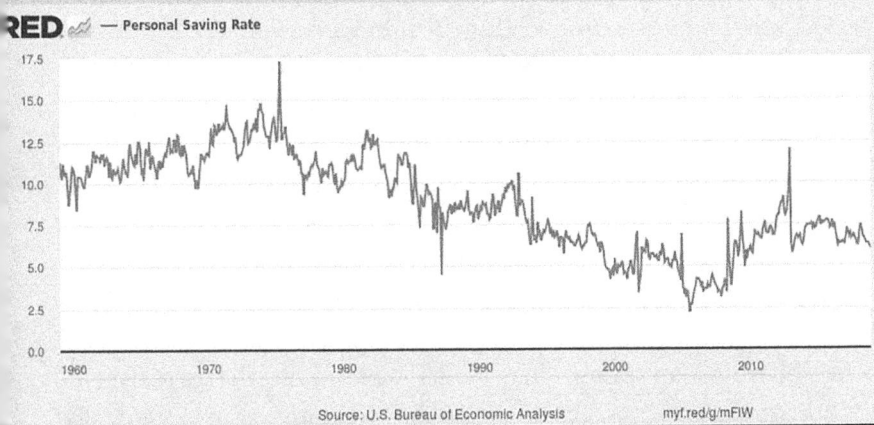

Figure 10. Personal Savings From 1960 Through Today

RED — Personal Saving Rate

Source: U.S. Bureau of Economic Analysis   myf.red/g/mFIW

income. This began to change in the early 1980s, when it started to trend lower. It bounced around a little, but stayed between 2.5 percent and 7.5 percent for most of the mid-1980s through today. The point of this is to further emphasize how hard it can be to save significant amounts of money.

It looks like a lot of Americans can take a page out of Nathalie's book. Save More is the second big cornerstone to becoming wealthy. Build the right skills and Earn More might be the first, but if you can't save any of the money you earn, you'll never be able to Invest More.

As we mentioned at the outset, studies show that almost fifty percent of Americans are living paycheck to paycheck. Even though Nathalie the Single Mom was able to be on the right side of that statistic, she had trouble figuring out what to do with her money.

When Nathalie was working at Target, she asked me what to do with her savings. She had only a savings account that she had built up little by little over several years. During those years of saving, she had seen her bank's advertisements about CDs, but with their very low interest rates, they never seemed very appealing. You usually have to lock your money in for certain time periods—for example, in a two- or five-year CD. If something happens and you need the money, you normally have to pay a fee to break out of it.

Nathalie ended up deciding it didn't make sense to put her money into a CD. As a millennial, she was starting her adult life right as the Great Recession occurred. She also vaguely remembered the tech bubble bursting in the early 2000s. Having heard stories about people losing their money, she was nervous about investing in stocks and scared to make a mistake. Like most people, she went about her life without giving very much thought to investing and always kept her money in cash or savings accounts.

There is an idiom that floats around in the investment industry that goes "cash is trash." Keeping your money as cash—sitting in a bank account or under a mattress for long periods of time—is a bad idea. There are plenty of alternatives where the money can grow faster. Like putting it into a CD, investing in stocks, buying a government savings bond, etc. It makes sense to have large amounts of cash only if you are planning to use it relatively soon—for example, if you are putting a down payment on a house in a month (or for hustling people in pool halls).

There is another reason "cash is trash" became axiomatic: inflation. We spoke a little about inflation at the end of chapter seven in relation to the cost of tuition going up over the span of a few decades. Inflation generally occurs when the price of goods and services increases over time. In 1974, a first-class U.S. postage stamp cost ten cents. In 2017, the same stamp cost forty-nine cents. This is inflation. If you have cash under your mattress, that money is actually *losing* value over time. Because inflation is increasing the cost of everything, your money will buy less in the future than it can buy today. If you put ten cents under your mattress in 1974, you still have that same ten cents in 2017, so in essence, you lost money because you can't buy a stamp anymore. If you are saving money over long periods, leaving it as cash is not a good idea.

CHAPTER TWELVE
RECAP OF NATHALIE'S STORY

"Beware of little expenses. A small leak will sink a great ship."

— *Ben Franklin*

Nathalie wasn't sure how to go about getting involved and taking part in the stock market even if she wanted to. While she had heard of stocks and bonds and mutual funds, she didn't know much about them or the mechanics of investing in them. Choosing her own investments was not something she wanted to risk doing. Nor was she even sure how to open an investment brokerage account. She didn't know if there were differences between Fidelity Investments, Vanguard, TD Ameritrade, or E*Trade. She didn't know if the small local advisors offered similar services or something else entirely. She also didn't know how much it cost to start investing. How could she be sure she wasn't getting ripped off?

The prospect of getting answers to these questions by calling investment companies or walking into a local office was daunting. It can be hard to open up about finances, which are deeply personal. And there is reluctance when people feel the amount of money they have isn't very much.

Trust is an important piece of any guidance or advice,

especially when it comes to finances. It's your hard-earned money—perhaps your life even depends on it. There are downsides and even barriers to simply giving money to someone else to manage. It can be hard to find the right financial expert to manage your money.

There is the possibility of outright fraud. Not everyone in the financial services industry is bad, but there has been a history of bad behavior and greed that always favors the finance guy or his firm while screwing the client (you). Of course, there are the mega screw-overs that make national news. Most people have heard about Bernie Madoff, Jordon Belfort (the *Wolf of Wall Street* guy), and the many big banks and mortgage companies who were putting people into home loans they couldn't pay—a scheme that led up to the Great Recession.

Smaller negative practices occur on an everyday basis. They aren't nearly as bad, but they are still taking money out of their clients' pockets to benefit the financial industry. The most common examples involve how money managers charge their clients. (Sorry, but I've yet to encounter a money manager who doesn't charge anything.) An investor's money can be used in a manner that drums up fees—making unnecessary transactions to make more money. Management fees can also vary between advisors. One may be charging too much; another may be putting clients into products that charge a lot of fees versus using a much cheaper alternative.

How do you determine what payment methodology is fair? The most common model of managed accounts (when you give someone your money and they manage an investment account for you) is fee-based on a percentage of the account value. Normal practice is that an advisor or investment manager will take around one percent per year of your total account. They'll usually take a portion of this fee on a daily or monthly basis.

Charging a percentage based on the assets is really the best way to go. Avoid anyone who manages money whose primary source of revenue is transaction fees. If they make money per transaction, that is a conflict of interest. Rather than success from the account growing, they will be inclined to trade as often as possible to generate revenue, otherwise known as "churning" the account.

Some financial advisors—these are harder to find—will charge an hourly rate, usually ranging from two hundred to six hundred dollars an hour. They will usually want to package several hours spread over a year; most won't meet with someone who is looking for only an hour of advice. Working with a financial planner who charges hourly could be a good idea if you can find one.

No matter how you break it down, when someone else is investing your money, they will need to pay themselves somehow. And because of how compounding works, reducing your investment returns by even one percent per year to pay for fees can have major consequences over time. This fact would've made Nathalie nervous. If the account didn't grow, or if it lost money, she would still have to pay fees to the financial advisor.

The industry is changing, but most money managers still have minimums for the amount of money a person needs to open an account. Where I currently work, the minimum is 500,000 dollars. Most investment advisors want to focus on big fish because they spend almost the same amount of time managing 2 million dollars as they do 200 thousand dollars, yet they make a lot more money on the 2 million dollar account. These kinds of limitations make investing through a financial advisor more difficult for the minnows like Nathalie. She would have felt self-conscious or unworthy calling or visiting asset managers, only to be rejected for not meeting the minimum investment size.

Nathalie had noticed investment professionals all had different designations or certifications. How was she supposed to know which were better than others? Would she want a financial planner, a financial advisor, or an investment advisor? Are they all the same? What's a stockbroker? What do the different letters after their name mean? Do they have to have those? What if they don't?

They all advertise that they are helpful, knowledgeable, and just what any investor needs. If you go into their office, they'll likely give you some pamphlets or packets that will put you to sleep faster than an Ambien. Nathalie is pretty bright, but had she collected literature and researched financial advisors I'm sure she would have had trouble understanding the differences between one and the next. Look at some of these financial certifications, for example:

CFA = Chartered Financial Analyst

FRM = Financial Risk Manager

CFP = Certified Financial Planner

AAMS = Accredited Asset Management Specialist

FMA = Financial Master of Arms

CIMA = Certified Investment Management Analyst

ChFC = Chartered Financial Consultant

CrFA = Certified Forensic Accountant

CFFA = Certified Forensic Financial Analyst

CIC = Chartered Investment Counselor

You get the point. They all sound the same. One of them I even made up. You wouldn't know. Did you guess the Certified Forensic Accountant (CrFA) was a fake? Then you'd be wrong. The Financial Master of Arms is the fake. Despite the bewildering designations, my advice is that a certification of some sort is probably better than none when you are looking for a financial professional to help you.

The good news is I'll show you how you won't need any of them. Once you've read this book, you'll easily be able to invest your own money and not have to pay anyone.

If only Nathalie had known how to invest on her own. If only. Let's do a quick exercise, as we did for Rob the Engineer, to prove how much money Nathalie the Single Mom could have had if only she knew how to invest on her own.

Imagine she went back in time prepared to invest. She could have invested directly in the stock market. She could have opened a brokerage account (which is free), moved money from her bank account to her brokerage account (which is also free), then bought the U.S. stock market index.

Remember, an index fund mirrors the stock market. The index fund will charge a tiny fee, but it's less than a tenth of one percent of the money she would use, and we'll therefore ignore it. The most common index for the U.S. stock market is the S&P 500, so we'll use the S&P 500 index.

Nathalie didn't make as much money as Rob, but we'll pretend she was saving $2,000 per year. Most of this money was sitting in a savings account at a local bank where it earned next to nothing. We will imagine that Nathalie's other investment choice was certificates of deposit, so we can see the difference between investing in CDs versus the S&P 500 index. Nathalie was working and saving money in 2005, which we'll use as a starting point. We will use actual, real-world returns of the S&P 500 and actual real-world returns of a two-year CD.

It is true that the risk profiles of CDs versus the stock market are very different (CDs are safer investments), but we are trying to show Nathalie's real-world options at the time. We'll also pretend her goal was to save up $20,000 for a down payment on a house. We'll calculate using both investment paths and see how far they get her to her financial goal. We will ignore taxes to keep it simple. First, if Nathalie had invested her money in the S&P 500:

Date	Value	Stocks	End Value
1/1/2005	$2,000.00	4.91%	$2,098.20
1/1/2006	$4,098.20	15.79%	$4,745.31
1/1/2007	$6,745.31	5.46%	$7,115.63
1/1/2008	$9,115.63	- 37.00%	$5,742.85
1/1/2009	$7,742.85	26.46%	$9,791.60
1/1/2010	$11,791.60	15.06%	$13,567.41
1/1/2011	$15,567.41	2.11%	$15,895.88
1/1/2012	$17,895.88	16.00%	$20,759.22

Sometime in year eight, she would have met her goal of $20,000. Next, using the Bankrate.com two-year CD rate, we can see what would have happened if Nathalie had invested in a sequence of two-year CDs for the same period. The CD rate used is the national average.

Date	Value	CD Rate	End Value
1/1/2005	$2,000.00	3.06%	$2,061.20
1/1/2006	$4,061.20	3.06%	$4,185.47
1/1/2007	$6,185.47	4.81%	$6,482.99
1/1/2008	$8,482.99	4.81%	$8,891.02
1/1/2009	$10,891.02	2.78%	$11,193.79
1/1/2010	$13,193.79	2.78%	$13,560.58
1/1/2011	$15,560.58	1.23%	$15,751.98
1/1/2012	$17,751.98	1.23%	$17,970.33

With CDs, after eight years, Nathalie is still short over $2,000. This quick example shows a few things. Nathalie could have met the $20,000 goal sooner by investing in the stock market. Remember, you have to pay a penalty to break a CD. So, if she needed the money or hit her goal of $20,000, she would not have been able to access it easily. Her stock index fund, on the other hand, can be sold at any time. You can also see how low the CDs rates became toward 2011 and 2012. Interest rates on bank savings accounts were even lower.

Halfway through the stock market example, there was a major recession. Despite the huge drop in value (-37 percent during 2008), things recovered quickly enough to still make it work out better than using CDs. In this hypothetical example, sticking to the S&P 500 plan while keeping in mind that stock market volatility is expected (including recessions), is still a superior way to make money over time.

This example shows us that when you are disciplined about saving money, you can make that money grow. Those were real-world numbers and real-world returns. Unfortunately, in real life Nathalie never ended up investing in the stock market. She felt too uninformed and discouraged and chose to keep money in her savings account, earning next to nothing. Fear of losing money is one of the greatest deterrents to investing. A great deal of this book will be dedicated to explaining how the economy works, and this will hopefully remove some of the fears you might have about investing and the risks involved.

Things still worked out nicely for Nathalie. She bought a house and is doing well. She was able to find ways to Earn More and Save More but stumbled on the Invest More part of the process. Let's recap some of the things we learned from her.

Plan ahead for meals, trips, or activities. This is a simple way to avoid unnecessary spending.

Be mindful of monthly "fixed" payouts on cable TV, Internet, phones, magazine subscriptions, gym memberships, car payments, etc.

Choose hobbies and make spending choices on things that give you good utility value. Utility value is the satisfaction you get from using a good or service.

Don't let pride prevent you from saving money or earning more money.

Use government resources where available—public parks, libraries, tax deductions, SNAP (food stamps), etc.

Here is a visual snapshot of Nathalie's financial situation:

	EARNINGS	SAVINGS	DEBT	INVESTMENT RETURNS
Rob	High	Low	High	Uninvested
Nathalie	Low	High	Low	Low

You can compare Nathalie to Rob and see how they lived very different financial lives. That takes us to your next homework assignment.

Reflect on your own spending habits. How does your spending compare to the habits Nathalie had? Think about your hobbies. Think about your planning and day-to-day expenses. Try to come up with one thing you can do to improve the amount of money you save. Write it down someplace. Write in this book if you need to. Write on your Kindle screen if this is an electronic version.

I know you probably thought about wasteful spending when you read about Rob, but when you think about Nathalie, think which of her habits you can copy. Find parallels in your life where you can take steps like those she took. Nathalie didn't need a six-figure salary to be able to accumulate money into a significant amount.

Nathalie found ways to Save More. She didn't replace clothes because they were a couple of years old or looked a little worn. But her boys never looked like homeless ragamuffins. She shopped at thrift stores and yard sales. But she went to department stores sometimes, too. She would take good care of her possessions and try to fix something before purchasing a replacement. But she had no qualms about spending money on what she perceived as good utility value. Nathalie had built an immunity from the constant bombardment of marketing and societal pressures of consumerism. And still she was able to take excellent care of herself and her children.

Now we'll take a look at someone who had a passion for investing: Mike the Car Guy.

CHAPTER THIRTEEN
MIKE THE CAR GUY'S
PRACTICAL CHOICES

"Talent is only the starting point."

— *Irving Berlin, American composer and songwriter*

Finally, we get to Mike, someone I met in a college investment club—a gathering where students worked together to invest money. A tiny sliver from the college's endowment fund was available to this student organization to invest. A professor supervised the group to make sure we didn't blow the money in some risky biopharmaceutical company or on oil drilling rights in the Indian Ocean.

The club was made up mostly of finance students, but others were welcome to join. Most members fell under some type of business major. Only a few students didn't. As an engineering student, Mike stood out as one of the non-business students.

While we are talking about investment clubs, it's worth pointing out they aren't only for college students. There are many community investment clubs across the country open to anyone who wants to learn about investing and enjoys social gatherings. If you hear Mike's story and get interested, Google local investment clubs in your area. Check out organizations like the NAIC (National Association of Investors Corporation).

The best way to characterize Mike is that he is a combination of Rob the Computer Engineer and Nathalie the Single Mom. Mike is easily one of the smartest and most resourceful people I've ever met. For example, he liked to embark on "do-it-yourself" projects that could save money. In college, he built a custom bed frame, mostly using two-by-fours from Home Depot. When he was done, most people thought it was something he had purchased—the quality was that good.

Like Rob, Mike elected to stay in college for five years, but with one major difference. It occurred to him that by taking the right courses, he could stay one additional year and earn a master's degree along with a second engineering bachelor's degree. Where Rob took five years to earn one degree, in those five years Mike earned a master's in mechanical engineering and a bachelor's in electrical engineering. This is a great example of utility value. It costs 100,000 dollars to earn one degree, but 125,000 dollars can get you one master's degree and an additional degree—that's not a bad deal.

That type of rational decision making was easy for Mike. He probably could have gone to college anywhere, but instead he chose an in-state school to take advantage of the "local" tuition rates. We covered this in chapter one when we discussed Rob's choice to pay out-of-state rates. Both Rob and Mike knew how much skills and education matter. Mike made the conscious decision to get these skills at the best possible value.

Mike knew he wanted to pay a low price to build skills that could earn him a high salary. Going to a boutique private school for 40,000 dollars per year when a public state school would be half that amount didn't make sense. He also didn't want to pay a lot of money for a degree that would lead to a low-paying job.

In July of 2015, CNBC published a news story called "Do Public Colleges Offer the Best Return on Investment?" CNBC reported the average cost of private college tuition and fees was three times the average cost of public four-year universities.[21]

Return on investment (ROI) is a calculation of the money you get back in wages versus the cost you paid for your education. PayScale, the online salary profile database, suggests the ROI for public universities is indeed higher than it is for private colleges. Using for their calculation the first twenty years of wages after earning the degree, PayScale showed that ROI averaged thirteen percent more for public university educations. The costs for a college degree are rising faster at private colleges compared to public universities. This has led PayScale to forecast that the ROI gets even worse for private colleges in the future. They estimate that by 2025 public universities will have a twenty four percent higher return on investment.

This practical money mentality used in determining education choices spilled over into other parts of Mike's life. It can be difficult to judge a college student by their spending habits because just about everyone is poor. From what I could tell, he didn't chase expensive fashion trends or spend money frivolously. He bought a lot of things secondhand, like golf clubs and furniture, rather than brand new.

He once purchased a wrecked pickup truck and fixed it. The truck had been in an accident and was considered "totaled." He purchased it for next to nothing and rebuilt the whole thing. It was near new when he was done with it. He had grown up in a mechanic's garage and knew his way around automobiles. He certainly wasn't lazy and didn't shy away from ambitious projects. His level of automobile expertise also led to saving money on maintenance costs. It won't knock your socks off, but stuff like oil changes, tire rotations, and tune-ups saved him money on a regular basis.

Even though he didn't have a background in finance and hadn't taken the same accounting and investment courses as most everyone else in the investment club, he more than made up for it with his intelligence and critical thinking skills. He had similar self-confidence and charisma as Rob. Instead of purchasing things that he would pay for in the future, though, Mike spent college looking for investment strategies to prepare to use the money he earned in the future.

The college student investment club was made up of investment novices. None of us had much prior experience investing. There weren't really rules, but students were encouraged to focus their investments on large, well-known U.S. companies. Students could invest in stocks or bonds, but the main focus was on stocks.

The members of the club would look at prospective companies by examining the financial statements these companies released (as all U.S. publicly traded companies are required to do). Members would make presentations explaining what they liked about a company and why it was worth their investment, or, vice versa, to sell.

The presentations from students were to persuade the group's members to agree with an investment course of action. More often than not, students would advocate buying stock of a company they personally liked and then cherry-pick positive numbers about the company as reasons to buy it after the fact. It was a little like putting the cart before the horse. An example would be a student who eats at Chipotle a lot and likes Chipotle burritos so he would propose the club should buy stock in the company. The student would then look at the company's income statements and balance sheets and then pick good numbers, but ignore any red flags.

Everyone in the club would vote on each proposal. The process was intended to give students a taste of investing rather than to really make money for the university. There were no consequences or rewards for the performance of the investments. Most members in the club didn't know what they were doing and ultimately approached investing like playing darts.

As you can probably already guess, Mike was the guy who

did everything right. He made the right choices to Earn More. He was already thinking about utility value and ways to Save More. He even chose to begin learning how to Invest More. We will go through some of the things Mike learned and some of the ways he thought like an investor when making decisions about money.

CHAPTER FOURTEEN
INTRODUCTION TO INVESTMENTS

"When I read about the evils of drinking, I gave up reading."

— *Henny Youngman, violinist and comedian*

Mike (and every other member) of the investment club learned firsthand that picking investments was difficult and there wasn't a magic rule or formula for success. It's like going to a self-serve frozen yogurt shop for the first time. There are a dozen different yogurt flavors and twenty or so toppings you can add to the yogurt. There are a million combinations at your disposal, and everyone has their own preferences. It's the same with stocks. Investors will look at countless options and have to decide among myriad stock combinations. Except for kiwi. Who puts kiwi on their frozen yogurt? I've never seen it. The frozen yogurt topping kiwi is the Sears stock of the investment world. Nobody wants it.

One of the lessons the members of the club had to learn about was which sources of investment recommendations could be trusted. Students would watch *Mad Money*, Jim Cramer's show on CNBC, or read articles from Suze Orman. It's tempting to follow advice from business world celebrities or even wealthy individuals. It's easy to fall into the trap of assuming because they are wealthy or on TV, they must have brilliant stock picking recommendations. If you follow their recommendation to buy something, make sure you keep track when they sell it too. You might buy stock in Apple because Warren Buffet bought it, but are you going to track when he sells it, too?

You should also consider how the person attained their wealth. Warren Buffet is known as a world-famous investor. He made his fortune more or less investing in the stock market so he is someone whose advice is likely pretty good, and you can trust.

I would exercise caution with some of the other often quoted investment gurus before following their advice. Suze Orman is a financial and business personality who has written several books, contributed to magazines, and had her own TV show for many years. When I look at her bio though, I'd guess most of her wealth has come from her successful writing and television career more than generating wealth from her own investing. While incredibly accomplished, her career in financial services doesn't appear to have a lot of in-depth stock or bond analysis. I would hesitate before following her specific advice on which assets to buy or not buy.

Jim Cramer, host of CNBC's *Mad Money*, is a famed stock picker known for his entertaining show and high intelligence. Mr. Cramer became a millionaire by running a successful hedge fund. His show is meant to be entertaining. He gives some prepared stock recommendations, but sometimes callers give him the name of a stock and he has to instantly make a buy or sell recommendation. It's hard for anyone to be very accurate with that format. Mr. Cramer himself says that he considers "mad money" to be money to invest speculatively and not for retirement. That is an admission of the risk of his stock recommendations.

Billionaire and owner of the Dallas Mavericks, Mark Cuban,

is another famous personality who expresses his opinion about certain companies. The children of Sam Walton, who inherited the Wal-Mart fortune, are also all billionaires. They didn't make their money in the stock market, so are they really experts on how to invest? My point: Don't automatically equate wealth with good investment advice. I've seen people follow terrible advice from a wealthy person. Their defense was always, "Well, they're a millionaire."

Take a minute and think about how a wealthy individual got their money. Was it from investing? Also listen to their explanation about why the investment makes sense and who the advice makes sense for. If you catch a sound bite and not the details, you might be making a mistake. If you end up deciding to buy a certain stock because you want to follow the advice of a famous person, put a portion of your money into it. Don't bet the farm on that one investment.

As Mike was diving into investing, he had to learn about the different investments available. Later in this book, I'll outline exactly which investments you will want to make and specifically how to do it. I'll also explain WHY I advise specific investments, which will help you make decisions for your personal finances.

We'll begin by looking at different investment classifications and what they are made up of.

When you think of food, there are many types you can choose to eat. It's the same with investing. In the same way food is classified into groups like vegetables, dairy, and grains, the investment universe is grouped in different ways to help classify types of investments. We'll look at the two main categories, starting with stocks.

Stocks

Mike's college investment club had the ability to invest in stocks. Another name for stocks is equity. When a person buys stock in a company, they are purchasing equity in it—in essence, a small portion of it. Usually a very small portion. For example, Microsoft's stock total worth is about 635 billion at the time of this writing. One piece or "share" of Microsoft stock is about eighty dollars. If you pay eighty dollars, you own part of that 635 billion value of the total company. Because the stock represents a partial ownership in the company, the value will go up if the company is successful and more profitable. If the company is less profitable, the stock value declines.

The price of a stock can be volatile, because stock owners tend to benefit the most from that company's upside but have the highest risk on the downside. This means they take good news very well and bad news very poorly, resulting in large stock price swings. If a company goes bankrupt, all the debts get paid first and debt holders have the first claim on the company's assets (property, equipment, etc.). After all the debts are paid, then stockholders get what is left (if anything). They usually end up with very little if a company goes out of business.

If a company is profitable, they may give money to stockholders. The company can pay dividends, which is simply paying cash to stockholders, or the management running a company may buy back shares of company stock from people who want to sell. Buybacks remove shares of stock from circulation. Fewer shares of stock in circulation reduces the total supply, ultimately driving up the price of the remaining available stocks. These are two ways stock owners can benefit from the success of the stocks.

You've probably heard people ask, "How's the stock market doing?" As I have mentioned, a category of stocks is measured using an index, which is a collection of assets with similar characteristics. Looking at one stock won't tell you how the entire stock market is doing, but looking at an index will. Illustrating this in a table will make it easier to understand. Here are some common index names and the type of stocks included within the index. You should be familiar with the first one.

Index Name	What it Measures
S&P 500	500 of the largest U.S. companies
Dow Jones Industrial Average	30 large U.S. companies
FTSE MIB	40 large Italian companies
MSCI World	Index of 1,600+ stocks from various countries around the world
Nikkei 225	Stocks of Japan's Tokyo Stock Exchange
DAX	30 large German companies

Most U.S. investment managers prefer the S&P 500 to gauge how the U.S. market is performing. In Mike's investment club, any stocks the club chose to buy would be measured against the S&P 500. Remember, Mike and the club members can invest directly in the market by buying an index. Therefore, their objective is to find stocks that will perform better than the index. There are standard indices for most countries. My focus has been on stocks and stock indices so far, but there are other asset classes we need to talk about. Stocks tend to be the "loudest" because of their volatility and the media's focus on them.

The U.S. stock market (S&P 500) has had an average return of 11.32 percent in the post World War II era. That's from 1946 to 2017.

Next, we'll look at another big category of investments—fixed income.

Fixed Income

Mike's investment club also had the ability to invest in bonds, another big category of investment assets (also known as fixed income). As the name suggests, these investments normally

113

have predictable, agreed-upon payouts. Think of a car payment or cell phone bill, except you are the one getting the monthly payment. A buyer of fixed income is actually lending an entity money. An example is a U.S. Savings Bond. When the U.S. government spends more money than it takes in, it has to borrow money for the difference. It does this by issuing bonds. If you buy a U.S. Treasury Bond or a U.S. Savings Bond, you are lending the United States government money.

It works the same way with a corporate bond. The Microsoft Corporation has stock you can buy, but they also offer bonds. If you buy a Microsoft bond, you are lending them money for a fixed period of time.

Fixed income instruments are favored by risk-averse people. Government bonds are backed by the government itself. If there is a bankruptcy, corporate bondholders are paid before stockholders. CDs at a bank, another form of fixed income, are insured by the FDIC. You can see how these types of fixed income are lower risk and generally considered safer.

However, fixed income, while safer, is not without risk. Bond values can fluctuate over time (depending on a host of factors we won't get into right now) and the value of a bond in a year could be less than it is today. Bonds are also only as sound as the underlying entity. For example, if a corporation or municipality runs into financial difficulties and has to default on its bond payments, bond investors could lose money.

There are fixed income indices just as there are equity (stock) indices, though they aren't as well known as the S&P 500 or Dow Jones Industrials. The main one is Barclay's Aggregate Bond Index, which represents the general bond universe. It is made of government treasury bonds, corporate bonds, and mortgage backed bonds (bonds that are made up of mortgage loans all combined together).

Let's look at performance now. The Barclay's Aggregate Bond Index data doesn't go back as far as the S&P 500 data. However, from February 1976 to November 2017, the annual return of this bond index was 7.43 percent.

Stocks Versus Bonds

Let's examine the difference between stocks and bonds. We know the average returns are 11.32 percent for stocks and 7.43 percent for bonds. The penalty for the higher stock returns is more volatility and stress for the investor. The cost of the additional safety fixed income provides is lower returns. The ever-changing earnings and growth prospects of a company can cause the stock price to really move around, like a cat chasing a laser pointer. Bonds, on the other hand, due to their fixed payouts, tend to have steadier prices. Someone young, like Mike, has a long time horizon that can withstand the ups and downs that stocks might have over shorter periods. Naturally, he was more interested in the stock category of investing.

Let's look at the ten-year returns for stocks and bonds from 2007 to 2017. We'll use the S&P 500 for stocks and the Barclay's Aggregate Bond Index for the bonds.

Year	Stocks	Bonds
2007	5.49%	6.97%
2008	-37.00%	5.24%
2009	26.46%	5.93%
2010	15.06%	6.54%
2011	2.11%	7.84%
2012	16.00%	4.22%
2013	32.39%	-2.02%
2014	13.69%	5.88%
2015	1.38%	.55%
2016	11.96%	2.65%
2017	20.49%	3.54%

As you can see, the returns from stocks vary a lot more than bonds. Look at 2008 again for stocks. That is a whopping -37 percent annual return! The worst drop bonds endured was in 2013 for -2.02 percent. That's a kiss on the cheek compared to the two-by-four across the face for the stock market in 2008. For the math nerds out there: In the post WWII period, bonds had a standard deviation of about 11.79 versus the standard deviation of stocks, 17.25. Standard deviation is a statistical term that measures the variation in a set of numbers. The higher the number the greater the variation. In this case, the higher standard deviation tells us what we already knew, which is that stock returns are more volatile year to year.

Learning about indices is a little dry, I know that. If somebody makes a movie of Mike's life, they'll leave out the part about his college investment club. Mike had attained skills he thought would lead to a well-paying job (Earn More—check). He also had a propensity to save money (Save More—check). He had begun learning to invest (Invest More—working on it). Will it work out for him? Well…yeah it will. By now you probably know I wouldn't have written about him if it hadn't.

CHAPTER FIFTEEN
MIKE'S LIFESTYLE

"One must be one's own inspiration."

— Tegla Loroupe, Kenyan long-distance runner and global spokesperson for women's rights

Mike the Car Guy connected with me again several years after college. When I moved to the city where he lived, we decided to get an apartment together. As you might be guessing, things went quite differently with Mike than with Rob the Engineer.

Mike had taken a job right out of college and had stayed with that same job. The salary he earned a few years out of college was similar to Rob's—somewhere around 75,000 dollars per year. This was incredible take-home pay for someone his age—easily putting him in the top ten percent of earners for his age.

It was a surprise to hear that even with the high salary Mike had been making since college, he had yet to buy a house and had rarely even leased an apartment. The city we were in had a fairly high cost of living, and Mike had therefore chosen to rent rooms from friends or relatives for most of the five to six years after college. He gave up a little privacy renting a room out of someone else's house, but certainly saved hundreds of

EARN MORE. SAVE MORE. INVEST MORE.

dollars per month.

Mike was unmarried and didn't have any children. He had a money-saving mentality that was similar to Nathalie's in some ways, just not quite as restrictive. He would look for ways to save money, but didn't live a Spartan existence. He would spend money on hobbies, travel, and entertainment.

When we were settling into our apartment, he advocated for not having cable TV. He cooked most meals at home, usually making big meals with several days of leftovers. He came up with ways for us to share meals and cooking supplies that resulted in both of us saving money. He didn't have coupon-o-phobia as Rob did. Mike would set aside coupons we received in the mail and used them where he could.

Mike was also not an impulse buyer. Things would never just "catch his eye" that he had to purchase on the spot. When it came to items like clothing, accessories, or electronic gadgets, he tended to have a mix of some nicer stuff for special occasions, but he wasn't brand obsessed. He was usually one or two iPhone models behind the current version.

He had a variety of hobbies. He joined local run clubs or played in noncompetitive amateur sports leagues. Mike would join volleyball or kickball leagues that normally play once or twice a week and then meet up at a bar to consume the liquid calories they'd just burned off.

Some of his other hobbies included hiking or camping (in a tent). He would also work out in a gym from time to time, but he didn't pay for a membership because he had access to a free gym through his work. Mike considered utility value when determining hobbies or activities. Traveling was one area he found worth the money.

Mike did a ton of traveling, more than most of the twenty-somethings I knew. He had been to Europe several times, Canada many times, to Mexico, and he traveled all over the U.S. pretty often. He would take a trip of some sort usually every few months. This was easily his biggest discretionary expense.

He had given up other hobbies like golf and skiing because he felt they weren't worth it, but for him, travel was worth the cost. Spending a thousand dollars on a weekend trip to Austin was a much better value than golfing ten times at a local golf course (which might cost about a hundred dollars per time).

When he did choose to spend money, it was usually on experiences rather than material goods—along with travel, he attended concerts and festivals and socialized in bars and restaurants. He rarely spent money on kitchen appliances, electronic gadgets, or even furniture. He was satisfied with plain, often secondhand stuff that was functional. The apartment didn't have a lot of style. It was filled with an eclectic collection of non-matching items. Interior design or feng shui were not at the top of the list. They weren't even on the list.

From Rob's story, we learned how earning more income is important in order to increase money for investments. With a goal of generating additional income, Mike considered working a part-time job. Rather than working as a bartender, driving for Uber, or waiting tables, he figured out a way to make money based on one of his interests. He used his auto mechanic background to move classic cars. He leveraged existing *skills* he had. We saw in chapter two how skilled labor will earn you more than unskilled labor. That also applies to part-time jobs.

Mike would go to car shows and car auctions. He would scour the Internet and look through car magazines to find cars at a good value. Every transaction was different. Some cars needed proper paperwork to verify their rarity, while others needed new parts or significant repairs. His ultimate objective with all the cars was to sell the vehicle at a higher price than he paid for it. A major key to his success was knowing exactly where and how to transact the vehicles.

Car auctions were one of the reasons Mike was so well-traveled. Every car transaction was unique. Sometimes he would buy a car only to relist it elsewhere and sell it within a month. He would pocket a few hundred dollars and move on.

In other instances, it might be a several-month process, during which he would order parts, make repairs, and hold the car for a specific auction. Most of the time he would make money, but not always. He would lose five percent in one transaction and perhaps two percent in another. Two percent is still a couple of hundred bucks when you are talking about a ten-thousand-dollar car. But more often than not, he would make money. After trying it out and having some fun, Mike estimated he could grow money at the rate of roughly fifteen percent per year with this venture. He figured that due to investing more money in his cars, the rate of return wouldn't fluctuate. He could buy more expensive cars or try listing more than one car for sale at a time but still taking the same ten to twenty hours per month he currently spent.

As he started to make money and get the hang of it, he slowly went to cars that cost a little more, between fifteen and twenty thousand. Then he moved on to having two cars simultaneously, sometimes a cheaper and more expensive one. The total value of the cars slowly grew over time, while Mike gave his car hobby the same ten to twenty hours per month he had before. Ironically, Mike found more success and enjoyment when investing in cars (something he had a passion for) than when he invested in the stock market during his investment club days.

Since he had established such good habits of saving money while at the same time maximizing his earnings, Mike had quite a bit of money to buy and sell cars. By the time we were roommates, he had built up to having several cars at the same time. He might have two or three that were ready to sell. One or two that he was working on. A couple that he was saving for a specific auction or to sell at a certain month of the year.

Since this was a part-time hobby, Mike decided managing five or six cars at one time was plenty. He didn't want to become a car dealership. With that five or six car limit, he grew his investments by increasing the value of the individual cars. Classic cars are highly valuable. They often sell for six figures at car auctions such as the Meccum auctions, which are televised. Mike bought and sold cars at events such as those.

Even back in college when Mike was learning about stocks and bonds, he was also learning to think like an investor. After several years of working a standard nine to five job, it became clear to him that compounding money had more potential than earning the same paycheck week after week. Mike was tired of working for annual raises of three percent. That wasn't nearly as much as some of the double-digit increases he knew were possible from investing.

One lesson we can learn from Mike is to invest in what you are comfortable with. Just because he had some money and wanted to invest didn't mean he couldn't be selective. During the period he and I were roommates, some friends wanted to purchase a small apartment building and were trying to pool together investors. Mike wanted nothing to do with an investment like that. He knew that wasn't in his wheelhouse. Perhaps if he had a background as a plumber, electrician, or carpenter he would have been more interested. He had urged this group of friends to try self-storage units or commercial garages instead of apartments. He would be interested in that type of real estate because he knew more about it. He occasionally stored cars in self-storage units and had spent time and done business in larger storage commercial garages. Mike had done well investing in things he was familiar with, so why would he change?

No matter how expensive or amazing his cars got, you'd never know it by the way Mike continued to drive his Toyota Camry around. Yup, he rarely drove his awesome cars just for fun. He would have a pristine 1969 Camaro sitting in storage while driving around his Camry. Sounds crazy, right? Most of the cars in storage, however, he was gearing up to sell (or already had them listed), and he didn't want to chance anything happening to them.

CHAPTER SIXTEEN
HOUSING: RENTING VERSUS BUYING

"A diamond is a piece of coal that stuck to the job."

— *Thomas Edison, inventor*

As Mike's roommate, I was curious why, even though he could afford it, he hadn't purchased a house and had been renting rooms for the previous few years.

Mike felt a house wasn't automatically an asset. For starters, it didn't generate an income stream. Houses cost money over time, due to maintenance or improvements.

Mike was well aware of the benefit to a homeowner of building equity (ownership) over time. He knew that paying rent did not offer any return or growth on the outgoing money. Many people view paying rent as the equivalent to throwing money out the window. He also knew you might make money when you sell a house if the value has appreciated, but until then, you are still paying out while you live there. An increase in property value doesn't give the homeowner any extra income and might actually increase your expenses if it causes your taxes to go up. Let's explore Mike's way of thinking about buying property a bit more.

Remember that debt payments can take away from the total cash you have available to invest. He was the first person to explain this to me mathematically. Let's walk through a math problem that will show you what I mean. I could feel you cringe when I said "math problem." Relax. It'll be about a third-grade difficulty level.

Mike broke down the cost of renting an apartment or buying a house into three categories, which we'll name definitive costs, optional benefits, and what I'll call X factors. Bear with me, it'll make sense once we get going. For our example, let's use the prospect of renting a condominium versus buying one. Luckily, the numbers are easy to find, because Mike was in this exact situation. We rented from a giant condo complex with hundreds of units. Although we were renting, there were plenty of units in the complex for sale that were identical to ours.

Definitive Costs

Definitive costs are clear-cut expenses that are known ahead of time and easy to define. We paid a total of 1,500 dollars per month. We paid for a few things like electricity, Internet, and rental insurance. Those would all cost the same whether we were renting or buying. Our rent covered utilities, trash removal, heating, indoor and outdoor maintenance, lawn care, snow removal, etc. Typical, right? Here is an exact breakdown of the definitive costs of renting at the time:

	Monthly	Yearly
Rent	1,500.00	18,000.00
Electricity (approx.)	75.00	900.00
Internet	75.00	900.00
Rental Insurance	12.00	144.00
Total:	1,662.00	19,944.00

We'll now compare this to the definitive costs of buying a condo. There are a couple of additional steps to figure this out for a potential property purchase. We knew at the time that the condos were selling for around 190,000 dollars. The mortgage loan interest rate and the amount of money put down can really change the costs. In our example, we'll say it would have been a three percent down payment with a mortgage interest rate of five percent on a thirty-year fixed mortgage.

Buying a condo has some additional fees. The mortgage payment will normally include property taxes and any property mortgage insurance (typical if you put less than twenty percent down; our figures will include those). At the time, our community had above average property tax rates of 1.79 percent. There was also a condo (or association) fee. This covered maintenance for the exterior of the building and grounds, trash removal, snow removal, water and sewer, and heating. It also included insurance on the building (but did not cover anything on the interior of the individual units). Because heating was included and the grounds had tennis courts and swimming pools, the condo fees were above average. In the case of this prospective condo, it was 400 dollars per month.

Homeowners also need to expect a reasonable amount of maintenance or repairs. The information on HGTV.com (yes, the HGTV channel is so great! I know!) advises to set aside one to three percent of the purchase price each year for maintenance on any real estate.[22] We'll say a condo is at the lower end, at one percent.

We now have enough information to figure out the definitive costs (finally!). The website mortgagecalculator.org can help with the detailed calculations for the mortgage payment. Remember, the mortgage includes private mortgage insurance (PMI) and property taxes (which are $283.42 per month):

	Monthly	Annual
Mortgage	1,349.57	16,194.84
Electricity (approx.)	75.00	900.00
Internet	75.00	900.00
Condo/Association Fees	400.00	4,800.00
1% toward Maintenance	158.33	1,900.00
Interior Condo Insurance	12.00	144.00
Total:	2,069.90	24,838.80

The bottom line: So far, the apartment has lower definitive costs. To recap, renting was 19,944 dollars for the first year. Buying was 24,838 dollars. This shouldn't be a surprise, right? Conventional wisdom is that buyers are partially paying off their loan each month (building equity in the home), so they will be better in the long run. We'll see if that works out in this case.

If Mike had been looking at a single-family home, several things would have been different. There would not be a condo fee. There might be an association or gated community fee, but it would probably be lower. The allocation toward maintenance costs would probably be higher than the one percent we used. Any upfront spending would need to be factored in (to buy lawnmowers, snow blowers, shovels, rakes, tools, etc.). The mortgage would probably require homeowner's insurance. All those sorts of things can be done in a calculation similar to the one we used for the condo. They would all be definitive costs of owning a home.

Optional Benefits

Now let's move on to the next, and harder to define, optional benefits. These benefits are in a gray area and usually depend on personal circumstances. Mike wanted to dedicate money toward investing rather than purchasing a home. Specifically, he wanted to use the money to invest in buying, upgrading, and selling cars.

He thought he could grow his money by about fifteen percent per year buying and selling classic cars. Whatever down payment Mike would make and whatever extra expense he had for a house meant money that he wasn't growing through buying and selling cars.

We have the brain power to calculate this effect. Let's consider the money made from investing an optional benefit of renting. We know the down payment would be $5,700 (three percent of

$190,000). We saw that the annual definitive costs of renting were cheaper than buying. Renting saved about $4,894.80 per year. If you add the down payment to those savings, you get $10,594.80 that can be used to invest if you are a renter.

We're going to turn all the savings into optional benefits.

Investing saved money ($10,594.80 x 15%) = $1,589.22

Did you follow that? The money not spent on the home purchase and saved on the cheaper cost of renting was used to invest where it could grow at Mike's estimated fifteen percent growth rate. Year after year, if he continued to invest, then this figure would grow and grow through compounding. Each year he would save $4,894.80 by renting. He could keep adding that to his growing investment pool.

Besides the optional benefit of investing the saved money, there is another significant benefit that we can't easily quantify. Renters have reduced risk because they aren't on the hook for a big bank loan. If an uninsured event happens and the property is heavily damaged, an owner is much worse off than a renter. Other downside risks could include nearby factories shutting down and the value of the property plummeting as a result. It's hard to quantify this reduced risk, but renters benefit from having less skin in the game.

You might be thinking I'm sounding pretty one sided. So far, it looks like the advantage to renting is winning the argument. Not so fast. Let's look at what benefits homeowners get that renters do not. We know homeowners build equity. That takes us to factoring the optional benefits for homeowners into this equation.

Homeowners pay off their loan over time with every mortgage payment they make. A portion of each mortgage payment reduces the amount of principal left on the loan. The rest of the mortgage payment is interest for the bank, possibly property taxes, home insurance, or private mortgage insurance. Mortgages are designed so that the portion of the mortgage payment that is actually paying off the loan starts off small and grows over time.

Using our example, the $190,000 purchase price had payments of $1,349.57 on the loan with a 3 percent down payment. The first few years of the mortgage payment works out to be about $2,719 of actual loan payoff per year. See what I'm driving at? Each payment you make in the early part of the mortgage loan is mostly interest and taxes, so the rate at which you actually pay off the principal in the loan (build equity) is very slow at first.

To look at it another way, if you are fifteen years into a thirty-year mortgage, you might think that since fifteen years is halfway through, you have paid off half the loan. Nope. You don't pay off an equal amount of the loan each year. The point I'm trying to make is that homeowners certainly benefit from building equity in the house, but not so much in the beginning.

Homeowners get the benefit of tax deductions. Home property taxes and the interest paid on mortgage loans are both tax deductible. There is no guarantee these deductions will last forever, but they are here now.

I don't want to get into a deep tax discussion (a math problem about tax issues—you'd just stop reading and throw this book in the trash). What your tax rate is and how many other deductions you have determines how useful these deductions are. For the sake of this argument, we are going to use a twenty-five percent tax rate and give homeowners the full benefit of the deductions.

Annual property taxes are $3,401.04. If you've managed to follow me so far, we are finally getting to quantify the optional benefits for a homeowner:

Loan Paid Off in Year 1	2,719.00
Property Tax Deduction	850.26 (3,401.04 x 25%)
Mortgage Interest Deduction	<u>2,288.25</u> (9,153x25%)
Total:	5,857.51

See? Owning has some benefits too! $5,857.51! Compare this to the renter's $1,589.22!

X Factors

Lastly, we'll get into what Mike called his X factors. These are situational factors that weighed on his decision. The first one is the intended length of stay. If you plan to stay somewhere for only a few years, it's probably more convenient to rent. Perhaps you are still learning about a new area and want to get the lay of the land before buying. If you expect a big promotion at work, maybe you want to wait until you know what you'll be earning before buying a home. Whatever your reasons, the length of time you plan to live in the house must be factored in. Remember, you don't build very much equity in the property the first few years.

The next factor is the additional work that comes from owning property. What's the price of laziness? How do you want to spend the spare time that you have? The additional maintenance and chores are something to consider.

The ability to come up with a down payment can matter too. If you simply have no money for a down payment, your decision is made for you. How easy is it for you to come up with the money? Will you have any left over for emergency funds? To come up with the money, do you need to borrow from friends, rob a bank, cash out your 401k?

Existing debt and lines of credit can limit your ability to come up with the down payment. Mike didn't have any debt, but if you have high interest credit card loans or high interest car loans, perhaps it's better to pay down debt instead of purchasing a house and increasing debt even more.

Or the reverse could be true. What if you plan to open a business or go back to college? Perhaps you want to refinance other loans you have. Housing debt will show up on credit checks and might make it harder to do those things. At the time

Mike was running his classic car business, he was considering purchasing a storage garage. If he had bought a house, it would have affected his ability to purchase a garage for storage.

The last X factor is the increase or decrease in property value. Of course, everyone purchases property hoping or thinking the value will increase over time. The reason this is considered an X factor is that the increase in value is both hard to predict and hard to get access to while you are living there. If you live in a house that increases in value by ten percent, that doesn't affect your income or the payments you make on your mortgage. If you sell the house or get a home equity loan, you can take advantage of that price increase in the property value, but it doesn't factor into the yearly costs very clearly. It's best to consider it on its own and not as a guaranteed part of the equation. The change in home values is also VERY location specific. Local economies play a big role in the changing values over time, so it's hard to rely on certain growth rates.

I listed some X factors that weighed on Mike's decision making. Basically, any outside factors that can't be easily quantified fall into that category. They can tip the scale if they are important to you.

Let's put it all together now. If the definitive costs and optional benefits of renting are greater than the definitive costs, optional benefits, and value of X factors for purchasing, then renting makes more sense. We'll summarize the annual figures from the example Mike was going through at the time. We'll take the costs and subtract the benefits to find the true costs. The cost is higher to buy versus rent in Mike's case.

	Rent	Buy (3% Down Payment)
Definitive Costs:	19,944.00	24,838.80
Optional Benefits:	1,589.22	5,857.51
Total:	18,354.78	18,981.29

You probably noticed a three percent down payment isn't very much. Even if we substitute for a loan with a twenty percent down payment and a slightly lower interest rate of 4.5 percent (due to the bigger down payment), it doesn't change the end result. There are no longer private mortgage insurance fees for the buyer to pay, and in that case, the monthly mortgage payment is reduced for the home buyer, but the flip side is that the down payment of $38,000 decreases the optional benefits for the buyer because they cannot invest that down payment.

It's a case-by-case basis, but in this example, the advantages to renting outweigh buying even if the numbers are run with a twenty percent down payment. This is where the X factors come into play. At that time in Mike's life, renting made the most sense. Had he planned on staying in the property for thirty plus years and figured the house's value would increase over time, that might have tipped the scales toward buying.

By now I'm sure you are sick of this example or have zoned out completely. The decision to buy a home versus rent is one that nearly everyone will have to make at certain points in their life. Refer back to this book when it's time for you to make that decision and try to calculate the definitive costs, optional benefits, and X factors according to your personal life circumstances.

CHAPTER SEVENTEEN
RECAP OF MIKE

"Where there is an open mind, there will always be a frontier."

— *Charles Kettering, American inventor and engineer*

After our brief stint as roommates, Mike the Car Guy and I kept in touch. The years that followed were crazy busy for him. It was one big life event after another. During his traveling for car auctions, he met someone special.

She lived hours away—by plane. They decided to try to make it work. At the time, Mike still had his engineering job during the week and was still doing his car thing nights and weekends. He lived frugally at home, but jetsetted all over the place for car stuff or just vacations. Traveling continued to be his biggest discretionary expense.

During his courtship with his special lady, they would take turns visiting each other. Mike would fly to North Carolina, where she lived, once or twice a month for weekend trips. Back home, his everyday life hadn't changed much. He kept his expenses low and was still doing a pretty good job of saving as much money as he could.

As the months fell off the calendar, Mike the Car Guy would send an update every once in a while. The long-distance dating became a serious long-distance relationship. The side investment of buying and selling cars became more of a focal point, and the nine-to-five day job became less of one. Plus, Mike's job had plateaued. He estimated it would take a decade or two of keeping his nose to the grindstone to get a promotion into management, which was the next rung in the ladder for him. Alternatives included looking for a different job or a different career. It wasn't long before he decided to quit his job and move to North Carolina to try to make the car gig full time.

An engagement, a wedding, a house, and then a baby all followed. When Mike moved down to North Carolina, he and his future wife shared a house with a few extra bedrooms. They saw eye-to-eye on the whole thrifty thing and decided to rent rooms out to friends. Much in the way that Mike rented a room years ago, he was now the one renting to others.

How was he able to make this happen? I don't mean the Cupid stuff, but traveling, quitting his job, moving to North Carolina, and trying to turn his hobby into a sustainable job? Earning More, Saving More, and Investing More.

Mike believed he'd never achieve the type of financial freedom he desired unless he focused his efforts toward investing for himself instead of working for someone else. If you look at national wage data, you'd see his theory makes sense. The Federal Reserve Bank of Atlanta tracks wages across the country. During the 2000s, wages have tended to grow between 1.5 percent and 5.5 percent per year. The average is somewhere between 3 and 4 percent.

Mike didn't see the wage tracker charts, and he didn't need to. He was able to notice this trend on his own. If he busted his behind one year, he might earn a 3.25 percent raise instead of a three percent raise . . . big whoop. If you compare this to the historical returns of stocks (11.32 percent) or bonds (7.43 percent), then investing begins to make a lot more sense as a way to spend your time and energy.

This is how an investor thinks. Can you focus your efforts

on a higher return than the 3 to 4 percent wage increases? Is it worth putting a down payment on a house or would it be better to use that same money to invest while continuing to rent? When buying a new car, do you use savings, investments or a loan? These are the types of questions someone who thinks like an investor asks.

Keeping your money invested and instead choosing to borrow can make sense when considering big purchases. Borrowing money at a low interest rate for a car, motorcycle, or boat are examples.

Say you have plenty of money available to buy a car. You can add the money to your investments and borrow money for the car, or you could pay for the car. If the car loan is at a three percent interest rate and your investment rate of return is averaging ten percent, it makes sense to borrow for the car. You'll pay three percent but make ten percent, so it's clearly better to borrow in this case. Since the investment rate of return is more unpredictable, I'd say the borrowing rate has to be pretty low to make sure this rule works out.

One of the tips I learned from Mike was not to change spending habits when he got a raise. It's easy to get a raise and then upgrade your cell phone plan, eat out more often, get your kids new toys, etc. Mike took the 3 to 4 percent pay increase and put all the money toward his car endeavor without changing his existing lifestyle. A common piece of financial advice, if you lack self-control, is to have your paycheck (or a portion of it) deposited directly into your bank account or investment account to avoid having the cash in hand. What you don't see, you don't miss.

Mike made a lot of smart choices on small things that individually didn't mean a lot, but added together they allowed him to build quite a bit of wealth for a person in his early thirties.

In the movie *Any Given Sunday*, Al Pacino gives his football team a pep talk before a big game. In the talk, he makes points that could just as easily apply to investing and that remind me of Mike's habits. He describes football (and life) as a game about inches. He encourages his team to play hard, to fight for every inch. When you add all the small things up (the inches), it can make the difference between winning and losing.

For investing, the "inches" that add up are the sacrifices and hard work that contribute to earning more. All the times you choose to reject a spending impulse or stay home and cook a meal instead of eating out. Saving more. Every time you do that, the inches add up for building wealth. It was a pretty intense speech. You should YouTube it. Al Pacino. What an actor.

Some of Mike's inches include the sweat and time he put toward rebuilding the totaled pickup truck, each late night studying in college for his dual degrees, renting rooms from friends instead of having his own apartment, and, of course, repairing cars in his spare time.

We should be able to put some numbers behind Mike's wealth. For most of the time I knew him, despite making close to 75,000 dollars per year, he lived more like someone making less than 45,000 dollars. We can conservatively estimate he had 20,000 dollars per year set aside. What would 20,000 dollars per year at his fifteen percent annual return get him?

	Starting Money	15% Return	Total
Year 1	20,000.00	3,000.00	23,000.00
Year 2	43,000.00	6,450.00	49,450.00
Year 3	69,450.00	10,417.50	79,867.50
Year 4	99,867.50	14,980.13	114,847.63
Year 5	134,847.63	20,227.14	155,074.77
Year 6	175,074.77	26,261.22	201,335.99

Wow. Those are some sexy numbers. You can see after six years we are talking about real money. The investments themselves are pulling over 25,000 dollars per year at that point. There is a reason we nerds in the finance industry call the power of compounding the eighth wonder of the world. Take note, because this an important concept: It might take many years of saving before you start seeing sizable returns on your principal balance. Time is your ally.

Mike's fifteen percent rate of return is higher than we should expect. Fifteen percent returns is a big assumption. Part of that is all the time and work Mike spent facilitating his car business. Unless you have a special skill like Mike's car knowledge, fifteen percent is an unreasonable expectation. Let's review the average annual return of a few common indices (remember those from before?). The U.S. stock market (S&P 500, SPX Index) has had an average return of 11.32 percent in the post World War II era. The Barclay's Aggregate Bond Index data from February 1976 to November 2017 had an annual return of 7.43 percent. The average return of gold from 1970 (just before Nixon took U.S. currency off the gold standard in 1971) to November 2017 was an annualized 7.8 percent.

These are a few common assets that people invest in and are more in the ballpark of what you should expect. The plus side is that you can have similar returns to those without putting in a lot of time or effort. You won't need a hobby.

Let's recap some of the things we learned from Mike.

Do-it-yourself projects could be an effective way to save money rather than paying a professional.

Consider the source of any investment advice. What is their background? If they are rich, how did they become rich?

Stocks have historically offered high but volatile returns. Bonds have historically offered lower but stable returns.

Think like an investor. Buying is not always better than renting.

Leveraging existing skills you have as part of investing is always something to consider. Skills that can be used to compound money can be valid investments.

Financial success is a game of inches. When it comes to earning and saving, small victories will all add up.

Here is a visual snapshot of Mike's financial situation:

	EARNINGS	SAVINGS	DEBT	INVESTMENT RETURNS
Rob	High	Low	High	Uninvested
Nathalie	Low	High	Low	Low
Mike	High	High	Low	High

You are doing so well reading this book. I'm so proud of you. Keep up the good work as you begin this next homework assignment. Yes, it's been a while, but this is an important one. Think back to your first homework assignment when you thought about your purpose for reading this book. You might have wanted to get a better understanding of investing or you might have wanted to find some ways to improve what investment choices you are making in your existing 401k. Or you might have planned to start your own retirement account (an IRA) or an investment account. Do you ever remember reading those *Choose Your Own Adventure* books back in middle school? "If you go into the dark cave, turn to page 75." "If you run, turn to page 52." Well, you are about to choose your own adventure right now. Adventure might be a strong word.

If your purpose involves your opening either your own retirement account or your own brokerage account, I'd like you to do that now. You can turn to chapter twenty-nine, "Opening an Account," to guide you. Use your purpose and motivation to your advantage now—don't wait until you finish this book. Take some time to open an account before moving forward. Once that is done, return to this section.

If you do not feel you need to open any new retirement or investment accounts, prepare for a less exciting adventure. Go to the page you are already on. Read the next section. (I told you it was less exciting).

CHAPTER EIGHTEEN
STOCKS VERSUS FUNDS

> "Beware of missing chances, otherwise it
> may be altogether too late someday."
>
> — *Franz Liszt, Hungarian composer, pianist, and conductor*

Now that we have learned the lessons Rob, Nathalie, and Mike have to offer us, we are going to dig deeper into the Invest More part of Earn More, Save More, Invest More. Not everyone will have a talent like Mike to earn a high return doing something unique. Most of us, including me, have to use the mainstream financial markets for investing.

While reading about Mike, we learned a little about stocks and bonds. I'm going to argue that you will want to have a very strong bias toward stocks over the next few decades, even if it defies the common adage of moving most of your money toward fixed income as you age. I'm going to argue that you will want equity (at least a sizable proportion) no matter your age, and I'll point you toward exactly which type of equity. I believe the strategy I outline will do much better than that of the average investor and even better than most investors whose money is managed by professionals.

Let's begin by looking at the average investor. J.P. Morgan

releases a quarterly *Guide to the Markets* that contains charts and some useful data on the current investment environment. It shows the average annual return of different asset classes over from the twenty-year period from 1998 to the end of 2017. It also includes the average annual return of typical everyday investors.

During this time, stocks (the S&P 500) averaged a growth rate of 7.2 percent per year. This is lower than the historical 11.32 percent figure since WWII, but remember this recent twenty-year period covers some big recessions. Over the same period, bonds averaged about 5.0 percent for their annual growth rate. International stocks of developed countries averaged a growth rate of 5.7 percent, represented by EAFE.[23] EAFE stands for Europe, Australasia (apparently that really is a word—who knew?), and the Far East.

You might be surprised that the average investor returned only 2.6 percent annualized during this period. Not very good, right? Barely better than inflation. There are many reasons why the average investor does so poorly. Most of them are psychological. It can include chasing hot stocks, not sticking to a strategy, following bad advice, etc. We'll come back to the 2.6 percent annual return later; meanwhile, keep that number in your head.

There is no reason for average investors to earn 2.6 percent when they can invest directly in those other asset classes. In addition, finding a way to have your investments more or less on autopilot would get an investor out of their own way. The growth figures also showed what we already knew: Stocks tend to have higher returns than bonds. Over the next few decades, not only will this trend continue, but future bond returns will be lower than their historical norms, diminishing their place as a suitable investment.

So, let's turn our attention to stocks and the different ways investors can get access to them. I'll outline the simple, no-hassle way for you to invest and earn above-average returns for below-average effort. I'm not saying you are lazy. Moreover, you made the effort to read a book about investing. But this book is a wimpy, quick read, so don't take too much credit. We will talk about three different ways to invest in stocks.

The first is to buy individual stocks of certain companies. This can be companies like Microsoft, Amazon, or Boeing. Essentially shares of any company that are publicly traded can be easily purchased on a stock exchange electronically.

The second way is to purchase a mutual fund or an exchange traded fund managed by an investment company and their portfolio manager(s). The portfolio manager will research and buy stocks to create a portfolio, perhaps between thirty and one hundred stocks. They will monitor this portfolio and change the makeup of it over time. Your money will be pooled together with all the other investors who have bought into the fund. A small fee is charged to pay for the portfolio manager and the operational aspects of maintaining the mutual fund or exchange traded fund (ETF). The investors sit back and hope the portfolio manager makes good choices and the money grows.

The third way is to invest directly in an index fund. We have gone over a few investment indices already like the S&P 500 or the Barclay's Aggregate Bond Index. Investing directly in an index attempts to get direct exposure to a market. The S&P 500 index, for example, is made up of 500 of the biggest companies in the United States. Investing in the index is buying a part of all 500 companies at once. The index fund mirrors the index as closely as possible.

The index fund will be similar to a mutual fund or ETF in that you're buying only one asset, but you get access to all the underlying holdings; your money is also pooled with that of all the other investors. It's like a big group hug with thousands of other investors. Index funds are cheap to invest in because there is no research and very little operational overhead; the fund simply copies an existing index. There is no portfolio manager to pay for. Investing in an index is referred to as passive investing, while investing in a mutual fund or ETF (where there is a portfolio manager picking stocks) is active investing.

Let's say you wanted to invest in the U.S. stock market. You could buy an index which mirrors the U.S. stock market, just passively owning all stocks available. Your returns will be exactly whatever the stock market does. Or you can invest in a mutual fund where someone (a portfolio manager) is picking stocks he or she thinks will have better returns than an average stock will. That is active investing. Mutual funds (active investing) try to beat the market. Index funds (passive investing) match the market.

Let's drill down into this a little more.

Picking individual stocks can be fun. Being able to say "I own part of Tesla" or "I just sold my shares of McDonald's" can make you sound smart—or like a pretentious fool, depending on the context. If someone comments on a Tesla driving by, you don't have to blurt out you own part of the company. Don't be that person. Picking your own stocks can give you a sense of purpose in managing your own money or conversation topics if you go to a lot of fancy cocktail parties.

But picking your own stocks can be time consuming. After researching and deciding what to purchase, those investments need to be monitored going forward. We established that you can invest directly in the S&P 500 through an index. It stands to reason if you are spending your time (which is valuable) choosing your own investment, you want to get some value for the time spent—you want to avoid a lower total return than the S&P 500. If you're getting a lower total return, that's not only money lost, but time wasted.

There are additional risks as well. One of the most common mistakes is to own stock in a company that the investor personally likes but might not necessarily be well-managed or well-positioned financially. A well-liked company (even one with a great product or service) might not be a great investment. I know it sounds ironic, but it's the truth. That's why, to properly protect their investments, investors need to do some sort of due diligence. They can review financial statements and follow the daily news and operations of the company. Does that sound very fun? Take a minute and think about how you might handle this situation. Even if you think it would be fun, it brings us back to the question of time. Do you want investing to take up a huge chunk of your time? Will this affect how many investments you own?

This could then lead to owning too few stocks. In the world of investing, the motto "having all your eggs in one basket" means it's unwise to own too few investments. You want to diversify the risk across assets to reduce the downside risk one single stock can have on your whole portfolio of investments. If you only had five stocks in 2017 and one of them was GE, it would have been worse than dropping a newly purchased soft-serve ice cream cone on the ground! GE was down 40 percent while the market was up 20 percent. There are also instances where employees of a certain company have their retirement account made up of the company's stock. That didn't work out so well for many Enron employees.

This is why you want to spread the risk around to more than five investments and why individual stock picking is tough for an investor who doesn't want to worry about building a portfolio of twenty or more holdings. And it's another reason people choose to invest in mutual funds or ETFs. Investing in a fund removes the time component for following and choosing individual stocks, but it also reduces the overall risk of the investments.

Yet another downside to amateur and intermediate investors choosing their own individual assets has to do with some of the psychological tricks our brains play on us. Investments that have made money in taxable investment accounts will have gains associated with them, and investors can be reluctant to sell a stock that has appreciated in value. Consider individual stocks like Wal-Mart and Proctor & Gamble, for example. If their prices increase and you sell them, you will then have to pay taxes on those gains. As long as you keep the stocks without selling, you don't have to pay for those gains. It is common for an investor to struggle to sell an appreciated stock. They don't want to pay extra taxes.

They may also have developed an attachment to their successful investment. This could lead to holding the stock for long periods of time while underperforming the overall market. Once an asset has grown in value, it can be psychologically difficult to sell. It becomes a case of the tail wagging the dog, because in actuality, keeping the investment can hold the investor back from making more money on better investments.

Stocks losing value can also psychologically impact an investor's choices (gain or lose, your brain works against you!). There can be a tendency to ride the stock right to the bottom. If an investor owned and grew attached to companies like Kodak, Borders, Blockbuster, etc., they might have held them as the price plummeted. Selling a stock at a loss is like admitting you were wrong—something people don't like to do. Investors may try to hang onto it hoping the price at least makes it back to what they bought it for. Like a gambler who is down and looking to "just break even."

I've said over and over that the investment strategy this book would advocate was not time-consuming or difficult. Researching, trading, and frequently monitoring dozens of stocks do not fit that description. If you are looking for a new hobby, then researching and picking stocks might be for you— but you won't find a lot of information about successful ways to do so in this book.

The second way to invest in stocks is in mutual funds or exchange traded funds (ETFs). Remember, these funds are actively managed, trying to beat the market. They are different from index funds, which mirror the market, known as passive investing. Mutual funds are an easy way to invest in a lot of stocks without all the work of picking them yourself. It's not as fun to talk about with friends. "I've added to my holding of the Fidelity Magellan fund" doesn't have the same ring as "I've done well on Microsoft this year." There is also a certain feeling of validation, like you've won something, when a single stock is successfully chosen. That feeling doesn't happen with mutual funds or ETFs as much. For someone looking to make money investing without spending time worrying about it, mutual funds and ETFs are not a bad option. The risk is reduced, and you don't have to worry or spend your time.

Any active mutual fund or ETF is still only as good as its quarterback (portfolio managers). Unfortunately, active funds still have a few characteristics that require monitoring. A mutual fund can change the way it works without the investors' noticing. The portfolio manager(s) could change due to retirement or changing roles within the organization. The fees on the fund might change. The style and way the fund invests might change as well. Admittedly, it's easier to pay attention to one or two funds than a collection of companies, as in successful stock picking. It's still less risky than individual stocks, but you could get burned if you don't pay attention. It's a risk of a minor burn, like a first-degree burn. You'd survive.

There is also the topic of performance. With a mutual fund or ETF, you will pay fees. Fees are typically deducted in tiny increments that reduce the existing investment. Investors are not sent a bill. Performance might be reported gross of fees (not including fees) or net of fees (including fees). Factoring in those fees, the fund must perform better than the passive index alternative. Otherwise, it is not worth paying fees when the index version, which can be invested in, results in better returns. A mutual fund can easily have a fee of .75 percent per year. That would mean the mutual fund has to beat the index by at least .75 percent per year to make it a viable alternative (give or take—usually an index has a tiny fee as well).

A CNBC article from February 2017 called "Active fund managers rarely beat their benchmarks year after year" helps explain how difficult it can be to beat index returns once fees are included for professional fund managers. Research from the article shows that only five percent of mutual funds investing in large U.S. companies that had beaten the benchmark for three years were able to do it over the next three years.[24] In other words, very few active mutual funds are able to beat the benchmark over time.

Another article, this time from *MarketWatch*, titled "This Is How Many Fund Managers Actually Beat Index Funds," presented even more data in favor of passive over active investing. Research done by Standard and Poor's showed that over a fifteen year period ending December 2016, ninety-two percent of active funds lagged the S&P 500 index.[25] These are staggering numbers.

The secret is out across the industry. Investors have taken notice, and they are responding with their money. In 2016, 264 billion dollars were taken out of active equity funds and 236 billion were added to passive funds. Over the last decade, over a trillion dollars have shifted to passive index funds. Most investment companies selling actively managed funds have responded by trying to lower their fees to compete with the growing investor trends toward passive investing.

Another estimate, by Dartmouth College's esteemed Professor Kenneth French, claims investors spend .67 percent per year in vain trying to beat the market in active mutual funds.[26] If beating the market is so hard to do, why even try? We have seen that the odds are long, and money will most likely be wasted in the attempt, so why not settle for the market returns that are already pretty good? We have seen the historical returns of the stock market that we can easily achieve without much effort.

Let's look at some numbers that might help show how powerful compounding is and how much fees cost over time.

Actively managed U.S. equity funds charge an average of .82 percent per year.[27] We can round that to one percent. We know that the U.S. stock market (S&P 500) has returned 11.32 percent per year since WWII. Let's hypothetically compare what 10,000 dollars would have done over twenty years at the historical market return versus a one percent lower return due to fees.

	Return of 11.32%	Return of 10.32%
Start	10,000.00	10,000.00
Year 1	11,132.00	11,032.00
Year 2	12,392.14	12,170.50
Year 3	13,794.93	13,426.50
Year 4	15,356.52	14,812.11
Year 5	17,094.88	16,340.72
Year 6	19,030.02	18,027.09
Year 7	21,184.22	19,887.48
Year 8	23,582.27	21,939.87
Year 9	26,251.78	24,204.06
Year 10	29,223.48	26,701.92
Year 11	32,531.58	29,457.56
Year 12	36,214.16	32,497.58
Year 13	40,313.60	35,851.33
Year 14	44,877.10	39,551.19
Year 15	49,957.19	43,632.87
Year 16	55,612.34	48,135.78
Year 17	61,907.66	53,103.40
Year 18	68,915.60	58,583.67
Year 19	76,716.85	64,629.50
Year 20	85,401.20	71,299.27

By putting in 10,000 dollars and letting it sit for twenty years, there is nearly a 15,000 dollar difference, all because of one percent. That is your 15,000 dollars. Why should money managers or advisors get it? This is a testament to both how much money you can save by investing on your own without an advisor and avoiding "active" funds that statistics have shown likely cannot beat the market consistently.

CHAPTER NINETEEN
INDEX FUNDS

"I am not afraid of storms for I am learning how to sail my ship."

— *Louisa May Alcott, American novelist and poet*

This takes us to investing in an index, or passive investing, which is the third way to invest in stocks, and what I'd consider the preferred method for our purposes.

Most indices are market weight. Let's use the S&P 500 as an example to explain what I mean. Within the index, more weight is given to a company depending on its size, which is defined by the total value of the company. At the time of this writing, Apple Inc. is the biggest company in the S&P 500 with a value of over 886 billion. Another company in the S&P 500 is Ford Motor Co. The total value of Ford is 52 billion. This means that the company Apple makes up a bigger proportion of the S&P 500 index. Apple makes up about four percent of the index because of its size. Ford is .21 percent of the index. Mathematically Apple's stock price movement affects the S&P 500 index more than Ford's stock price movement.

Rather than going out and buying all the different stocks that make up an index, you can buy one index fund that buys all the underlying stocks in the index for you. Large mutual fund or investment companies can sell index funds for a very cheap price. Anyone can buy a Vanguard S&P 500 index fund or a Fidelity S&P 500 fund. The fund maintains the 500 stocks, so you don't have to. Index funds don't have a lot of operational expenses or highly paid portfolio managers and analysts. All they do is make trades to mirror what the actual index is holding. An investor typically pays less than .10 percent per year for an index—much cheaper than regular mutual fund management fees.

For instance, the company Charles Schwab offers an S&P 500 index fund that has an expense ratio of .09 percent. This means it would cost 90 cents per year to invest 1,000 dollars. It also doesn't cost anything to buy or sell the fund.

Within the index fund universe, there is another distinction you need to know about. Even though the S&P 500 is a market cap weight index, there exists an equal cap weight version as well. This means that every company in the index is held at an equal value. For an index with 500 stocks, each one would be .2 percent of your money. In the S&P 500 market cap weight index, Apple would make up about 4 percent of your investment. In an equal weight index, it would be .2 percent just like the 499 other companies.

The most important point to keep in mind is that for the S&P 500 *the equal weight index has had better performance historically.* Let me say that again. The equal weight index has had higher returns than the market weight index for the S&P 500. And remember, the market weight index S&P 500 represents the U.S. stock market. So, if the equal weight version of the index historically outperforms, using an equal weight index alone means you should have a way to outperform the stock market. The equal weight index was created in 2003, but the company, Standard & Poor's, has performance information back to 1990.

From the start of 1990 until the end of 2017, the equal weight index averaged a return of 11.31 percent per year compared to 9.80 percent for the market cap weight S&P 500 index. Over the entire twenty-seven-year period, this additional 1.51 percent of extra return really makes a big difference. Look where you would have ended in 2017 if you started with 10,000 dollars in 1990.

Index	Start Amount in 1990	Ending Amount in 2017
Equal Weight S&P 500	10,000	191,161.00
Market Cap S&P 500	10,000	127,392.00

The total return is over 60,000 dollars more for the equal weight market cap, even though it only averaged 1.51 percent more per year.

Let's recap what we read in simple terms. The S&P 500 index is the U.S. stock market, right? It is a market weight index. But there is a different *version* of the S&P 500 index that is an equal weight index. This different version has outperformed the regular S&P 500. If it were simply that easy, everyone would then buy equal weight indices, right? Why would anyone buy the market cap weight version?

One reason is that the market cap weight index is the default version. Many investors would rather mirror the market exactly. The returns of an equal weight index have outperformed historically, but it's not as simple as beating the market by 1.51 percent every year. That is the average outperformance, but it's not guaranteed every year. There are years where the market cap weight will win, years where the performance will be nearly equal, etc. But over time, the equal weight index will win. My grandmother makes the best molasses cookies I've ever had. If she made a batch that didn't come out right one time, I wouldn't change my opinion of her cookies. One bad year for the equal weight index wouldn't change the fact that it wins *most* of the time.

If the equal weight index always did better over every single time frame, then it would truly be a no brainer. Since that isn't the case, many investors are happy to settle for the default version of the index.

Take a moment to realize the makeup of the equal weight versus the market cap weight index. The market cap weight will have more of its money in the largest, most mature companies, like Exxon or Apple. Most of these companies are global, well-established, and already hold a powerful market share in whatever business they are in. By comparison, the equal cap weight has more of its value in mid-size companies that are well-established but still going through high growth that the biggest companies normally aren't.

The equal weight version of the index has another great feature. It recovers more quickly from recessions than the market cap weight index. This better bounce coming out of recessions has to do with the heavier proportion in the equal weight index of smaller companies, which benefit more from renewed domestic economic growth than the mega, mature corporations who tend to have a higher portion of their revenue generated outside the U.S. The big guys need the whole globe to begin recovery where the medium-sized companies are more nationally focused.

Basic math also works in favor of an equal weight index. If you think of the general mechanics of how an equal weight index works, the outperformance will make sense. Wise investors know their goal is to "buy low, sell high." That is classic investing advice. That is exactly how an equal weight index works. In order to keep .2% of every stock, the index has to buy stocks that have gone down and sell stocks that have gone up. It's common for an index to do this once a quarter. This means, naturally, they are selling stocks that have gone up (selling high) and buying stocks that have gone down (buying low). This process sells the winners that have made money and buys the losers, which offer better value.

Unfortunately, it can't be all sunshine and rainbows. There

are arguments against an equal weight index. The first is volatility. The equal weight index will have slightly higher volatility than the market cap weight index. This means that when the market goes down, the equal weight index will go down slightly more. And the same is true when it goes up. Because the equal weight moves more drastically, investors would do well to exercise patience. Through the more volatile price movements, the average performance over time is what matters. Particularly during stock market downturns, because you know in likelihood the recovery will also happen more quickly.

Looking at actual return figures might help to see exactly what I mean by the volatility differences. Here are the returns over the ten-year period beginning in 2008 for each type of index.

Year	Equal Weight	Market Cap	Difference
2017	18.90%	21.83%	-2.93%
2016	14.80%	11.96%	2.84%
2015	-2.20%	1.38%	-3.59%
2014	14.49%	13.69%	0.80%
2013	36.16%	32.39%	3.77%
2012	17.65%	16.00%	1.65%
2011	-0.11%	2.11%	-2.22%
2010	21.91%	15.06%	6.85%
2009	46.31%	26.46%	19.84%
2008	-39.72%	-37.00%	-2.72%

It is also often pointed out that the equal weight index pays a lower dividend yield, and that is considered a bad thing. I'd argue that it's actually a good thing. Dividend yield is the payout investors get from a stock; a fund or index passes along dividends to the investors. The equal cap weight index tends to have a payout ratio of around 1.5 percent. The market cap weight is slightly higher, at around 2 percent.

There isn't a correlation between a company paying a dividend and its having a higher return. In other words, stocks that pay dividends don't necessarily have higher returns than stocks that pay smaller dividends or no dividends. Google is one of the most valuable companies in the world and doesn't pay a dividend. Famous investor Warren Buffet's company, Berkshire Hathaway, also does not pay a dividend.

Warren Buffet's reasoning for not paying a dividend matches my reasoning for why the lower dividend yield of an equal-weight index is not a disadvantage. Dividend payments count as income for most investors, so you will have to pay taxes on dividend payments. I'd rather pay taxes only when I want to. Rather than being forced to pay taxes on dividend income I might not need, I can sell portions of stocks or an index fund when I want money and pay taxes only on my schedule. Knowing companies that pay higher dividends don't necessarily have higher returns, I don't see why having a lower dividend yield should be held against equal weight index funds. From the perspective of the investor, they are more tax efficient.

The next argument raised against equal weight funds is its greater expenses. Because the equal weight fund is trying to maintain that .2 percent per position, the fund has to do a lot of rebalancing of the underlying stocks. This means more trading costs associated with an equal weight index. There is slightly more overall operational expense, but the difference is not very large. One of the most common S&P equal weight index funds is administered by the company PowerShares. The fund currently has an expense ratio of .20 percent per year. This compares to the high single digits of most market cap weight funds. Both are still very cheap when compared to the average "active" equity fund which is .82 percent per year as of 2016.

Trading and administrative costs are decreasing over time

across the industry. Investors have been moving their money toward lower cost funds and ETFs. Even a few years ago, that same PowerShares fund (run by Guggenheim at the time) was .40 percent each year. The costs have been cut in half since a few years ago (down to .20 percent which we pointed out). As technology continues to improve and there is increased scalability for these investment companies, I'd confidently predict that the gap between market cap and equal cap weight indices will shrink over time.

Out of all the arguments against equal weight indices we covered, there is only one I have some agreement with. An equal weight index might be too low for the technology sector. A lot of the structural trends we discussed throughout the book have to do with improving technology. Technology is currently the biggest sector in the economy, and I'd guess it will continue to play a crucial role in the future. Some of the biggest companies are Alphabet (Google), Microsoft, Apple, Amazon, Facebook, Intel, and Cisco. These companies are so big they are causing the technology sector to be underrepresented in an equal weight index. One way to address this is that a sector-specific tech fund could be added along with the equal weight fund to construct a more complete investment portfolio. We will discuss which investments will create a solid base and the suitable add-ons, like tech funds, in the next chapter. The upcoming section will explain the exact investments to grow your money.

CHAPTER TWENTY
SPECIFIC INVESTMENT CHOICES

"It always seems impossible until it's done."

— Nelson Mandela, former President of South Africa

Put your finger on a spinning globe and it will most likely land on a country or region that has an index you could invest in. For my money, there is still a lot to like about the United States, even though other countries might be having higher growth rates. Most of my analysis has focused on the post World War II period. Still, throughout that time, there have been reasons to think the U.S. would lose its economic superiority.

In the late 1970s and through the 1980s, Japan's economic growth and technological prowess led many financial experts to advise clients to favor Japan over the United States. The booming Japanese economy, they predicted, would grow to surpass the United States. We know that isn't how things worked out. Japan went on to have a couple of decades of flat growth and muted stock returns.

Next, during the 1990s, the talk was about the "Asian tigers"—countries like South Korea, Taiwan, and Singapore.

Emerging markets that had high growth rates and cheap labor. After a big crash and currency crisis in the late 1990s, that investment theme faded away.

In the 2000s, investors were encouraged to consider BRIC countries (Brazil, Russia, India, and China). They had big populations and a lot of potential for growth. Their size and scale equaled that of the United States. Perhaps the jury is still out, but so far, the investment track record has been spotty for these countries.

As far as regions of the globe and their investment prospects go, I see a lot of promise for the U.S. over the next few decades. The U.S. economy is still the largest in the world. On a per capita basis, America's wealth remains relatively high, while continuing to grow. People who have been invested in the U.S. stock market are clear beneficiaries. The vast resources and dominant market share across the globe in important industries make it hard to unseat America as the top economic country. About half of the twenty largest companies in the world are American.

The American economy is also insulated from much of what goes on across the globe. Between the domestic resources that are enabling energy independence and the ability to produce nearly everything needed within its borders, the U.S. is able to survive on its own better than most other countries. Since the dollar functions as the world's reserve currency, the U.S. is also less vulnerable to changing currency risks than other countries. This basically means the dollar is used to grease the wheels for a lot of international commerce. Global commodities like oil and gold are also commonly priced in U.S. dollars.

America is a leader in global science and technology. Its higher existing wealth allows it to continually attract the best and brightest and maintain a monopoly in this realm. The United States has some of the best higher-level learning institutions in the world.

The U.S. has a lot of influence across the globe. America's

values and wishes go a long way in shaping the global economic, financial, and political makeup of the world.

For these reasons, constructing an investment base from U.S. stocks is a wise move. Particularly from large companies from the S&P 500. These diverse companies tend to make money in a variety of ways and have the scale and market share to weather negative economic periods. This means they are safer than smaller companies that might be completely reliant on one product or line of business. Most S&P 500 companies are international sellers as well. The average company in the S&P 500 makes almost half of its sales outside of the U.S. This also makes them less exposed to downturns or poor sales in a single country.

Now that we also have an explanation supporting our country bias, we can put together some investment recommendations. Of *exact* investments. Yes, it's finally here. I provide you with both the name of the suggested funds and the ticker symbol you would need to place actual buy or sell trades for the fund. For readers who want a specific walk-through on how to use tickers to place a trade on an exchange, that will be outlined in chapter twenty nine.

Bonds

Generally, invest none or very little of your money in bonds. Due to low expected returns, the rewards, even for the low risk bonds, is simply not worth it. If you feel you need some, own less than conventional wisdom suggests. There is an investment adage that goes "The portion of your investments in bonds should be your age." But fifty-year-old people don't need fifty percent of their investment in bonds. If you are going to need the money within the next few years, then certainly, some amount in a safer investment like bonds makes sense.

At most, bonds should make up fifty percent of your investments. If you need money during a stock market downturn, you can sell bonds to allow time for the stocks to recover. During recessions or stock market downturns, bonds tend to hold their value or even *increase* in value. Wise investors sell bonds during a recession if they need money before they sell stocks. If long-term growth of investments is your goal, however, bonds will disappoint you in the coming decades. Here are some inexpensive and successful bond funds if you need them:

Ticker   Fund Name
VBILX   Vanguard Intermediate Term Bond Index
VICSX   Vanguard Intermediate Term Corporate Bond Index
VFICX   Vanguard Intermediate Term Investment Grade Fund

Equities

Equities are a better investment than bonds for the foreseeable future. Over the next few decades, the higher risk of equities still makes them a good value, due to the very low returns of bonds. Since we're lukewarm on bonds, we'll play hot on cold for the different types of equity investments.

Individual Equities are warmer than bonds, but for the reasons I've previously outlined, they're not my recommendation for personal investors who want it simple and easy.

Equity Mutual Funds are heating up. While a better strategy than individual stock picking, they still have components that need to be monitored. Empirical evidence shows mutual funds have trouble beating the returns of the general stock market.

Index Funds. Hot. Simple. Easy. Cheap. Yes, I'm describing index funds. If most mutual funds fail to beat the market, let's simply invest in the market's mirror, index funds. I will outline some choices. There is not a lot of difference between them, but I like to provide options. Tickers with three letters are exchange traded funds (ETFs), five letters are index and mutual funds.

Ticker	Fund Name
VOO	Vanguard S&P 500 ETF
SPY	SPDR S&P 500 ETF Trust
IVV	Ishares Core S&P 500 ETF
VFINX	Vanguard 500 Index Fund

Equal Weight Index Funds. Scalding. Lava level hot. Or magma. Whatever. Equal weight will not do better all the time; it will underperform over certain periods, but historically has done quite better than the market weighted S&P 500. I can't speak for other countries or every index of stocks ever created. I am only advocating for the S&P 500. I do not know the data behind other equal weight index funds. Here are some choices for equal weight variations of S&P 500 index funds:

Ticker	Fund Name
RSP	PowerShares S&P 500 Equal Weight ETF
INDEX	Index Funds S&P 500 Equal Weight Fund

This all leads to a simple and relatively safe investment strategy. Investing in an S&P 500 index should be the main (or even entire) part of your investments. Simply putting money in this index will be a good investment for decades to come.

If you feel the overall market index is not enough, you can add some specialized investments, too. Certain sectors like technology or healthcare fit some of the structural themes in the economy. Certain countries or regions outside of the U.S. might also appeal to you. I'll suggest a few, but you can always Google additional funds or themes on your own. Look for index funds. Companies like State Street (they will usually have "SPDR" in the name of the fund), Blackrock (might have Ishares in the fund name), Vanguard, and Fidelity tend to charge the lowest expense ratios. An index fund should always be less than .25 percent unless it is international, then it might be a little higher. I'll save you some research and give you some suggestions for the Technology sector and Healthcare sector.

Tech Sector:

Ticker	Fund Name
XLK	Technology Select Sect SPDR
VGT	Vanguard Info Tech ETF
FTEC	Fidelity Info Tech ETF

Healthcare sector:

Ticker	Fund Name
XLV	Health Care Select Sector
FHLC	Fidelity Health Care ETF
VHT	Vanguard Health Care ETF

I'll leave it up to you if you want to invest in foreign countries or regions. Funds like Ishares MSCI India ETF, ticker INDA, are examples of what types of index funds you can find from Blackrock or the other big companies I've named.

I will suggest some ways you can combine the funds outlined over the past few pages. Of course, the level of sophistication you choose is up to you. My recommendation is a strong foundation of ticker RSP or INDEX – at least 50 percent of your investments. Here would be a few suitable combinations:

50% RSP, 25% SPY, 25% VICSX
90% INDEX, 10% XLK
50% RSP, 10% VBILX, 20% VGT, 10% XLV, 10% INDA

I have provided you with the knowledge and even specific suggestions for you to get the most out of the investments in your existing 401k, 529 plan, or any investment account or retirement account you decide to open on your own. If you only have limited options in your 401k at work, remember to bias toward equity. Pick less fixed income. Stick to low-expense ratio equity funds, or, better yet, index funds if available. Choose an equal weight index fund for the S&P 500 if you can, but if one is not an available option in your employer's specific 401k plan, settling for a normal S&P 500 index is still very good.

Investing on your own is really that simple. Reread this chapter if you are still unclear about the specific strategy and investment choices. You might be wondering, "What about all the other types of investments out there?"

Shorting stocks (profiting when a stock goes down in price), investing in stock options (arranging to buy or sell at a previously agreed-upon price), and other alternative ways to access stocks are for sophisticated investors. Without a lot of expertise and work, novice investors tend to have poor performance pursuing those strategies on their own. We'll consider those practices to be beyond the scope of this book and save ourselves the complication.

Precious metals, namely gold and silver, are always an investment option, but I prefer investments that offer better returns. Gold and silver have a reputation of doing well during recessions or during periods of high inflation. However, most of the research I have seen doesn't agree with this. The relationship between gold and inflation isn't as strong as it's touted to be.

Historically, gold and silver go up when the economy enters a recession and fear increases among investors. Gold is regarded as an investment safe haven. It is a tangible asset that fearful investors flock to if they think the companies backing stocks or bonds might collapse. On the flip side, during economic expansions, gold investment returns tend to be lackluster. I like to classify gold or silver more as a currency than an investable asset. If you own a stock, bond, or CD, the value of these is tied to something—either a series of interest payments you receive or profits the underlying company is making. With precious metals, that isn't the case. Their value is not tied to any income

EARN MORE. SAVE MORE. INVEST MORE.

or profitability.

One other caution I have for gold investors is to consider that the technology for mining is ever-improving. Mining for nearly all metals and commodities has become much cheaper and easier. This in turn could increase supply, and higher supply typically means lower value. I am not anything close to an expert in gold or silver. I can only speculate.

Speaking of things that are currency-like . . . let's take a look at cryptocurrencies. I doubt anyone can accurately predict how cryptocurrencies will play out over the next few years or decades, since they are such a new type of investment. Governments generally dislike them because of the difficulty in tracing the transactions. This means they are favored by people who transact illicit goods or otherwise try to obscure their dealings from governments across the globe. At the very least, I'd expect governments to regulate or otherwise find a way to insert themselves into the process over the next few years.

The purpose of cryptocurrency is to be a currency, not necessarily an investable asset. A currency whose price moves around significantly over short periods of time isn't a good currency. Transactions are difficult because the currency can be ten percent higher or lower at the end of the day. Right now, rather than being used as a currency, it seems to be used mostly as a speculative investment. Like precious metals, there aren't any underlying cash flows associated with it. This makes me reluctant to call it a real investment. Its function is to be a currency.

While we are talking about speculative investments, I want to mention collectibles. This could include coins, sports cards (or memorabilia), art, classic cars, or antiques. Collectibles could be worth exploring as an investment if you have a passion for them. My only words of wisdom are to not bet the farm on the results. Generally, I'd say the same as I have about precious metals or cryptocurrencies. If you are inclined to invest in these categories of "investments," I'd recommend keeping at least fifty percent of your invested money in stocks, bonds, or even real estate (depending a bit more on your circumstances). For all the collectible goods that made people wealthy, there are many that had poor results. I seem to remember that Cabbage Patch dolls, Beanie Babies, POGS, and Norman Rockwell plates were all supposed to be valuable collectibles. They weren't. Not to mention Hot Wheels, various types of trading cards, marbles . . . the list goes on.

That also goes for any "hot" stocks you'd like to invest in. I've spent much of this book explaining what I think is a better way to go about investing, but if you want to invest in one of your favorite companies or a popular stock, try to make it only a portion of your investments. A good rule is to keep any specific stock under ten percent of your investments. Put the bulk of your money toward an equal weight S&P 500 index fund and let it grow.

The bottom line is that you don't need those extra types of investable assets. I outlined the 11.32% stock market return since World War II. That is more than enough to build wealth. I'm not an expert on precious metals, cryptocurrencies, or coin collections, but can confidently say stocks have a good track record and don't require a lot of legwork.

Other than that, using whatever skills you have and investing in yourself is always a good idea. Mike the Car Guy's knowledge and abilities allowed him to walk a less common path by fixing and trading classic cars. Having mechanical skills is similar to having carpentry, plumbing, or electrical knowledge. Skills or specialized knowledge in those areas can benefit you, for example, in real estate investing and real estate management. These are the types of investments that I feel make sense and can offer strong returns, but they require time and work. The strategies we went over for investing in the stock market require little to no effort at all. Easy as pie.

The investments I previously outlined should do well for

decades to come. You can keep adding to them over time without needing to sell or rearrange anything. It's an easy strategy that can be set and mostly forgotten. One of the prior homework assignments asked you to open a brokerage, retirement, or 529 account if you didn't already have one. Chapter twenty nine outlines how to place a trade in these accounts, or you can simply call whoever houses your investment account and tell them you'd like to place trades to purchase the ticker symbols I outlined above.

CHAPTER TWENTY-ONE
DEBT EVERYWHERE YOU LOOK

"We all learn by experience but some of us
have to go to summer school."

— *Peter De Vries, editor and satirist*

D id you ever see the television show *Beyond Scared Straight?* It was about adolescent teens who had committed crimes and a new "therapy" to correct their behavior. Law enforcement teamed up with the Federal Bureau of Corrections to bring the teens into prisons. They would get a tour of the prison, see what life was like, and meet some of the inmates. Convicts would speak/scream at the teens in an attempt to "scare" them into correcting their behavior. The show was on the A&E channel.

This chapter is going to work exactly the same way. And by "exactly the same way," I mean a little bit that way. Maybe you've lacked the self-control to set money aside or haven't been convinced of worthwhile reasons to invest money—prepare to be frightened.

High U.S. debt levels and changing demographics will impact economic growth and investment returns. These are both major structural forces acting on the economy. If you currently have trouble setting money aside, looking at how these forces will play out is supposed to scare you into saving money. Understanding the different influences these forces have on the economy will also support the investment choices we went over in the last chapter.

We'll begin with debt. The word is enough to send shivers down my spine. Debt. *Brrrr, shiver.* We looked at debt on an individual level when we talked about Rob the Engineer. High amounts of debt can hinder the flexibility you have with your money because so much of it is already earmarked for car payments, student loan payments, home loans, credit cards, etc. When it gets bad enough, all the money you make is spoken for, trapping you so that you are working mainly to pay off things you already purchased. It's hard to break out of a cycle like that. You spin away on a hamster wheel but never build assets.

Corporations work in a similar way. A company, like a person, can borrow money to do things like expand their business, make renovations to existing buildings, pay their owners, or buy out another business. The more debt a company has, the more it can hinder its available options. Corporations can also find themselves using all their profits to pay existing debt. Like an individual, a company will struggle to get ahead if it doesn't control its debt.

Governments work the same way. The more overall debt governments have, the more difficult it becomes for them to provide intended services. More and more of their revenue (income taxes!) must be put toward debt. If too much revenue goes toward debt, how can a government cut taxes or build new bridges or fund a space program? Too much debt held either by individuals, companies, or the government will affect a nation's ability to grow.

Historically, the United States hasn't grown as well when the government has higher levels of debt. Other developed countries around the globe have had the same tendency. In case you don't believe me, I'll show you. Let's look at the total debt in the U.S. economy and how it has changed over time. If we add up all the debt in the United States, we can compare it to economic growth. Adding all the debt owed by households, non-profit organizations, corporations, and government agencies will give us the total debt. The Bank for International Settlements (BIS) publishes this data. BIS is an international financial organization made up of sixty central banks that has been around since 1930. It's based out of Switzerland. Since tennis legend Roger Federer is from Switzerland, I trust the data.

When looking at a number like total debt, we need to first put it into context. It's hard to define what is considered a lot of debt. Jeff Bezos, the CEO of Amazon, is worth about 100 billion dollars. If he had one million dollars in debt, it wouldn't be very much for him. If Fred the mailman had that same million dollars of debt, he would be in a "world of hurt" (to quote Bull Hurley, from the 1980s movie *Over the Top*). Sorry, Fred. That is why when we look at debt, we'll compare it to the size of the country's annual economy. We'll use Gross Domestic Product (GDP) to represent total output of goods and services of the United States. And voila (figure 11):

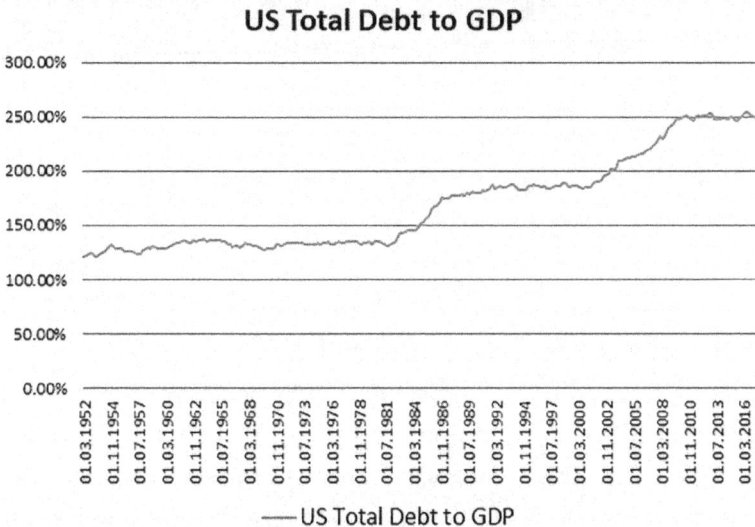

Figure 11. Total US Debt Compared to Gross Domestic Product

Putting the Bureau of International Settlements data into a chart shows that current debt levels are about 250% of GDP. The data goes back to 1952 as you can see from the dates on the X axis. The chart shows that total debt is right around its highest levels of the past seventy years. Looking back, you can see that over time debt has risen at a faster pace than economic growth. Sometimes it's slow and steady and sometimes there is a sharper incline upward, but the trend is clear.

This has caused a downward trend on overall growth. We know this because we can put GDP growth by itself on a chart over the same period, from 1952 to 2017. The annual GDP growth rate kind of bounces around like a pinball machine, especially in the 50s, 60s, and 70s but the overall trend of GDP growth is clear (figure 12)[28]:

Figure 12. Growth of US GDP from 1952 to 2017

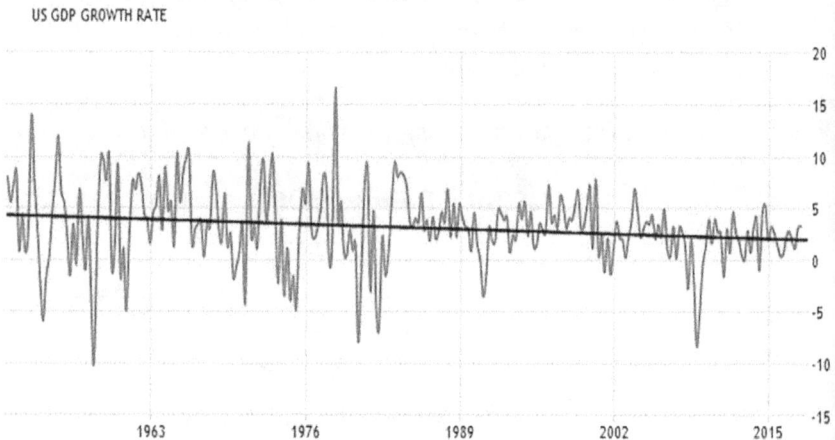

US GDP GROWTH RATE

SOURCE: TRADINGECONOMICS.COM | U.S. BUREAU OF ECONOMIC ANALYSIS

The gray frantic line is the annual GDP growth for the United States. The straight line is the average, following a trend that illustrates my point. GDP has usually been between -5% and +10%. The downward slope of the straight line over time means GDP growth has gone down. It looks like GDP growth averaged just under five percent in the 1950s down to around two percent today. From the previous chart, we know that overall debt has gone up at the same time this GDP has been slowing down. I do not believe this is a coincidence.

Similar trends can be found in Japan and Western Europe, so this debt/growth relationship is not new and is not only a U.S. problem.

The total debt as part of that 250% total debt to GDP ratio from figure 11 is about 47 trillion as of mid-2017. Remember, that is a mix of corporate debt, household debt, and government agencies. Whew! Wipe that sweat from your brow. Don't worry, companies and other people own most of it. Not the federal government. Out of the 47 trillion in debt, *only* 18.6 trillion, give or take, is government debt.

How does the U.S. government owe so much? What do they spend their money on? Here is a chart using the Congressional Budget Office's data that showed how 2017's federal spending compared to revenue.

Figure 13. US Federal Spending Compared to Revenue

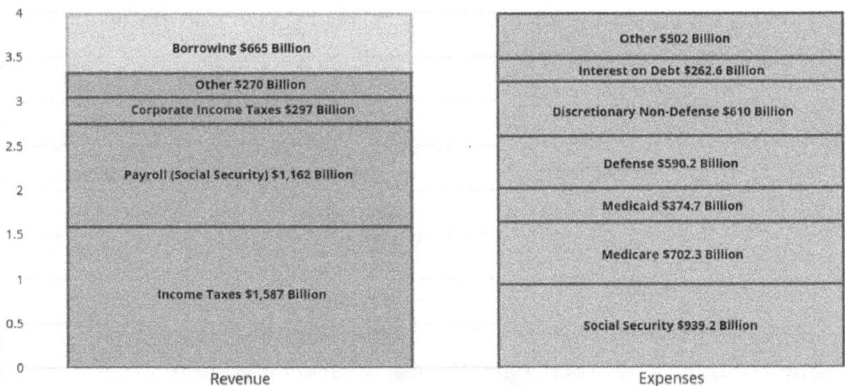

171

The right side of the chart shows much more spending than the revenue on the left side, with the difference made up by borrowing. The hole is getting bigger. We know total debt compared to GDP has gotten quite high, but is government the problem like everyone always says? Is the 18 whatever trillion a lot? I mean, I know it seems like a lot. But remember we need to compare it to the size of our economy (like Jeff Bezos owing a million versus Fred the mailman).

That information is easy to figure out. The quick answer is yes (sorry, that wasn't suspenseful). Yes, it is a lot of debt for this country. The government's portion of debt is a big share of GDP when you compare it to historical figures.

The last time government debt was so high compared to GDP was in the late 1940s, after World War II. Has there been another world war going on that I didn't hear about? We saw from the last chart that debt is growing . . . and the Congressional Budget Office forecasts it will get worse in the years to come. Why will it get worse?

It has to do with promises. And I don't mean pinky promises. It has to do with the promises the U.S. government has made to pay for certain programs like Social Security, Medicare, and Medicaid. The cost for these programs, sometimes referred to as "entitlement programs," is going to grow bigger and bigger in coming years. I hate to be the bearer of bad news, but those programs will cost more as the baby boomer generation continues to enter retirement.

Social Security and Medicare have serious demographic and reliability issues. As you work through your life, you are supporting the elderly by paying their Social Security and Medicare. When you retire, the working population will be supporting you. That was the theory behind these programs. The problem we will be encountering over the next few decades has to do with demographics. The baby boomers didn't have the huge families that their parents did. That means there are fewer workers to support the boomers in retirement. Someone has to pay for this.

A bipartisan budget advocacy group called The Concord Coalition put together this chart (figure 14) to show what I'm talking about.

Figure 14. Baby Boomer Social Security Demographics

Americans are Living Longer and Having Fewer Children

Consequently, fewer workers are available to support each Social Security and Medicare Recipient

1960: 5 to 1   2010: 3 to 1   2030: 2 to 1

Source: Social Security Trustees, June 2016.

THE CONCORD COALITION

You can see that the ratio of workers to retirees changed from 1960 to 2010, and see what is projected for 2030. There is a higher proportion of retirees compared to citizens in their prime working ages. Longer life expectancy means people live longer after retirement, too. It could mean if Medicare was once needed to cover a person's insurance needs for fifteen years, it must now do so for twenty-five years. Those extra years cost the government a lot more. The same goes for Social Security. Projected life expectancies have grown by about ten years since the late 1940s.

Don't get me wrong. This is wonderful on a personal level. I'll get to eat plenty more of Grandma's molasses cookies. However, on a grander scale, for an entire society, it cannot be ignored. The spending issues it creates for Social Security and

Medicare could become a crisis.

Before we get too much off track, how does this relate to investing? The short answer is that bond returns will be low (to be covered in more detail in chapters twenty three and twenty four). For now, keep in mind that the federal budget, which is already heavily indebted, has a lot of Social Security and Medicare promises to pay out. Stay in the rabbit hole a bit longer, Alice.

It is difficult for the U.S. government to cut Social Security and Medicare. Really, how can you pull the rug out from the sick and elderly whose lives depend on these programs? Not to mention these are people who *always* remember to vote.

As the debt to cover these mandatory programs grows, so will borrowing. This means more federal revenue will go toward interest payments on the extra borrowing.

Buy some umbrellas. I'm afraid this rain on the parade is only going to keep going. If federal spending is already spoken for on these mandatory programs, it's likely other government spending will need to take a haircut. Departments like education, transportation, agriculture, and veterans' affairs will have a harder time getting funding. Same for the military.

But wait... there's more! Just like the ShamWow commercials that throw in an extra mini ShamWow at the end, I'm throwing in more promises that need to be paid for. That's right! Even more debt! State and local governments have public pensions for their employees. And you guessed it, they haven't been funding these pensions to keep up with the promises they've made. A pension is a retirement program that will pay employees when they retire. We already have projections for what employees will need to be paid. Long story short, many states are underfunded to pay their future retirees as things stand right now.

The Federal Reserve compiles data to track how state and local pensions are funded. As of this writing, the latest data they have is for 2016[29]. The total pension assets of all state and local pensions combined were over 3.8 trillion dollars! That's good news. Four trillion is a lot of assets.

On the other side of the equation are the liabilities (what is owed). That is the amount of promises these pensions are projected to have to pay out. The bad news is that the liabilities are significantly higher than the assets. Nobody knows exactly how this will play out. States and municipalities don't need to keep assets equal to 100% of their pension liabilities. They can remain underfunded over time. There might come a point, as some government pensions have experienced, where taxes need to be raised, pension benefits reduced, or state and local workers in the pension laid off.

Because it's fun to think our state is better than other states, here is a breakout of funded state pensions (figure 15). Let's all make fun of New Jersey and Kentucky now.[30]

Figure 15. Breakdown of US Pensions by State

Funded Ratios for State Pension Plans, 2016
Only 4 states had at least 90% of the assets needed to pay promised benefits

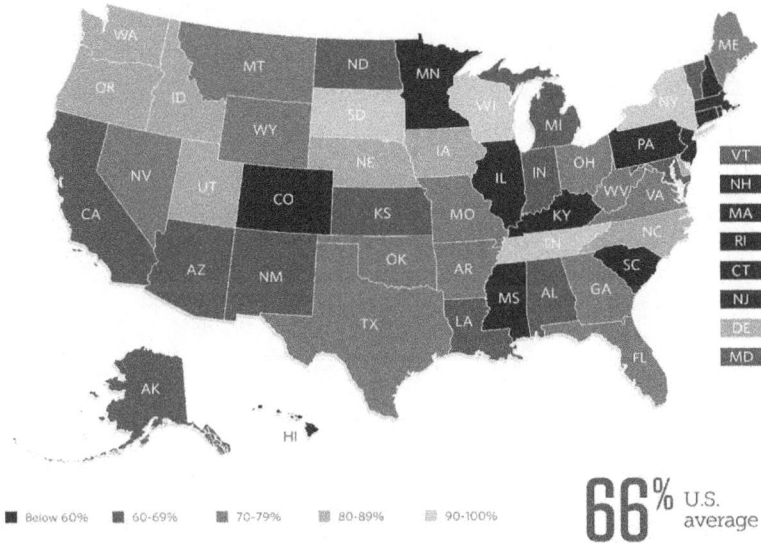

■ Below 60% ■ 60-69% ■ 70-79% ▨ 80-89% ▨ 90-100%

66% U.S. average

Note: Percentages reflect 2016 Governmental Accounting Standards Board reporting standards.

Sources: Comprehensive annual financial reports, actuarial reports and valuations, other public documents, or as provided by plan officials

© 2018 The Pew Charitable Trusts

The situation shows that every part of the economy—personal, corporate, and government—has extraordinarily high levels of debt. Can you rely on Social Security and Medicare to be around when you're ready to retire? Instead, why not use this as a reason to build your own investments? Build a security blanket to reduce your reliance on these programs.

CHAPTER TWENTY-TWO
STRUCTURAL CHALLENGES

"He who awaits much can expect little."

— *Gabriel Garcia Marquez, Columbian novelist,*
screenwriter, and journalist

I can recall grabbing a beer with Rob the Computer Engineer back in 2012, I believe, at some bar where the TVs were covering a news story about the budget. The two political parties of the United States were arguing how to best handle the never-ending budget issues. One side wanted to raise taxes. The other side wanted to cut spending. To be honest, Rob and I weren't very informed on the issues. Rob expressed his desire to cut government spending; he didn't want to entertain the idea of higher taxes.

It struck me as a little funny. Rob—the guy who couldn't control spending—expected the government to control their spending? Besides the irony of the situation, I wondered which of the two political parties would win their argument. It wasn't too long after Rob and I enjoyed that night out that breaking news showed both political parties had agreed to a compromise.

They agreed to keep spending at the same level but also to *not* raise taxes. Say what? It was decided raising taxes or cutting spending were both bad. I equated their solution to someone who wants to lose weight and must decide if they want to improve their diet or exercise more and they can't decide which to do—so they do neither. Episodes like that 2012 "compromise" are why the U.S. is in its current position—historically high levels of debt for the size of the economy.

What options do governments have to fix the current debt and future promises they've made? One option is to reduce the debt. Make debt reduction a priority at both the federal and state level. It's certainly not the flashiest or most rousing public policy platform. Admit it—you are half asleep right now from those past few sentences.

Since 1970, there have only been three years where the U.S. government had a budget surplus (taking in more money than spending). That is three years out of nearly fifty years. Both political parties have had their chance in the White House or have had control of Congress. They can share the blame on this one.

If debt reduction isn't the strategy, can the U.S. grow its way out of this debt? Sort of like the Jeff Bezos example earlier, where one million of debt wasn't a lot compared to his vast wealth? Can the U.S. grow so large that forty-seven trillion of debt is easier to manage? Color me skeptical.

We saw from the prior section that high levels of debt usually stunt economic growth. All the retiring baby boomers are exiting the workforce over the next couple of decades. Due to the lower birth rates in the U.S. (currently less than two children per woman according to the World Bank[31]), the influx of new workers is at lower rates than it used to be. The other source of a growing labor force would be immigration. It's a hot button political issue, but without immigration, significant labor force growth is doubtful.

J.P. Morgan's *Guide to the Markets* is a quarterly release of various investment and economic data. Part of their December 2018 release illustrated changes in the working age population.

From 1978 to 2007, the working age population, ages 16–64, was increasing by over one percent per year through a combination of immigration and natural population increases from native born Americans. From 2008 to 2017, there was a significant change in this growth rate, downshifting to half a percent per year, meaning the growth in workers is slowing.

The U.S. Census Bureau uses population trends to project the future population of the United States. This is their projection for 2016 and 2040[32]:

Year	Working Population	Native Born	Immigrant
2016	199,611,000	165,294,000	34,317,000
2040	215,571,000	174,634,000	40,936,000

Over the course of the twenty-four projected years, the working population is projected to grow by almost sixteen million. The annual rate of growth of this segment of the population averages about .33%. This is lower than it was for the decades that the JP Morgan's *Guide to the Markets* illustrated (1 percent), meaning that the growth rate of the working population has been slowing and is projected to slow even more.

Aging employees might work beyond retirement. Perhaps people will work more hours or take second jobs. The unemployment rate might reach new historical lows. But a burst in workers probably won't be in the cards.

As we talk about these structural impediments in the overall economy, try not to be frightened. Try to think about how these are serious problems that make you want to invest your money so that you will be protected.

The retiring baby boomer generation (seventy million strong) has made demographics a headwind to economic growth. Besides the larger number of people using entitlement programs, older people are naturally in a more conservative part of their lives. Their levels of production and consumption go down (a negative for economic growth). And the proportion of people in the labor force is a smaller part of the whole population. Future obligations for retirement and medical benefits will come due.

The United States isn't the only industrialized nation facing these issues. Japan, China, and Western European countries are in similar boats. Japan has embraced robotic technology to cover their labor shortages. China is following suit and is currently a leading purchaser of robotic technology to offset their decline in workers as their population ages. The disruption caused by technology screws workers at times, but it helps an economy's labor issues.

Technology in robotics and artificial intelligence (AI) will help to make up the labor pool shortages. What is the other solution? Everyone work until they are eighty? Better make room for more nap pods. More workers or more productivity is really the only way to grow the economy substantially.

Historically, technological innovation has created new jobs while destroying existing ones. ATM machines and online banking replaced a lot of bank tellers, but there are more jobs in the overall banking industry than ever. Previously in this book, I used examples in the agricultural industry to show how eliminated jobs were replaced by other jobs. The people who had their jobs eliminated still had to find new jobs or learn new skills. These are real people. If someone loses their job to a machine at a jeans factory, they have to find a new job. In many cases, a lower paying job. Perhaps jeans now cost five cents less per pair, but that gives this one real person very little comfort. Technological changes seem to be happening faster and faster.

To avoid being one of the "left behind" workers whose job gets eliminated and then has trouble finding a similar job, begin thinking about Rob the Engineer, Nathalie the Single Mom, and Mike the Car Guy for ways to funnel more money toward investing. Taking control of your finances and building an investment nest egg is a good way to avoid being left out in the cold if Johnny No. 5 takes your job (an obscure reference to the

80s movie *Short Circuit*).

The tech revolution continues to happen whether you are ready for it or not. McDonald's and Burger King have been rolling out more and more self-service ordering kiosks to replace the cashiers. Amazon now has over 45,000 robots in its warehouses doing work previously done by humans. Charles Schwab "robo advisors" are now managing more than 20 billion dollars in money.

Theoretically, cutting Social Security and Medicare benefits, or cutting pensions that state and municipal workers rely on (or plan to rely on), might help stop the debt monster. But simply put, it would be political suicide for policy makers to enact changes like that. I doubt any of the major political parties would embrace the idea of making significant cuts. It usually takes incredibly dire situations to force reforms of this nature. Greece experienced a financial crisis triggered by the turmoil of the Great Recession in '08/'09. Attempting to emerge from the crisis required multiple austerity packages, like increasing the retirement age and reducing public pensions. These reforms were met with nationwide strikes and massive protests.

Part of the argument is that people already using those programs may not have anything else to live on. And they likely wouldn't be able to go back to work if they are already deep into retirement. They'd be, in a word, hosed. Same for the people on the verge of retirement. It's hard to tell someone who is a few years from retiring that their Social Security payments will be slashed or delayed. The more likely option is to come down harder on current workers. People currently in the workforce have time to change their behavior (i.e., Save More).

Time to put all these structural happenings together.

There is a ton of current debt across all parts of the economy. Debt, even as a percentage of our economy, is at near record highs.

The current demographics of an aging population with longer life expectancies means many of the social programs may not deliver on promises without adding significantly to the existing debt.

This debt, along with lower birth rates and less immigration, likely means subdued economic growth on the horizon.

Earlier, you read that consumers don't have much in savings. Half of households with people aged 55 and over have no retirement savings at all. Many households live paycheck to paycheck.

Technology is going to cause a lot of job insecurity and disruption.

These structural changes relate to your personal investing in multiple ways. These are solid reasons for you to take matters into your own hands and get your personal finances in order. You were given amazing, wonderful, specific investment ideas earlier in this book. If you don't have any sort of retirement account, you best get cookin.' Try to get your investments going before you finish this book. If you have a 401k or other retirement program at work, use it. Or you can set up an individual retirement account (IRA). With either of these, you can take advantage of investing money for retirement on a pre-tax basis. That *saves* money. Save More, remember?

Despite the relatively slower economic growth of the past ten years, the stock market is at or near record highs (S&P 500 index). So, despite the subdued economic growth and growing debt, investors who have participated in the stock market have done well. Add that to the reasons to get involved in investing: don't be left behind.

CHAPTER TWENTY-THREE
THE FEDERAL RESERVE AND
BOND YIELDS

"Have patience. All things are difficult before they become easy."

— *Saadi, Persian poet*

Throughout this book, I've advocated for investing in the stock market as opposed to investing in bonds. In this section, we'll explore why bonds have had such low returns recently and why that might continue.

I recall being at a summer bonfire with Nathalie the Single Mom and some other friends back in 2013. Nathalie made an offhanded complaint about banking. Her savings account interest rates were paltry. She wanted to know why interest rates were so low for people trying to save money.

I did a really bad job of trying to explain how interest rates are set by central banks. In the case of the United States, our central bank is called the Federal Reserve. Two minutes into my explanation, her eyes sort of glazed over. When I finished my poor, rambling explanation, she politely smiled and tried to play it off like she understood, saying something like "Oh, okay" before changing the subject.

She still did much better than the character played by Mark Wahlberg (one of the world's best actors by the way) in the movie *The Other Guys*. He plays a cop alongside Will Ferrell, and they get involved in a case investigating financial crimes. Wahlberg's character can't wrap his head around the concept of the Federal Reserve. A few times in the movie, he refers to it as a prison, and even threatens an accused perpetrator with locking him up in the Federal Reserve. Will Ferrell, the nerdy cop, shakes his head in response and mutters under his breath, "He still doesn't understand the concept."

I'll try to do a better job explaining it here than I did to Nathalie back in 2013. It's important to at least "understand the concept" so you can agree with me about future bond returns being lower than a snake's belly.

The Federal Reserve (the "Fed") is a central bank for the United States. Central banks are government institutions that manage the currency, the supply of money, and interest rates. In many cases, they also oversee the commercial banking industry of their respective countries. Their basic purpose is to maintain a stable economy. Other central banks include the Bank of England, Central Bank of Brazil, Bank of Canada, People's Bank of China, State Bank of Pakistan, etc. You get the point. Central banks are common around the globe.

In 1913, in an attempt to prevent the severe financial crises that occurred throughout the 1800s and in 1907, the Federal Reserve was created. Over the years, the scope and power of the Fed has increased (usually after a crisis). The Fed has two main objectives, often referred to as its dual mandate: to maximize employment and maintain price stability. Let me repeat that, because it's the important part of what we are talking about. The Fed's main job is to keep unemployment low and to keep the price of things stable (control inflation).

The Federal Reserve also provides a lot of economic research (some of it has been cited in this book). We'll keep our focus on the dual mandate and the tools the Fed uses to control the unemployment rate and keep inflation stable.

One of the important tools the Fed uses is to control how easy it is for people to borrow money. The Fed doesn't approve or decline our credit card applications, or give loans to regular people like you and me. Instead, it makes borrowing money easier or harder for banks and other financial institutions, and that impacts the banks' customers, like you and me. The Fed is like a bank for banks.

If unemployment is high (lots of people out of work), the Federal Reserve can make credit easier to get so more people can buy things or start new businesses. This can stimulate the economy. In turn, a growing economy will lead to more jobs being created and a lower unemployment rate.

The flip side is when the economy is running too "hot." If workers are scarce (very low unemployment), companies tend to pay higher wages to keep them from leaving. If resources and materials are also in short supply, their prices go up (uh oh, remember the Fed wants stable prices!). This increase in wages and prices can lead to higher and higher inflation, so the Fed will attempt to reduce lending in the economy. Like your dad taking away your allowance, the Fed makes it tougher for financial institutions to lend money. When it's harder to borrow money, the economy should cool off. This prevents the prices of food, housing, transportation, energy, and everything else from growing too fast. Slowing down the economy is how the Fed meets its second mandate of maintaining stable prices. This push and pull, of stimulating the economy and slowing borrowing, is the theory behind the Fed in a nutshell.

You probably aren't asking yourself this, but let's imagine you find the Fed interesting and want to know how? How do they make things easier or tougher for banks? Good question. Pat yourself on the back. I'm going to oversimplify things from here on because I don't want to get bogged down on details about the inner workings of the Federal Reserve.

One way the Fed influences credit is by controlling some

of the interest rates financial institutions use. This ends up translating to what interest rates banks charge to borrowers and how they reward savers. Low interest rates encourage people to borrow to buy cars, houses, or start businesses. They also penalize savers by not giving them a very big reward (like earning very little for having money in a savings account). High interest rates reduce borrowing and increase the incentive to save. This is the most important Fed tool. It has a couple of other tools to control credit, but we'll focus only on this one, controlling short-term interest rates.

The Fed uses tools to make lending easier or harder. If there is only one part of this discussion you want to remember, that should be it. Controlling the interest rates has a big influence on the economy. The Fed's actions are a driving force behind the economy, arguably more so than the actions of the U.S. president or the U.S. Congress.

The ability to influence interest rates can be a powerful tool for the president and/or the ruling political party in the United States. That is why the Fed was designed to be an independent institution. It probably doesn't make a lot of sense for a president to decide to lower interest rates right before an election. "Guess what everybody, I made interest rates lower so you can refinance your home mortgage or car loan to save on your monthly payment. I did that. Me. But sure, go vote for the other guy."

Thankfully, all the monetary policy (the credit and interest rate policy of a central bank) decisions are handled by a twelve-member committee. No president can make or remake the committee because of the long tenures each committee member has. The president appoints a chairman. Some chairpersons you might have heard of are Alan Greenspan, Paul Volcker, and Janet Yellen. President Trump appointed Jerome Powell as the current chairman.

The twelve-person committee will tighten credit (mainly by raising interest rates) if inflation starts to go up (to control inflation). Or they will loosen credit (lower rates) if prices are

stable but there are high levels of unemployment. Let's look at
how rates have moved historically so you can see what I mean
between the relationship of interest rates and inflation rates.

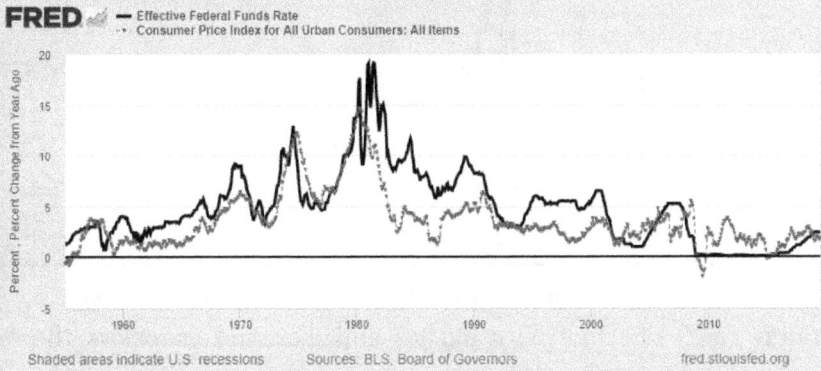

Figure 16. Federal Funds Rate in Comparison to Inflation Rates

The solid black line is the Federal Reserve's federal funds
rate—the interest rate they influence. The dotted line with mini
triangles is the inflation rate. It's the Consumer Price Index
(CPI). The Fed looks at other inflation measures as well, but we'll
stick to CPI for simplicity. The chart goes back to 1961. You
can see the correlation between the lines in the chart. Raising
rates (making the solid line go higher) would be the Fed's way of
lowering the dotted line (inflation).

The reason the correlation isn't stronger has to do with
juggling the second part of the mandate – unemployment –
as well as the delay of effect on the economy of interest rate
decisions. The U.S. economy is complicated. It is a difficult,
slow, and cumbersome ship to steer. Over the past few decades,
the Fed has sometimes chosen to raise rates when it anticipates
inflation beginning to rise, but as you saw in the previous chart,
recent inflation has never come close to where it was during the
1970s and early 1980s.

Now that we've seen how interest rates are changed to combat
inflation, we can also see how they combat unemployment.

Figure 17. Federal Funds Rate in Comparison to Employment Rates

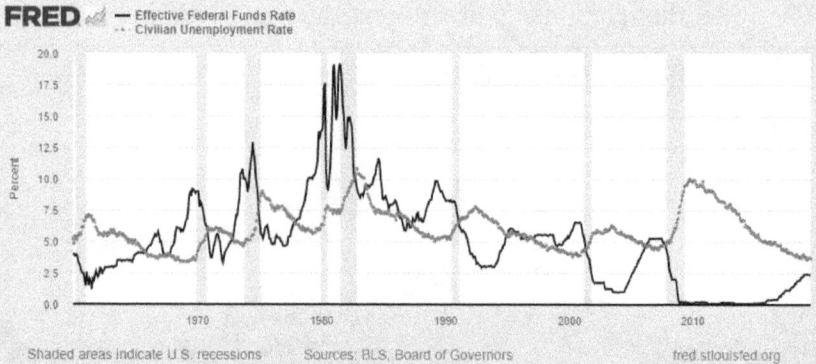

The solid black line is the same as before, it's the federal funds rate. The line with dashes and diamond shapes is the unemployment rate. As unemployment rises, the Fed might lower rates to stimulate the economy. That is why in much of the chart a rising dotted diamond line (unemployment) is followed by a downward solid line (interest rates). Like inflation, the relationship isn't perfect. But the trend is still clear: Generally, if unemployment is high, interest rates (solid line) are lowered until the unemployment rate (diamond line) starts to go down.

Now you should be getting a better idea of what the Fed is at least trying to do. You can see from the last chart that right after the Great Recession in '08/'09, the Fed brought its rate down to zero to try to stimulate the economy and get people back to work (the unemployment rate was 10%+).

By now you must be getting *fed* up hearing about the Fed. We're almost through it. Consider how these interest rates can affect your life or how they might have affected your life in the past. If you have taken out a loan within the last decade, it's likely been at a lower interest rate than a similar loan would have been during the 1980s. One example is a thirty-year fixed rate mortgage. From 1970 to today, we can look at the historical rates (figure 18).

Figure 18. Average of 30-Year Fixed Rate Mortgages in the US (1970 -)

You can see the rates correspond to what the Fed has set for rates. When the federal funds rate was higher (as in the early 1980s), the thirty-year fixed mortgage rate was higher.

The flip side is for the savers. When the Fed has a low rate, this translates into low rates in savings accounts, CDs, U.S. Savings Bonds, and other bond investments, such as mortgage bonds. Most mortgages are bundled and then sold to investors. If you are paying a low rate for your mortgage, it stands to reason that the investor buying your mortgage is also earning a low return. This logic applies to investors and individuals who buy any type of bond (from the U.S. government, corporations, and municipalities). Putting it all together now: Returns for bond investors are also be affected by the Fed's rates.

Let's look at what's been happening to the federal funds rate the last few decades (figure 19). Recognize a pattern?

The vertical gray bars signify recessions. As the economy starts to heat up, the Fed raises interest rates. That is why you normally see rates increasing leading up to a recession. Then the rates are lowered to stimulate the now-in-a-recession economy. Take a closer look from the period starting in the early 1980s leading up to today. The rates appear to be on a longer term bottoming-out process with lower lows and lower highs.

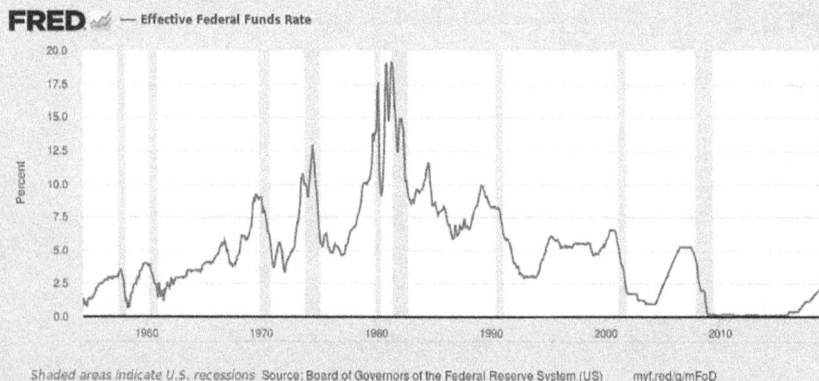

Figure 19. US Federal Funds Rates Beginning in 1960

Bond investment returns have followed a similar pattern to the Fed rate. Remember when I talked about how the Barclay's Aggregate Index measures bond returns? Here are the returns by decade:

1980s: Averaged 12.10% per year

1990s: Averaged 7.71% per year

2000s: Averaged 6.31% per year

2010 to end of 2017: Averaged 3.61% per year

From what we know about inflation and the federal funds rate, this should make sense, right? Back in the 1980s when rates and inflation were much higher, bond owners had higher returns. As the federal funds rate went down, returns went down. Inflation, the federal funds rate, and bond yields have been trending one way since the 1980s: lower.

This is not a new phenomenon. There have been other instances of 30+ year rate bottoming processes like this. Leading up to the Great Depression, through it, and up until the 1960s was another 30+ year rate bottoming process. Something similar occurred in Japan. From the late 1980s through today, Japan has been going through a multi-decade-long rate bottoming process.

There is yet another chart I'd like to show you that might help illustrate what I mean. It's probably the nerdiest chart of the book. This chart uses ten-year government bonds. The chart shows how long these rate bottoming processes can take. It compares current U.S. rates to Japan's experience and the U.S. experience through the Great Depression.

Figure 20. Long Rate Bottoming Processes in both the US and Japan

Long Rate Bottoming Processes

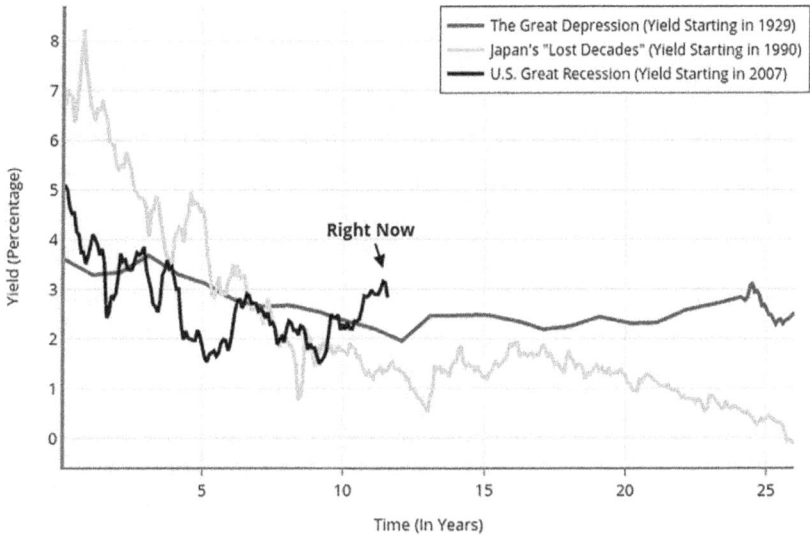

The black line is the current process of U.S. bonds, and I've identified where rates were at the end of 2018. The other two lines are the rate cycles of Japan and the Great Depression which took decades to resolve. There is a precedent for having low rates over long periods of time. This could mean that bond investors are looking at another fifteen years or more of relatively low returns!

Ten years after the 1929 stock market collapse, ten-year government bonds were yielding just 2.2%. We are about ten years past the Great Recession and today's ten-year bonds are around 3%. A quote attributed to Mark Twain is, "History doesn't repeat itself, but it often rhymes." Where today has the shared economy and robotics, the 1930s had machine tool and metalworking improvements and agricultural innovations like refrigerated trucking.

I hear realtors, bank lenders, and even economic "experts" predict that higher rates are around the corner. And they aren't talking about one or two percent higher. They think rates could march higher and higher and higher. Maybe even back to double digits. "When I bought my first house, the interest rate was fifteen percent on the mortgage." I hear people all the time refer to prior years when interest rates were much higher. They expect that since it happened before, it will happen again. My view is that the Fed might not be able to raise rates back to those elevated levels so quickly. It's really not so simple, because the structural challenges today are different from the early 1980s. We might have another decade or two of lower than normal interest rates. There will be Fed rate hikes, sure, but they are temporary moguls on a bigger downhill ski slope (oh look, another winter comparison).

CHAPTER TWENTY FOUR
STRUCTURAL TRENDS
REDUCE BOND YIELDS

> "Defeat is not the worst of failures. Not to have
> tried is the true failure."
>
> — *George Edward Woodberry, literary critic and poet*

Let's relate some of the real-world structural issues back to the Fed's ability to raise interest rates. Remember how the total debt in the U.S. economy has been going up and up? The total debt to the GDP is over 250% which is a record for the post WWII era! Whenever the Fed increases interest rates, debt becomes harder to pay. Obviously, the more debt you have, the bigger a burden higher interest rates will be. Because there is so much debt out there, it will take fewer rate increases than usual to slow economic growth.

Think back to Rob the Computer Engineer. So much of his money was going toward paying his debt (and the interest on it), he wasn't able to do other things with his money, like come up with a down payment on a house. He also used to keep rolling his debt from one car to the next, right? Well, what if the next car has a higher interest rate? That means it's harder to pay for. Or maybe he has to actually wait longer than he normally would to buy that next car. That is the type of thing that slows down economic growth.

If you take the existing high levels of debt and add the future debt (trillions) that will incur from promised Social Security and Medicare, the magnitude of every interest rate change will have a greater effect. A simple math problem can illustrate what I mean. We'll use a five-year loan paid monthly.

DEBT	OLD RATE	NEW RATE	OLD PAYMENT	NEW PAYMENT	DIFFERENCE
50,000	2.00%	2.25%	876.00	882.00	6.00
200,000	2.00%	2.25%	3,506.00	3,527.00	21.00

The example shows that if you already have a lot of debt, a slightly higher rate will be more expensive. The payment for the higher debt increased by twenty-one dollars. Relating this back to the U.S., our large existing debt load (and future debt load) will mean bigger debt payments from small increases in interest rates. This means anytime interest rates go up, they will slow the economy more than they have in the past. This will constrain the Fed from ever raising rates too quickly or too high. We saw in the last chapter that bond returns were lower when the Fed rates were lower.

When you look at the structural changes happening in the U.S. economy, retiring baby boomers ensure there will be plenty of bond buyers. If there weren't any buyers, perhaps bonds would have to be offered at better returns. But that won't be the case, due to the baby boomers. Buyers will keep a roof on bond yields, preventing them from getting much higher than they currently are. As investors age, they prefer fixed income because of the steady payments and low risk. They'll accept a low-return, low-risk investment with payments they can count on.

Typical investment advice is to increase your proportion of bonds as you age. The idea is that a 30-year-old can take more risk because they don't need the money to keep a roof over their head. A retired 70-year-old might not have many sources of income, so they need their investments to fund their day-to-day expenses. The basic concept that people tend to purchase safer investments as they age is an important consideration with current demographics. The baby boomer generation is going to continue shifting their investments to bonds as they age.

The shift in how the boomer generation is invested will be staggering. An article titled "Elders and equities: How much stock should retirees own?" from CNBC discussed this shift.[33] A popular investment product called target date funds is basically a mutual fund with a year or retirement "target" date in the name of the fund. If you plan to retire in 2040, there is a target date fund offered specifically for someone retiring in the year 2040. An example would be the Vanguard Target Retirement 2040 Fund. The investment company managing the fund assumes you'll be aged sixty-five in 2040. (Why else would you own the fund?) The CNBC article talks about how Vanguard's target date funds will be ninety percent equity and ten percent bonds until the investor is aged forty. The ratio shifts to fifty-fifty up until age sixty-five. Then it shifts to seventy percent bonds and thirty percent equities from age sixty-five and beyond.

Re-read those past few sentences if you didn't grasp it. The funds began ten percent fixed income, but by age sixty-five, shifted to seventy percent fixed income. This strategy for their target date funds is a very common one. Most financial advisors follow a strategy for their clients similar to the one Vanguard follows for their target date funds.

Most of the economic power still resides with the baby boomer generation. Millennials may be the biggest generation ever, but the wealth and influence is still with the boomers. According to the AARP, 10,000 baby boomers turn sixty-five every day[34]. This will last into the 2030s. This will influence spending and saving across the entire economy, including the investment markets. The changing ways they spend money (and stop earning as much) will have deflationary effects across the economy. Expect them to live more frugally. As we've pointed out a few times, almost half of them have less than 100,000 dollars in assets to live on during retirement. They can't spend what they don't have. (They aren't the U.S. government, har har har.)

The Bureau of Labor Statistics releases consumer expenditure data that tracks how thousands of people of different ages spend money. A few highlights from the 2014 data show these spending ranges:

Age	Average Annual Spending
50	$70,000
55–64	$56,267
65–74	$48,885
75+	$36,673

The trend of the data is unmistakable. Fifty-year-olds spend an average of 70,000 dollars per year and then it decreases as people get older. That is why we won't see high inflation. And without inflation, the Fed is meeting its mandate and won't have to raise interest rates. The boomers are just starting to turn seventy. There are over 70 million people in that generation.

Demographics in developed countries around the globe are mostly the same, which is further evidence of one thing: Low bond yields are here for a while longer.

Boomers aren't the only cause of low inflation. Let's reinforce some of the low inflation evidence we can see in the economy around us. We tend to hear a lot about increasing education costs or increasing healthcare costs. If we read the tea leaves, what can we predict about inflation?

Education and healthcare have indeed been outliers for inflation, but even these areas are changing. For all the talk about increasing education prices, the Consumer Price Index shows the rate of increase has been slowing down. Costs are only increasing about 2.3% per year as of the end of 2017.

Healthcare has been a little higher. Nevertheless, costs that were rising more quickly have since slowed down. I won't offer any opinions as to why, but costs from the 1980s through 2018 have trended down. It is now closer to three percent per year. People commonly cite education and healthcare as "high inflation." Two to three percent per year is high?

Just hear me out for a minute. Consider where you spend your money. I don't need data to back up how the price of electronics has come down and continues to come down. Name brand smart phones might be the exception, but their quality, power, and capability has increased. You might be paying more, but you are getting a better product than before. TVs, computers, and other gadgets have more features and cost *less* than they did in years past. They are objectively better and cost less money. Food prices aren't going up very fast and probably won't. Advances in agriculture have made it much cheaper to produce food in modern times.

Energy prices? Relatively low. Ever increasing competition and new technologies are likely to keep it that way. Extracting oil through fracking and improving efficiencies have lowered the cost of obtaining energy sources, which are being passed onto consumers. Costs for renewable energy resources continue to get cheaper as well. This leads me to believe inflation on energy costs will be manageable. And lower energy costs should keep transportation costs down, too. Not to mention the deflationary effects of the "sharing" economy. What's cheaper, an Uber ride or a taxicab ride?

Cell phone plans haven't been going up. Cable or Internet plans aren't increasing very quickly, either. In some cases, they are going down as different forms of competition, such as Netflix and Hulu, arise. Department stores and clothing companies aren't seeing high inflation either, per their

Consumer Price Index (CPI) figures. Amazon, online shopping, and technological improvements in logistics are keeping all these costs down. I wouldn't bet on much inflation in this space either.

Shelter costs for housing and apartments, depending on the location, are real. But even housing, per the CPI, is trending in the three to four percent price increase range per year in big cities. As we saw earlier, U.S. population growth isn't out of control, so I wouldn't expect anything of that nature to suddenly cause drastic housing inflation.

Amazon itself is a huge price deflator, shaking up the whole retail sector (and other sectors may follow as rumors swirl of Amazon eyeing other industries). They are changing the entire retail industry, much as Wal-Mart did for decades. Many competitors fell by the wayside because they couldn't compete with Wal-Mart's low prices. Business media outlet *Investor's Business Daily* ran an article titled "Here's One More Thing Amazon May Be Killing" referring to Amazon's effect on inflation[35.]

Amazon is also a big proponent of incorporating robots, artificial intelligence, and drones into their operations. The future effect robots and drones might have on Amazon and other businesses is still difficult to predict precisely, but I can guarantee its effects will be deflationary. These tools along with 3-D printing, are the types of new technologies that put massive cost cutting pressure on industries.

Let's even go ultra-basic for a minute and look at the materials used to actually make things. These prices have been relatively steady. Bloomberg has an index of all sorts of commodities. Things like energy (oil, natural gas, diesel), grains (corn, soybeans, wheat, sugar, coffee, cotton), metals (copper, aluminum, zinc), and livestock (cattle, hogs) all captured in the index. At the end of 2017, the index value was actually lower than it was in 1991.

Ask yourself this question. If the cost of the materials to

make things has gone down over the past 25+ years, is it really surprising inflation is so low?

There is a reason inflation is crucial for investing. Inflation is one of the strongest factors in determining bond yields. If inflation is low, it means the Fed doesn't have to raise rates. If investors think inflation will stay low, they will accept buying a low return bond.

Back in 2007 as the economy was heating up, inflation hit almost five percent. That seems very high compared to today. Even when it nearly touched five percent in '07, we saw the Fed raise interest rates to counteract it. After the Great Recession, inflation vanished to practically nothing. In late 2017, even with unemployment down to four percent, inflation still slowly reached over two percent.

The Fed's dual mandates are to keep employment high and prices stable. At nearly a four percent unemployment rate, as of this writing, check off the box for the first mandate. At this point, the Fed expects the second mandate, stable prices, to become a concern. They are not alone. Many of the "experts" and gurus in the economics, business, or financial services industries have been saying inflation will appear soon. Always soon. Right around the corner.

The Federal Reserve releases what is called "dot plots," which are their prediction of future interest rate changes. They make forecasts going several years out. We can track these forecasts over time and compare them to the actual rate hikes completed by the Fed committee (figure 21).

The chart is a little "busy." Lines everywhere. All the dotted lines show what the Fed's committee predicted for rate hikes. The black line on the bottom, the very bottom, shows what actually happened. In some cases, they weren't a little bit off—they were way the hell off. In 2014, for instance, they couldn't hit water if they fell out of a boat. The Fed projected a rate over three percent by the end of 2017. It was 1.5% at the end of 2017. Inflation never materialized, so they kept rates low.

Figure 21. Fed Prediction of Future Interest Rates Versus Actual Rates

Fed Expectations Versus Reality

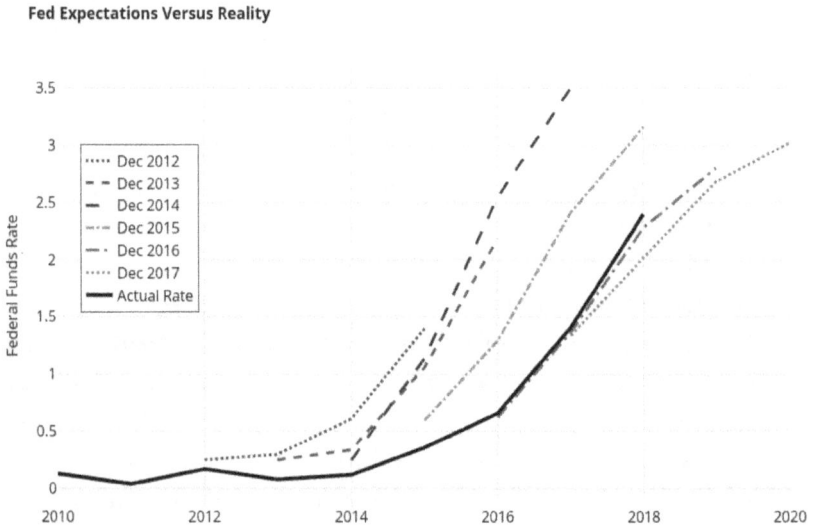

Yes, these predictions are by the same committee that manages the rates. Recent rate predictions have been more accurate. But you can see in prior years there was an optimism about how the overall economy would grow, how inflation would grow, and, in turn, the need to raise rates. You can also see from the most recent predictions that the optimism has been toned down. Predictions from late 2016 and late 2017 have tempered the pace of future rate hike expectations.

Despite how supremely smart the committee members are, as baseball player Yogi Berra jokingly said, "It's tough to make predictions, especially about the future." Structural forces at work are keeping inflation down, and these same forces have a way to go before they resolve themselves.

By now, it's probably clear as day that I have very little faith in bond returns over the next couple of decades. So, if the bond side of the coin doesn't make for a great investment, we bias toward the equity side of the coin.

The technological changes keeping inflation down have also been increasing the profitability of companies employing those technologies. If the money from better profitability isn't being passed along as wages, where is it all going? Well, if it isn't going to employees, some of it must be going to business owners and investors. This increased productivity is going to bring more income to someone; investing will make sure that income goes to you. This is also one of the reasons I highlighted the technology sector as a good long-term investment.

After exploring some of the big structural themes, next we will look at market cycles. The U.S. economy works in cycles. These are usually called business cycles. That is why you hear of the market booming followed by the eventual busts.

CHAPTER TWENTY-FIVE
MARKET CYCLES

"Always focus on the front windshield and not the rearview mirror."

— *Colin Powell, retired U.S. Army General and Secretary of State*

Earlier, we talked about Nathalie the Single Mom and the fear she had of investing. Her biggest fear was losing money in a recession. She remembered the housing crash and stories of people who lost money from retirement or investment accounts. Nathalie didn't know exactly what a "stock market crash" was, but she had certainly heard of them, and they frightened her.

Like most people, she thought a recession could start at any time. She also thought any investment value lost would be lost forever. She didn't know that the economy naturally moves in cycles and that a recession is a normal part of an economic cycle. Don't get me wrong, recessions suck. They are every investor's nightmare, but if you understand they are a normal part of investing, you shouldn't fear them. Once you understand they are normal, you will know to be patient and let your depreciated asset values recover with time. Nathalie was paralyzed by her fear and never got involved with investments.

Learning about market cycles will help you figure out how the economy works. It will help you overcome some of the fear that many investors (or prospective investors) have. You will keep a level head and sleep well during a booming economy or a recession.

As we discuss market cycles, the first thing we have to get into is the Federal Reserve. The Fed's importance in market cycles is critical. But talking about the Fed is like a medication for insomnia, so we'll only remind you they influence interest rates and that they try to keep unemployment and inflation low.

You can see the cycles reflected in the stock market. Here is the chart of the S&P 500 (the common proxy for the U.S. stock market) from 1946 to today. Since the value of the S&P stayed below 100 until 1979 and has since gone to a value of over 2,600, the early values of the chart would not be helpful unless we use a logarithmic scale to look at the index. (A logarithmic scale uses exponential not linear increments.) Doing this allows us to see how the economic cycles have affected the stock market more clearly.

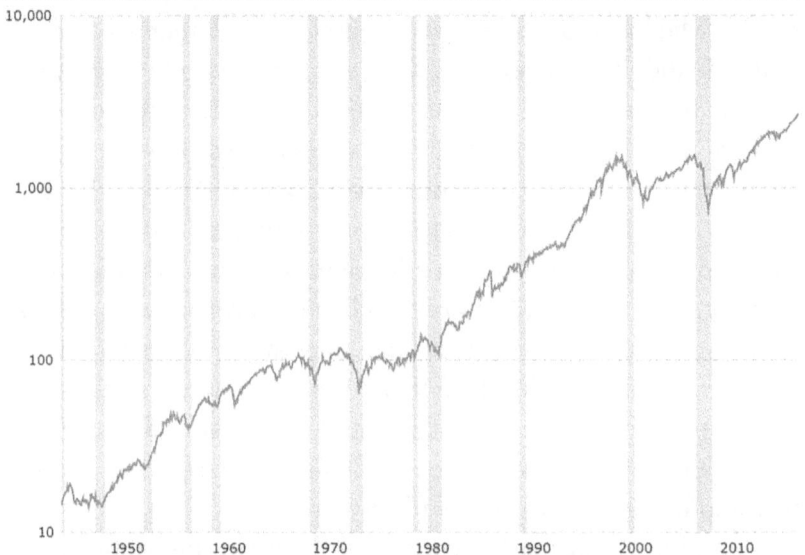

Figure 22. Value of the S&P 500 in Comparison to Recessions

The vertical gray bars indicate recessions. You'll recognize the stock bubble burst of the early 2000s and the housing bubble of late 2008. During each recession, unsurprisingly, the stock market tends to go down. And then, as the market troughs, it begins a new upward climb until the next recession. Going back all the way to 1946, you can see a somewhat regular cycle pattern of going up for a while and then down and then continuing to climb upward.

No business cycle is exactly the same. Unfortunately, each cycle is not a checklist to be filled out before beginning the next one. That is why even economists or financial advisors who study the economy every day can't figure out exactly when a recession is coming. We can talk about some of the patterns and trends that have defined most cycles, but unforeseen global events or big economic shocks can have unplanned influences on the economic cycle.

Economists typically break the market cycles into four phases. We'll organize the parts into early, mid, late, and recession. The four phases of a business cycle go something like the following graphic:

Figure 23. The Four Phases of the Economic Cycle

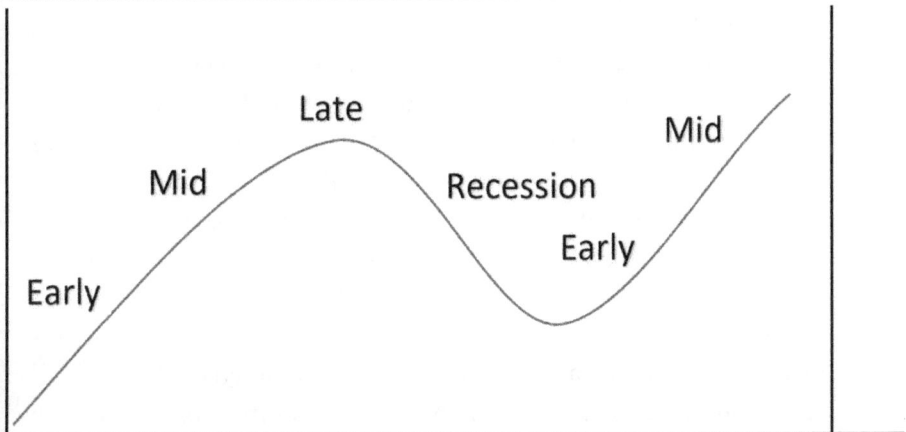

The first phase is the early phase, usually when the economy is emerging from a recession. There is typically a change from negative to positive GDP growth, and then accelerating growth. The Fed will create or maintain easy monetary policy, making credit easier to attain. They will lower their federal funds interest rate. Company sales and profits begin to grow, but their inventories are usually low. Unemployment is high, but not worsening. The costs of raw materials and wages for workers are relatively low for companies. Consumers like you and me are feeling hopeful and relieved that the economy seems to have turned a corner.

The mid cycle phase is normally a period of further growth. It is typically the longest lasting phase in a business cycle, when the economy builds on the early phase gains. The Fed might start to tighten their credit policy (making borrowing a little tougher). Businesses and consumers are borrowing and investing. Sales and inventories are growing. Companies generally have sound profitability. Overall business volume across the economy grows, and different industries and regions are sharing in the growing activity. Employment and incomes grow. Consumers feel optimistic and eventually excited about the economy. Toward the end of the mid cycle phase, investors are usually pretty thrilled, and they start to become greedy.

The late cycle phase is usually when the economy starts to run too "hot." Unemployment is low and companies have difficulty finding qualified and available labor. The Fed is raising interest rates to make credit more difficult for borrowers as it attempts to control rising inflation. The economy slips to slower and slower growth. Sales begin to decline, and corporate profit starts to weaken. The Fed's tightening credit conditions lead to an increase in loan defaults as some people or businesses struggle to maintain the now higher debt costs. The thrill and confidence consumers had now turns into anxiety or even denial.

The only phase left to discuss is the dreaded recession phase. Economic activity is contracting. Profit declines further, and the Fed reverses its policies to try to make credit more accommodating. But remember, there is a big lag to steering a ship the size of the U.S. economy. Sales are low, unemployment is growing as employees are laid off, and some companies close their doors for good. Business pessimism sets in. The late cycle feelings of denial have turned to fear and desperation. Consumer spending decreases. Many investors panic and sell stocks.

Let's take a quick look at the economic cycles we've had over the last several decades and you'll be able to see I'm telling you the truth. You'll see. The research on business cycles of the National Bureau of Economic Research (NBER), a nonprofit that has been around for about a hundred years, is commonly used across the investments and economics profession. Here are their measurements for business cycles.

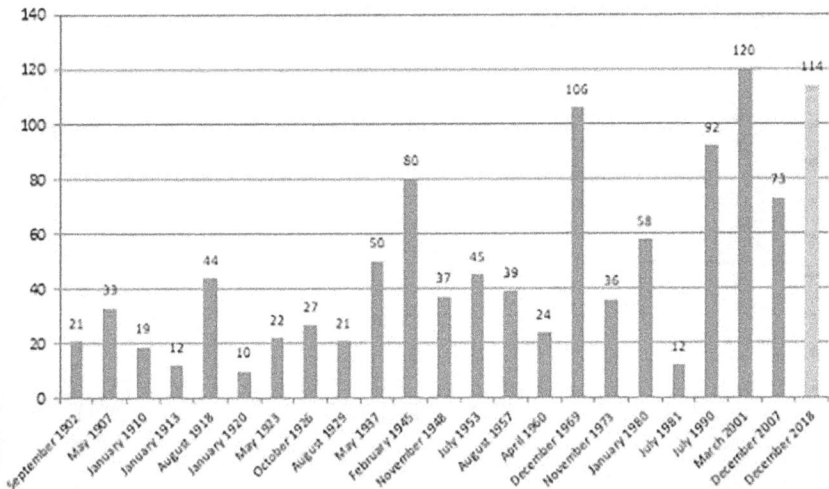

Figure 24. The Four Phases of the Economic Cycle

Monthly Duration of Business Cycles

Going all the way back to 1900, we can see each business cycle and how long it lasted (in months). Each bar on the chart measures how long the cycle lasted, from the trough of the cycle all the way to the peak. The dates on the bottom of the chart indicate the peak of the cycle. We can see that the business cycle we are currently in has gone on for 102 months and counting as of December 2018. It is now the third longest-running expansion since 1900. The one observation we can make is that it seems like the cycles are growing in length. It's not always the case, but you can see the tendencies of more recent cycles seem to last quite a bit longer than the cycles from the early 1900s. More often, they are in the five to ten year range instead of the one to five year range of the earlier cycles.

Time to make an important point. Pay very close attention. Economic cycles are a normal part of investing. Booming economies are normal. But so are recessions. Recessions are a normal part of market cycles.

Small stock market dips or corrections can occur every year without the economy's entering a recession. These will be temporary and usually recover over weeks or months. They naturally occur even within the early, mid, or late phase of the economic cycle without signaling that a recession is near. Outright recessions can really whack the stock market and take months or years for stock prices to recover.

CHAPTER TWENTY-SIX
WHERE ARE WE IN THE CYCLE?

One of the tricky things about investing in anything—classic cars, stocks, bonds, gold, real estate—is they all have ups and downs. Economic expansions and recessions impact every type of investment. There isn't a type of investing you can do that only goes up all the time. Unless you want to assume no risk and see very low returns. Learning how to read some of the signposts will help you figure out where we are in the business cycle and will add to your investing confidence.

Whenever I've been physically lost, it's usually for one of two reasons. The first is when I've got no clue where I am and I'm "way the heck lost." This can be stressful, irritating, and even scary. The other type of lost is when I have a general sense of the direction I'm going or the area I'm in. I don't panic or need help. I know I can get my bearings with a little patience and that everything will eventually be okay. Understanding how market cycles work should help you keep your bearings and never be "way the heck lost" when it comes to your investing.

The goal of learning these market cycle signposts is not so

you can determine when to sell all your stocks at market peaks and buy back in during recessions. Moving investments "all in" or "all out" is tricky and not a strategy I advise.

First, observe daily life. By observing and listening to what people talk about and paying attention to the big "can't miss" type of headlines in the news, you'll get a sense of where the U.S. economy is. Remember: Every cycle is different. We are going to look at certain telling signs, but they won't work like clockwork for each and every cycle. Even knowing the indicators, you won't be able to simply declare when it's "recession o'clock," or when a recession is about to begin.

Observe how greedy people appear to be. As the economic cycles enter the mid and later phases, people will start to earn higher wages. They'll have made money in their retirement and investment accounts. Their home values will be higher. This all tends to lead people to excessive risk taking. If you see high levels of greed setting in, that should be a red flag. Are more people you know buying houses that seem out of their price range? Is there a general sense that the value of everything is going to keep going up? Do you hear people talking about investing in things they haven't researched or in areas they haven't shown previous interest? Are people purchasing things that don't seem reasonable, and part of their explanation includes, "It's an investment"?

When you observe people borrowing money to "make investments," that is a clear red flag. Especially borrowing for a real estate investment or a business that seems sketchy.

If you notice that spending and investing habits seem a bit overleveraged, that usually indicates we are later in the economic cycle. When people spend or invest cautiously, it is usually earlier in the economic cycle.

Second, pay attention to the job market. This is one you will hear the media cover pretty well, since it's universally considered a barometer for the economy. The U3 unemployment rate is reported monthly by the Bureau of Labor Statistics (BLS), and is used as a common measure of the job market. High unemployment rates are consistent with the early part of the business cycle. As the rate gets lower and lower, it means the economy is progressing toward the later part of the cycle.

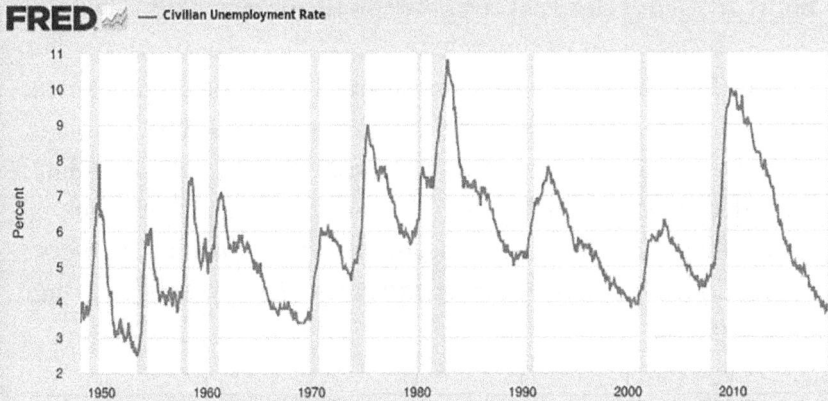

Figure 25. US Unemployment Rates

Source: U.S. Bureau of Labor Statistics

The gray bars indicate recessions. The chart shows the unemployment rate going all the way back to 1948, so about the last seventy years. You can see the U.S. unemployment rate doesn't go much below four percent. And when it does, it doesn't last for too long. Perhaps this will change slightly with the changing demographics in the U.S., but historically, once the unemployment rate hit five percent, the economy was at least past the early phase of the business cycle. And as pointed out, anything four percent or lower would probably indicate that we are later in the cycle.

At the same time as unemployment starts to decrease, wages should start to increase. I use the term "should" because technological changes and the reduction in the power of labor unions might have a dampening effect on wage rates compared to historical standards. It does stand to reason that if labor becomes scarce (low unemployment rate), employers need to pay more. Rather than give any figures, I'd say if you notice or hear the media talking about accelerating wages or wage growth rates going up, take note. The combination of rising wages and low unemployment is what is important. Rising wages on their own might not mean anything. Low unemployment and high wage growth would indicate a later point in the cycle. Low wage growth (or shrinking) would mean recession, or early cycle.

One indicator that goes hand-in-hand with unemployment is the difficulty employers have filling job openings. The National Federation of Independent Business (NFIB) collects data provided by small businesses. One of the things they track is how difficult it is for a small business to find qualified workers. If they can't find good workers, the economic cycle is entering a later phase.

Figure 26. Percentage of US Businesses with Very Few Qualified Candidates

Businesses With Few or No Qualified Applicants (in Percentages)

You can see how this played out the last two to three economic cycles. The gray bars indicate recessions. It shows when employers have trouble filling jobs, the economy is probably in at least the mid part of the cycle. As jobs become harder to fill, businesses cannot expand, and their growth is constrained.

To observe this indicator, you don't have to hear directly from CEOs or hiring managers. Pay attention at your own place of employment. Is your company able to fill its job openings with qualified people? Have any of your friends or family members been complaining about the quality of people recently hired? I'd be careful about taking just one or two examples as gospel. A common refrain among your friends, family, and co-workers will be how their place of employment "can't fill open positions" or find "good" new hires. If you think you have never noticed it in the past, it's probably because you weren't looking. Keep your ears open and the next time someone you know talks about it, you'll recognize it.

Another way to figure out where we are in the cycle is to pay attention to the Fed and the changing direction of interest rates. If interest rates are going down or have recently been lowered quickly or successively, that might indicate the economy is in the recession or early phase of the business cycle. When rates are going up, that might indicate mid or late parts of the cycle. Since each cycle is different, there isn't really a certain level that means a high or low interest rate. We can't say, "Rates hit five percent. That means it's late cycle."

You might be wondering how you are supposed to keep track of interest rate movements. You don't need to do any research online or go out of your way to find it. When the Fed moves interest rates, it makes the news. Even if it's something you ignored in the past, you'll notice it in the future. Remember, rates going up means the cycle is not just starting out but is probably in the mid or late stage. Rates going down quickly or successively means the cycle is probably earlier. The other good indicator is your savings account interest rate. If it goes up, it's because the Fed raised rates. Same for its going down.

Avoid getting speculative interest rate direction from auto lenders or mortgage lenders. They tend to make a lot of assumptions. They'll typically always think rates are going up (or at least tell you that) because they want to sell you something now. They are trying to convince you it's better to buy now before rates go up in the future. Stick to monitoring your savings rate at the bank or paying attention to a headline like "The Federal Reserve Raised Interest Rates Another Quarter Point Today," or something to that effect.

Raising rates attempts to slow down the economy so it will be mid to late cycle. It makes borrowing more expensive and forces more money to be diverted toward loan payments rather than spending to boost the economy. We can again use the chart that we saw in chapter twenty three showing the Fed's interest rates over the past seventy or so years. The gray vertical lines are recessions.

Figure 27. Federal Reserve Interest Rates Over Approximately 70 Years

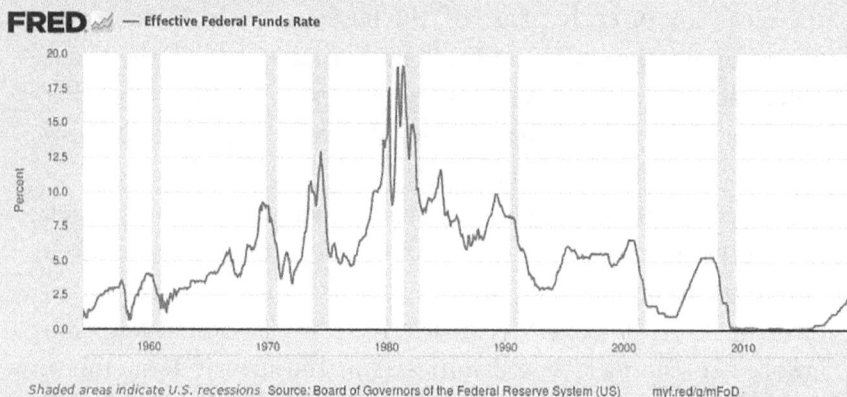

Shaded areas indicate U.S. recessions Source: Board of Governors of the Federal Reserve System (US) myf.red/g/mFoD

Started Hiking	Ended Hiking	End in Recession?
October 1955	August 1957	Yes
September 1958	September 1959	Yes
December 1965	November 1966	No
November 1967	June 1969	Yes
March 1972	September 1973	Yes
May 1977	March 1980	Yes
March 1983	August 1984	No
January 1987	May 1989	Yes
February 1994	February 1995	No
June 1999	May 2000	Yes
June 2004	June 2006	Yes
December 2015	December 2019	TBD

You can see that once the Fed starts to successively hike rates, it tends to lead to recession. Monitor if rates are going up or down to determine where the U.S. might be in the economic cycle. This indicator doesn't bat a thousand, but the track record is pretty good.

Related to the Federal Reserve's hiking rates is the eventual yield curve inversion, another helpful indicator. This is one of the nerdiest concepts of the book and is not something we need to delve into deeply. Briefly, I'll explain that yield curve inversion is when short-term yields are higher than or equal to long-term yields. If a two-year CD yields the same as a ten-year CD, it's late cycle. We're going to skirt around the concept because getting into the weeds on this would just be painful. As the Fed hikes rates, short-term yields are directly affected. Longer term yields in the fixed income market will not rise as much as short-term rates will. Eventually, short-term yields equal longer-term yields. It just happens. And it's an indicator of being late in the cycle.

Yield curve inversion is a pretty good forecaster, but how might you hear about it? It will make the front page of the papers and televised news will certainly mention it. Electronic news outlets will write about it, too. Trust me, they will mention it. In the economics and finance world, yield curve inversion is one of the most famous indicators foreshadowing a recession. Maybe your savings account is paying you close to what car dealers are offering for a loan or what a home loan's interest rate is. This one is a little tough to follow, but keep your ears open for mentions of the "yield curve inverting" or being flat. Only when it actually inverts or becomes flat does it matter. A flattening curve or coming close to flat doesn't matter.

Another cyclical indicator is auto sales. Coming out of a recession, auto sales begin to pick up as the economy heals and consumer optimism improves. Once auto sales peak and begin declining, it normally means we are at least mid to late cycle. Auto sales are a helpful indicator but are not as precise as some of the others. Here is a chart that shows domestic auto sales over the past 50+ years. The vertical gray bars are the recessions.

Figure 28. Auto Sales of the Last Fifty Years

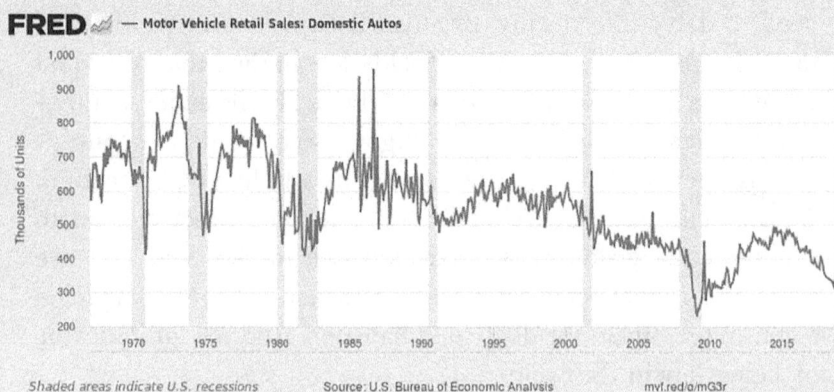

Shaded areas indicate U.S. recessions   Source: U.S. Bureau of Economic Analysis   mvf.red/o/mG3r

Using your powers of observation, you might notice many of your friends or family members purchasing vehicles around the same time. Consider some of your friends, family, or co-workers and ask yourself how old their cars are. You might notice a pattern and start thinking to yourself, "Geez, a lot of people I know are buying new cars," or "Interesting, everyone I know seems to have bought a car within the past few years." That's one way to think about auto sales.

Another way to see everyday changes is by noting car dealership advertising. Once car sales pick up in the mid cycle phase, dealerships greatly reduce their advertising because they won't need any—they are already growing company profits. Radio ads can be a pretty good barometer of this. Once auto sales peak and begin declining, there is a noticeable increase in radio advertisements from car dealers. If you ever catch yourself thinking "Hmm, there are all kinds of car advertisements on the radio," that should signal to you that car sales may have peaked, sales are now declining, and the dealerships are trying to bring people back in.

If cars are an economic indicator, it should come as no surprise that housing sales are too. Similar to auto sales, housing sales tend to move cyclically. They rebound after a recession, hit a peak, and then start to decline before the recession sets in. The most memorable housing bubble collapse was leading up to the '08/'09 recession. You can see in figure 29 that housing sales began to significantly decline in 2006. The housing sales decline began well before the recession actually set in.

That is why housing sales can indicate where we are in the economic cycle. If housing sales have peaked and are declining, it's likely the business cycle is at least past the midway point. As I've said multiple times, every cycle is different. Try to think of the people you know who are buying or have bought houses recently. Pricing alone is tough to use as a gauge, because some of the migration going on within the U.S. can affect pricing in strange ways. Stick to your observations. Pay attention to

Figure 29. Housing Sales of Last Fifty Years

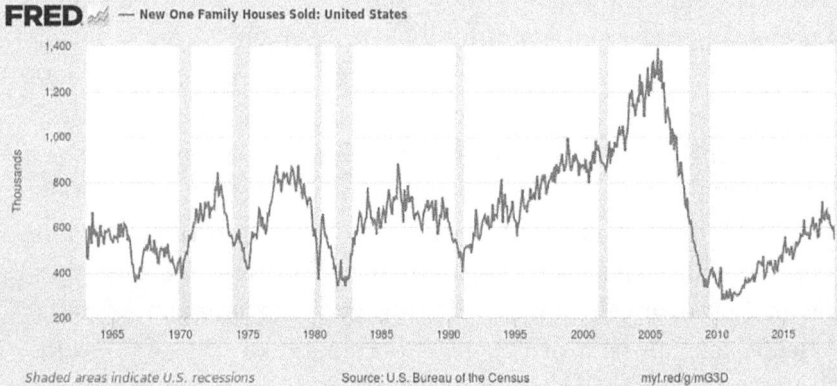

FRED — New One Family Houses Sold: United States

Shaded areas indicate U.S. recessions   Source: U.S. Bureau of the Census   myf.red/g/mG3D

declines as they occur over longer periods of time. If you hear on the news housing sales declined for one month that might not mean anything at all. If sales have been going down for six months straight, that is a sign housing is beyond its peak.

Several consumer confidence measurements keep track of how the average person feels about the economy, such as the Conference Board Consumer Confidence Index, University of Michigan Consumer Sentiment, and Bloomberg Consumer Comfort Index. You can see graphically how the Conference Board Consumer Confidence Index goes up and down over time (figure 30). When the number hits its cycle peak, recession has tended to follow within a year or two.

This makes sense for a variety of reasons. Usually, if everyone is very confident about the economy, the stock market will probably be pretty high. People who have confidence in the stock market will be buying stocks, not selling, right? It's when people think the economy is bad, during the recession phase of the cycle, that stock prices are low. This one is a little easier to observe. Confidence is high when you start hearing

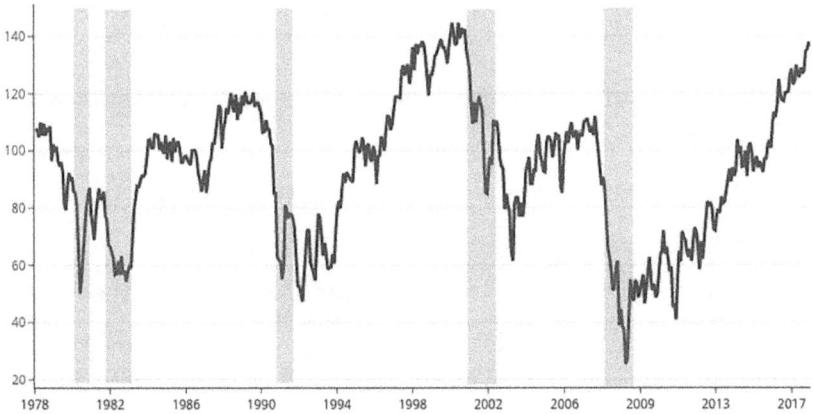

Figure 30. Consumer Confidence Beginning in 1978

just about everyone comment on the economy. At BBQs and ball games you might hear people talk positively about it. Politicians will be trying to take credit for how good things are. Toward the peaks in consumer confidence, just about everyone, and I mean everyone, will be saying the economy is going well. When everyone thinks the economy is in great shape, all this confidence is already baked into stock prices.

These indicators will help you to determine where the U.S. economy is at in regard to phases of the economic cycle. The point is that recessions, while scary, are a normal part of the investment process. They tend to occur after housing sales, auto sales, and confidence levels have peaked. They tend to occur once the unemployment rate has bottomed out and employers are having difficulty finding qualified workers to fill openings.

Indicator List

Level of greed. Visible by excessive borrowing or speculative "investing."

Unemployment rate. Which direction is it going, and is it very low?

Wage growth. Large raises across the economy mean labor is scarce.

Qualified workers. Can businesses hire anyone good?

Interest rates. What direction are they going?

Yield curve inversion. Look out for this phrase in the news or media.

Auto sales. Aggressive ads? When did friends/family last purchase cars?

Home sales. When did friends/family/coworkers last purchase homes?

Consumer confidence. Is everybody happy and talking about how great the economy is?

Do not use market cycles as a way to "time" the stock market—that is, trying to buy during recessions and sell at peaks. Even Wall Street economists have a hard time telling exactly when a recession is coming. The *Wall Street Journal* surveyed economists in summer 2007 on the potential of a forthcoming recession. They put the odds at twenty-three percent that a recession was coming. A major recession started about six months later.

If Wall Street economists who get paid lots of money and spend all their time monitoring the economy can't predict when a recession is going to begin, it's probably not a bet that average investors should be trying to make.

Once you understand how the business cycles work and are

able to get a sense of how early or late the economy is into each cycle, you can still use the information to your advantage. Let me outline a few examples. If you are looking to sell a piece of property, maybe a camp or something, later in the cycle is a good time to do so. Same with your *New Kids on the Block* memorabilia. Your only chance of selling that is late in an economic cycle. Nobody is buying Jordan Knight's signature on a T-shirt during a recession.

Late in the cycle is not the time you want to upgrade your house. Avoid selling your house just to buy a bigger, more expensive one. Avoid borrowing for big purchases late in the cycle. Don't become overleveraged.

The average investor tends to invest more in the later stages of the cycle because the fear of missing out starts to set in. The media generally becomes more of a cheerleader, reporting on how great the economy is doing. Greed can be a powerful emotion and the average investor will buy at high prices, chasing returns. Greed clouds the judgment of investors and really sets in at the later stages of the business cycle.

Famed investor Warren Buffet offers this gem of wisdom: "Be fearful when others are greedy and greedy when others are fearful." One of the few emotions more powerful than greed is fear. And when recessions come, and they will, fear will take over as investors all rush for the exits. You will tend to panic just like the other investors as stock values plummet. Recessions are normal—just keep reminding yourself of that. Remember the cycles. Remember the charts from this book. Try to overcome the fear. Hold on to your investments and refrain from selling. If you can, take advantage of the lower prices in the market and add to your investments during a recession.

One piece of cautionary advice: It's very hard to tell precisely which phase of the cycle the economy is in and the exact moment things are changing from late cycle to recession. If it were easy, economists and investment managers would be the overlords of the world. Use this information to understand how the economy generally works. Don't be stupid enough to think you are smart enough to "time" the market cycles perfectly. Do not use market cycles as your all-in or all-out timing tool for investing.

Attempting to do that is incredibly difficult. You can try to be cute with portions of your money, but if you try to time the market with all your investable assets, you are going to have a bad time. It's a fool's errand to try timing the market exactly. Rising stock markets can last longer and go farther than people expect. So if you sell out of the markets, you can miss out on a lot of continued growth. One such example was 2017, where many investors were compelled to exit the stock market, only to miss the more than twenty percent growth for the year.

When in doubt, continue investing incrementally—perhaps a certain amount per month or a certain percentage of your paycheck and just stick to it. We've discussed how the cycles can last different lengths of time. It might be five years and it might be ten years, so it doesn't make sense to sit on the sidelines waiting for a recession.

I'll close out this section by saying that sometimes doing nothing is the hardest thing to do. As the market dips five to ten percent here and there or, worse yet, enters a recession, fear will tell you to sell. And when the stock market is late into the cycle, greed will tell you to buy more. Remember how cycles work. Recessions are normal. Be patient. Be disciplined. Sometimes doing nothing at all is the best action. That is what makes for a successful investor.

CHAPTER TWENTY SEVEN
POLITICS AND INVESTING

"Politics is for the present, but an equation is for eternity."

— *Albert Einstein, science nerd*

I've saved the least for last (or nearly last). I'm referring to a big topic you surely aren't tired of hearing about—politics. We've talked about economic cycles and how so much of the economy is influenced by the Federal Reserve. The president's influence on the economy is usually exaggerated. A lot of fiscal policy and budget is determined by the legislative branch, not the president.

In the current hyper-partisan environment, many people allow their emotional connections to politicians or political parties influence their investment making decisions. Don't just take my word for it. Nicknamed the "Oracle of Omaha," Warren Buffet knows a little about investing. He said in February of 2017, "If you mix your politics with your investment decisions, you're making a big mistake."

Particularly with either President Obama or President Trump, many investors predicted doom and gloom and missed out on positive stock market returns. Let's take a look at the last several presidents to see how their reputations and plans actually played out for the economy and stock market.

We'll start with President Reagan of the 1980s. He generated a lot of investor excitement because his policies of deregulation, small government, and tax cuts were going to cause a stock market boom. What many people forget is that the American economy entered a recession within two years of Reagan's presidency. The stock market was down about twenty-five percent. After that rocky start, things turned around and President Reagan presided over a big economic expansion. There were massive fiscal deficits, but stock market prices did very well. Still, a lot of investors who were excited at the prospect of President Reagan had the wind knocked out of them the first couple years.

Then we get to President Reagan's vice president, who succeeded him, President George H. W. Bush. He was supposed to extend the big rally that President Reagan had started. Again, investors who invest based on politics were certain the expansion would continue. President Bush ended up having to raise taxes, the economy slowed, and a recession began within a year or two. Didn't turn out quite like the Reagan years for the stock market.

Next came President Bill Clinton. He was elected without the expectation of high stock market returns. President Clinton had the goal of reforming healthcare and didn't have a business background; many people painted him as a socialist. Despite these low expectations, an eight-year economic expansion ensued after Clinton was elected. The stock market tripled and welfare reform passed, along with deregulation. The government budget began running a surplus. Few predicted how great the economy would be under President Clinton.

George W. Bush followed President Clinton. Part of his platform was a renewed focus on America with less expensive overseas intervention. He was a fiscal conservative and was going to continue the deregulation that began under President Clinton. Wall Street and many investors figured him to be a positive for the economy. President Bush enacted tax cuts, but because of wars in Afghanistan and Iraq, in addition to increased public spending, budget deficits occurred. By the end of his second term in 2008, the country was in deep recession and the stock market was thirty-five percent lower than it was at his inauguration eight years earlier.

You can probably see where I'm going with this. Our characterizations about politicians, their platforms, and their political party don't always play out in the stock market and economy as people expect or predict. President Obama was elected based on promises to put average people ahead of Wall Street (it was the recession, and there was a big backlash on Wall Street and the big banks). President Obama wanted expansive healthcare reform, causing many to dub him a socialist. As we now know, it didn't happen as many predicted. The recovery was not strong by historical standards, but the stock market tripled. Obamacare also passed and the banks were bailed out, but not many thought the economic expansion would be so long or that the stock market would do so well.

The jury is still out on how the stock market will fare under President Trump as of this writing. Some investors peg him as unpredictable and chaotic and fear he will singlehandedly cause a recession. On the opposite end of the spectrum, people see a successful billionaire businessman who will get GDP back to four percent or more while mirroring Reagan's stock market growth. In his first three years, the stock market returns have been mixed, two stellar years and one lackluster year.

Rather than invest based on the president or one political party over another, pay more attention to the economic cycles and structural changes going on in the economy (demographics, interest rates, technology, etc). Those effects will have a larger influence on the stock market.

CHAPTER TWENTY-EIGHT
WHAT NOW?

"Procrastination is the thief of time."

— *Edward Young, English poet*

We've covered everything you need to get started with investing or improve how your current assets are invested. Now it's up to you to follow through. The next chapter of this book is a guide to how you can open an account at a large financial institution. All of these institutions have investment accounts, retirement accounts, and 529 college savings plans available. The guide will show you how to open the account, move money into it, and place actual trades.

Actually, one of the homework assignments earlier in the book was to open an account if you didn't have one already. I know you didn't blow off those homework assignments, right? No, of course not. In case you did, turn to the next section right now, and then come back here.

Let's talk about retirement accounts for a moment. Choosing the right retirement account can be confusing. Is a Roth IRA better than a normal IRA? Of course, the answer depends on your situation. A 401k plan or an IRA will require you to pay income taxes when you take the money out in retirement, but you are allowed to fund the accounts with money before it is taxed at your income tax rate. These accounts also require you to take distributions once you get to a certain age (currently age 70).

A Roth IRA, on the other hand, must be funded with after-tax dollars. If you wait until after you are fifty-nine when you take the money out, you are not taxed on it. There are also no required distributions by the government.

To determine which type of retirement account is better for you, you need to think about your income tax rate now versus your expected tax rate in retirement. You need to think about other sources of income you might have in retirement and when you would need money from a retirement account. Are you in a high income tax bracket? Then you have an advantage using a 401k or regular IRA because of the amount of money you save on taxes. If your tax rate will be low when you retire (i.e., not many sources of income, low Social Security payouts), then a 401k or regular IRA will also make sense, because when you take money out of your IRA, it is taxed at your income rate.

If you plan on having large sources of income later in life (perhaps a pension or very large Social Security payments), a Roth IRA might make more sense because you'll be in a high tax rate, so getting tax-free Roth IRA income helps you. Or if you might not need the money until your eighties, a Roth IRA might make sense since it doesn't require distributions. If you still aren't sure, my advice is to pick one and get started. If your situation changes in ten years, you can always open a new type of retirement account and shift where you add your money.

For your planning purposes, I've included the account type, the typical purpose of the account, and whether it is funded with pre-tax money. Pre-tax means money can go directly from your paycheck before you pay federal income taxes on the money.

ACCOUNT	PURPOSE	PRE-TAX DOLLARS
Brokerage	Regular Investment Account	No
529	College Saving Account	Yes
401k	Retirement Plan through Employer	Yes
IRA	Individual Retirement Account	Yes
Roth IRA	After-Tax IRA	No

Just to nudge you along, I have dispelled common excuses people use to not invest:

I don't have enough money to invest. You can invest with as little as ten dollars to get started.

I don't know what to invest in. You were provided the exact, specific ticker symbols for the index funds that will make for good investments. You were also told types of funds or investments to focus on.

I don't have time to invest. It takes about twenty minutes to open an account and none of the recommended investments require monitoring or changes. There is virtually no time required at all.

I don't know where to start or open an account. Specific companies are mentioned earlier in the book. You need only an Internet connection.

I'm scared to lose money in a recession. We covered that recessions are a normal part of the economic cycles. Given time, economies recover from recessions.

Lastly, think about Rob the Computer Engineer, Nathalie the Single Mom, and Mike the Car Guy.

Think about your spending or generosity with money. Is your spending wise, or is it wasteful? What ways can you increase the amount of money you earn? Find ways to Earn More.

Think about utility value when you spend money. Find hobbies or activities that provide good value to you for the money spent. Plan your expenses better and try to keep as much of your paycheck as you can. Find ways to Save More.

Think about putting as much money as possible toward investing. Be practical, and remember that every inch of Earning More and Saving More counts. Think like an investor. Make practical decisions with your money. If you think like an investor, Earning More and Saving More will lead you to Invest More.

CHAPTER TWENTY NINE
OPENING AN ACCOUNT

"If you could get up the courage to begin,
you have the courage to succeed."

— *David Viscott; psychiatrist, author, and media personality*

Time for the walk-through on how to open an account. You can skip this entire section if it doesn't apply to you.

For everyone else, you need Summer School (this last section). Let's go through the process of opening an account at a brokerage house. Most of the big investment brokerage houses are fairly similar. None have upfront costs or costs to keep an account open. Users only have to pay to make trades (many trades are free). The prices to make trades will be approximately the same. I'll outline a list of some of the famous financial institutions where you can open an account for a traditional or Roth IRA, brokerage investment account, or 529 plan.

- E*Trade
- Fidelity Investments
- Vanguard
- Charles Schwab
- Morgan Stanley
- TD Ameritrade

All these companies have phone apps that you can use to manage your account, great customer service departments, and more features on their website than you will need (or want). If you feel so inclined, you can research them a bit on your own.

Scenario 1: Keeping it Simple

For the first example, we'll return to one of our old friends, Nathalie the Single Mom. Suppose she doesn't have a personal computer. She finally gave in and got a smart phone with Internet capability and a data plan. She wants to set up an account using only her new smartphone.

With a full-time job, a house to maintain, and growing twins, the last thing she wants is more work. Nathalie will keep it as simple as possible by sticking to the recommendation of investing only in an equal weight S&P 500 index. She will start with 500 dollars that she had in her savings account. From there, she will put twenty dollars per week into the account directly from her paycheck. These twenty dollar installments are not automatically invested, they stay in the account as cash until Nathalie uses those funds to place trades (more on that coming). She might notice the smaller paycheck at first, but after a couple of months, she figures she will be used to it.

Then, every once in a while, she will go into her brokerage account to check things out and invest this money that is building up. Nathalie figures that putting at least twenty dollars per week is better than nothing, and it's a good start. In some ways, putting the money into the investment account directly from her paycheck is prioritizing investing and prevents her from spending the money. She also wants all dividends to be reinvested back into her investments. She figures it can earn more being invested than sitting around as cash. Thankfully for Nathalie, it will be more of a rainy day fund. She doesn't have any spending plans or needs that she knows of, but would rather the money grow as much as it can.

Nathalie also has no preference as to which brokerage account she uses. They all seem the same to her. For this example, let's say she chooses Charles Schwab. Schwab does allow free transactions for ticker RSP, the equal weight S&P 500 index fund. Nathalie would begin by using her smartphone's browser to go to the website to open the account. There is an app available for both Android and Apple iOS that can be used to make trades or monitor the holdings in the account. The site Nathalie would use is www.schwab.com to open the account.

After searching the various toolbar options, Emily finds a dropdown will open where she can choose the option "Open an Account."

Nathalie would then click on "Brokerage Account." A new section asks whether this is an individual or joint account. You can make your own choice, obviously, but Nathalie just needs a simple individual account.

Users are asked if they want additional complementary features like "Schwab Trading Services." No. Nathalie will elect not to take part in that. Nathalie wants a hands-off approach and has no intention of getting deeper into investing, reading business news, or dealing with any extra bells and whistles. She is busy enough as it is. After bypassing that option, new account users are shown a summary of basic information they will need to provide—for example, Social Security number, address, and employer's name and address (if applicable).

The next screen requires users to fill out their personal information. It should take only a couple of minutes. Nathalie zips right through it.

After that is done, she is asked to create a Login ID and password to access her account. There is also a security question. After filling that out and clicking "Next," she is then asked to fill out her address and phone number. Moving on from there, another screen will ask for some work-related information. If users have a job in financial services, they may be asked to answer a couple of additional questions. After that, Nathalie will have some identity-verification questions.

Hang in there, we are almost done.

Then there is a page that asks for the purpose of the account and the source of funds (where does the money funding this account come from). There are a few checkboxes to choose from. "Won the money in a dance off" is surprisingly not an option. Nathalie chooses the first option from each list: All the funds come from her normal day job.

The next screen will have a few more checkboxes to add any additional account features (*yawn*). Nathalie wants none of it; she'll remove any additional features. There is also a section about switching to a paperless account and receiving everything through email. Of course, Nathalie wants paperless. Remember all that time she spends in state parks? Let's conserve this beautiful planet one paper mailing at a time if we have to.

Terms and conditions are next. I'm sure you'll read them with bated breath. Once Nathalie gets through all that, the account will become open. Boom! The whole process probably took about ten minutes. Just ten minutes? Geez, some of you readers spent more time watching cat videos on YouTube today.

There are still another few minutes of work to get money invested. Once her account is open, Nathalie sees her account number and options for transferring money or assets into the new account. When you open the account, you technically don't need to put money into it right away. You can leave the account open with $0.00 until you are ready to go forward, and it won't cost you a dime to do so. But Nathalie thinks, why wait? Let's do it now and be done.

Most of these brokerage accounts are a little like your other banking accounts in the way they receive or distribute money. The account can be funded in multiple ways. You can send in a handwritten check to put money into a brokerage account. I know there are people who got a thousand free checks when they opened their checking account fifteen years ago and they are determined to use every last one. You can also use mobile deposit and take a picture of a check, or you can send money electronically directly from banking, savings, or other investment accounts. Payroll direct deposit is another option.

Users can also transfer all the securities and cash they have at one financial institution over to a different one. So, if Nathalie got tired of Charles Schwab, she could always open a new account somewhere else and transfer everything without having to sell the assets. None of this applies in Nathalie's current situation, so it won't be explored further.

This account setup process is admittedly a little work. But I swear to you, once you get through this initial junk, the rest is smooth sailing. The plus side is that these institutions have very good customer service representatives who can help Nathalie if she hits any roadblocks or has questions. The customer service also tends to be actual people rather than automated.

Back to funding Nathalie's account. She wants to link her bank account to her new Schwab account to transfer the initial 500 dollars. The money is coming from her existing savings account, remember? She can do this by continuing on from the account opening completion.

Schwab's mobile site has a green button that reads "Enroll Online" to get the ball rolling. Nathalie will only have to go through this process once for each account added or linked. Once Nathalie's account is added, money can be transferred from her savings to the new brokerage account. In this case, we are doing a one-time 500-dollar transfer. Depending on the banks you use, it could take a day or two for that 500 dollars to arrive and be available in the Charles Schwab account.

In case you forgot, Nathalie also wanted to set up a direct deposit, which means part of her paycheck would automatically be deposited into the new brokerage account. Whoever does your payroll at work should be able to help set this up. We'll have to use our imagination and pretend we were there for Nathalie's quick and boring conversation with her payroll department to request twenty dollars per week be deposited into the account.

It is also worth mentioning that not only can you set up a one-time transfer from a checking or savings account, most of these brokerage institutions allow setting up a recurring transfer. Charles Schwab allows monthly, quarterly, annual, twice a month, and other automatic deposits from outside accounts to the brokerage account. Instead of the twenty-dollar direct deposit, Nathalie could have set up her brokerage account to grab that much money from her checking or savings.

Once Nathalie sends the 500 dollars to her investment brokerage account, she can begin the actual investing part. Finally, right? From the Charles Schwab phone app, she'll be able to see her homepage or summary page showing the brokerage account balance.

From here, the Schwab menu in the upper left has different options that are available. "Trade" is one of the options. It's really the only option Nathalie cares about. After selecting that option, she will see the screen where users buy and sell stocks, exchange traded funds, options, and mutual funds, etc.

In this case, Nathalie wants to buy ticker "RSP," the PowerShares S&P 500 equal weight index. After entering in the ticker, the Schwab phone app auto populates the fund name and current market prices. Since this is a buy transaction, she will obviously select "Buy." Then there is a dropdown to turn on dividend reinvestment, which we've discussed briefly.

Nathalie wants to turn this on. Different funds or stocks sometimes make dividend cash payments. Certain funds also make capital gains payouts (usually at the end of the year). Users can elect to automatically purchase more of the asset that paid out instead of accepting the cash. When RSP pays out a dividend of ten dollars, for example, Charles Schwab will instead use that ten dollars to buy ten dollars' worth of more RSP instead of putting it into cash. Ten dollars might not be enough to buy one share of RSP, but Charles Schwab will buy a fraction of one share. Over time, Nathalie might see she owns

5.25 shares of RSP because of these fractional reinvestments. Since Nathalie has little use for cash sitting around in the account, she'd rather keep it invested to contribute to the growing account.

The next decision is whether to make this transaction a "market order" or "limit order." Market orders make the trade at current market prices and limit orders make the trade at a price the user needs to specify. For assets that are well traded, market orders are fine. They are also simpler, so Nathalie sticks to market orders. The trade will be summarized once all the inputs have been made.

The trade summary shows that there is no commission for the RSP fund! This means Nathalie is trading for this at zero cost. Wow! Once the trade is made and done, there will be a screen showing the completed trade order.

There you have it, champ. Nice going, Nathalie. She is done. Account opened. ETF now owned. Dividends will be automatically reinvested. Twenty dollars per week will be added to the account, so that every few months, Nathalie will log in and invest the accumulated cash. She can do this during a break at work, or waiting in line at the grocery store, or watching her kids play at the park. It takes only a few minutes. Other than that, let the security grow. Selling assets and moving cash back out of the account is very easy. It's a simple transaction to sell and then transfer the funds back to the savings account. It takes two days for the sale proceeds to land in the investment account and then probably another day to move to those funds to a savings account.

Scenario 2: Planning for Retirement

In this second scenario, we will try opening an IRA account and use a different financial company to house the account, Vanguard. To make things a little more relatable, we'll say it's our old pal Rob the Computer Engineer who wants to open the account. Rob has a little extra time and has decided he wants to take some risks. He wants to own a variety of assets; some will be ETFs and some will be mutual funds. We will also make sure that every asset reinvests dividends and possible capital gains payouts from certain funds. It is better to put this back into the investment that paid out rather than have it sit in cash. Vanguard is a good place to open an account if the plan is to use a lot of Vanguard ETF or mutual funds.

Let's also assume Rob will use a desktop computer. He sits at a desk all day for work, so it's more convenient for him to access his account there. He'll open his account using the desktop version of Vanguard's website.

To get started, simply go to Vanguard.com. Click on one of the links for "Personal Investors." The current version of the website has an option toward the upper right that reads "Open an account." Let's also pretend Rob is not moving an existing account over to Vanguard, but starting from scratch. On the updated screen, click on the red button that says, "Open a new account." There are several funding options, but Rob is going to fund the account from an existing bank account. He would select that option and click continue.

Next, the site tells users what is needed in the account opening process: bank numbers to eventually transfer money to this Vanguard account and some personal information. Nothing unusual. Rob would continue from there to the choice of which type of account to open, in this case, a retirement account.

Rob already has a 401k, which is basically the same as a regular IRA, so in the dropdown, he decides to choose a Roth IRA. He then fills out the required personal information. It won't take more than a couple of minutes. Then comes the part about how the account will be funded. After filling out the required information, Rob decides to start with 2,000 dollars. Every year, he plans to put his annual bonus and tax refund into this Roth IRA.

After choosing to send over 2,000 dollars from the bank

account data previously entered, Rob chooses to reinvest dividends and capital gains rather than have them paid out in cash.

Next comes a quick summary of all the info you have entered so far and then a few questions to verify your identity which will take a couple minutes. After a quick electronic signature . . . and the riveting terms and conditions, Rob needs to come up with a username and password.

After more user agreements, confirmations, and more bland blah blah blah stuff, you get to the account homepage. The 2,000 dollars Rob added to the account during the set-up process will take a couple of business days to be fully available, but in certain cases, Vanguard may let you buy securities now with the funds (they restrict certain securities).

Now it's time to place some trades with that two thousand bucks. Let's go with one of the equal weight S&P 500 index funds as the asset base for this account. Users can use multiple options to execute a trade. They can go through the "My Accounts" option from the red option bar up top and select the option "Buy & Sell." There is also a "Buy and Sell" option on the "Balances and Holdings" screen, as well.

Rob will start by purchasing 1,200 dollars of the ticker INDEX. This is an S&P 500 equal weight index fund. To do this, he'll select the "Trade non-Vanguard funds via FundAccess" option. On a quick side note, Vanguard funds will have the word "Vanguard" in their name, so it is easy to tell them from non-Vanguard funds.

The fee is twenty dollars for the transaction. All future interest payments and capital gains payouts (the transaction gains mutual funds pay out) will be reinvested into this fund at no extra cost. And since this is an IRA, none of the capital gains payouts or interest payments will be taxed.

Rob reviews the trade and submits it.

Next, Rob will put in a few other trades. We previously discussed how the equal weight S&P 500 index has outperformed historically but has a smaller allocation specifically to the information technology sector of the economy. With all the big structural changes we have talked about, some investors are inclined to add money specifically in this area. Rob is one such investor. For the next trade, he'll put one share into ticker VGT. This is the Vanguard Info Tech ETF. It trades for free on Vanguard.

Additionally, he adds one share to ticker VHT, which is Vanguard Health Care ETF. As with information technology, there are certain structural changes, namely the aging baby boomer generation, that might make the healthcare sector a good investment. This ETF also trades for free in this account because it is a Vanguard ETF.

Lastly, Rob has a strong desire to invest in an ETF that follows the economy of the country India. He wants to invest in ticker INDA, which is the Ishares MSCI India ETF. Rob wants to put about 250 dollars into this India investment. The rest of the money will remain in cash in the account for the time being.

Even if there is a slight dip in the stock market, short-term day-to-day changes should not cause any panic or reaction at all. It's a normal part of investing. Rob still has a couple of decades until his planned retirement.

Remember, in any brokerage account, investors can also purchase individual stocks or set up automatic investing if they choose. If Rob was inclined to buy a single name stock like Microsoft, he could go ahead and do so. Throughout this book, however, I have recommended sticking to low-cost funds. As for the automatic investing, Vanguard allows you to do that only with Vanguard mutual funds. Unfortunately, most of these big brokers have their own rules for which assets can be invested automatically and how it's done.

You just read a whole book. See what you can accomplish? Investing your own money is another obstacle you can easily handle. You are now ready to invest on your own. You have been shown a "set it and forget it" strategy that should outperform the overall stock market over the next twenty to thirty-year period. You have also been shown the tools to invest without having to pay expensive mutual fund fees or fees to investment advisors, likely saving you one to two percent returns each year. Thank you for taking the time to read this book. The investment strategies I have outlined are ones I truly believe in, as these are the strategies I follow for my own investments.

EPILOGUE
CHECK YOURSELF

Tear this list out of the book. Stick it on your fridge. You've just taken the time to read this book—now make sure you get something out of it. Here is a checklist of action items to make sure you follow through on what you just learned, in order of priority.

☐ Open an IRA or brokerage account if you do not already have one. This should be your only focus. Do it right now. Don't wait until tomorrow or next week. Don't make excuses. Just do it. Use any of the investment companies discussed.

☐ If you have an existing IRA, 401k, 403b, or other investment account, now is the time to switch the investments. Bias to index funds and equity.

☐ If you recently opened an IRA or investment account, put money in it now, even if it is less than a hundred dollars and place some trades for the investments recommended in this book. You want to get started ASAP to increase your chances of following through.

☐ Set up an automatic deposit into your investment/ retirement account. Use either payroll direct deposit or periodically pulling funds directly into your investment/retirement account from your bank account. Even if it's just ten, twenty, or fifty dollars.

☐ Examine your family's spending habits. Consider things like your hobbies, eating habits, travel, and transportation among others. Come up with ideas to reduce spending. Consider utility value.

☐ Set up a reasonable plan to reduce spending. If you try to cut back on everything at once, nothing is likely to stick. Try to cut back on one or two things. The point is to use a gradual approach reducing one or two things at a time.

☐ Pay off any high interest loans like credit card balances, payday loans, or car loans. Before you put money toward investing, pay off anything with an interest rate of 7 percent or more.

☐ Examine your main source of income. Can you work harder for the next promotion? Are there any licenses or certificates or training that could increase your salary? Are there any educational courses (perhaps even paid for by your employer) that might increase your salary?

☐ Consider if there is a part-time job you wouldn't mind doing. Or a hobby you have that could be monetized.

☐ The biggest and most difficult undertaking is a career change. Consider your situation and if this path needs to be explored further. Online research or making phone calls to talk to job counselors and college admissions personnel can be done for free. Borrowing money to invest in your education or skill building is usually a good investment.

☐ Come up with a plan to increase your earnings. Make sure it fits your situation and isn't overly ambitious. You still want to enjoy life.

☐ Are there any government programs or tax breaks you are not taking advantage of? Are you eligible for housing, childcare, or food assistance? Are you taking advantage of every tax credit or tax deduction available?

☐ Incrementally increase how much money you add to your investments once you begin saving and earning more. Automate your investing if possible, especially the reinvestment of dividends.

☐ Investments in your retirement or brokerage accounts WILL grow. Be patient. Stay the course. The growth will be uneven and unpredictable. Increase your income, reduce your spending, put your new cash flow into your investment accounts. Follow that recipe.

Appendix A:

Bureau of Labor Statistics Job List

From "May 2016 National Occupational Employment and Wage Estimates United States." Bureau of Labor Statistics, March 31, 2017. Occupational Employment Statistics.

OCCUPATION TITLE	ANNUAL MEAN WAGE
All Occupations	49,630.00
Accountants and Auditors	76,730.00
Actors, Producers, and Directors	90,570.00
Actuaries	114,120.00
Adhesive Bonding Machine Operators and Tenders	34,610.00
Administrative Law Judges, Adjudicators, and Hearing Officers	95,240.00
Administrative Services Managers	98,930.00
Adult Basic and Secondary Education and Literacy Teachers and Instructors	55,140.00
Advertising and Promotions Managers	117,810.00
Advertising Sales Agents	63,660.00
Advertising, Marketing, Promotions, Public Relations, and Sales Managers	136,020.00
Aerospace Engineering and Operations Technicians	71,070.00
Aerospace Engineers	112,010.00
Agents and Business Managers of Artists, Performers, and Athletes	86,560.00
Agricultural and Food Science Technicians	40,470.00
Agricultural and Food Scientists	70,470.00
Agricultural Engineers	77,330.00

OCCUPATION TITLE	ANNUAL MEAN WAGE
Agricultural Equipment Operators	30,430.00
Agricultural Inspectors	44,260.00
Agricultural Sciences Teachers, Postsecondary	96,630.00
Agricultural Workers	25,570.00
Agricultural Workers, All Other	35,120.00
Air Traffic Controllers	118,200.00
Air Traffic Controllers and Airfield Operations Specialists	100,190.00
Air Transportation Workers	93,560.00
Aircraft Cargo Handling Supervisors	51,900.00
Aircraft Mechanics and Service Technicians	61,190.00
Aircraft Pilots and Flight Engineers	131,250.00
Aircraft Structure, Surfaces, Rigging, and Systems Assemblers	52,530.00
Airfield Operations Specialists	52,380.00
Airline Pilots, Copilots, and Flight Engineers	152,770.00
Ambulance Drivers and Attendants, Except Emergency Medical Technicians	25,600.00
Amusement and Recreation Attendants	22,000.00
Anesthesiologists	269,600.00
Animal Breeders	42,340.00
Animal Care and Service Workers	25,110.00
Animal Control Workers	36,600.00
Animal Scientists	72,890.00
Animal Trainers	34,580.00
Announcers	47,000.00
Anthropologists and Archeologists	66,440.00

OCCUPATION TITLE	ANNUAL MEAN WAGE
Anthropology and Archeology Teachers, Postsecondary	91,940.00
Appraisers and Assessors of Real Estate	58,030.00
Arbitrators, Mediators, and Conciliators	72,730.00
Architects, Except Landscape and Naval	84,470.00
Architects, Except Naval	81,920.00
Architects, Surveyors, and Cartographers	76,260.00
Architectural and Civil Drafters	54,290.00
Architectural and Engineering Managers	143,870.00
Architecture and Engineering Occupations	84,300.00
Architecture Teachers, Postsecondary	92,890.00
Archivists	54,570.00
Archivists, Curators, and Museum Technicians	52,460.00
Area, Ethnic, and Cultural Studies Teachers, Postsecondary	84,590.00
Art and Design Workers	52,660.00
Art Directors	101,170.00
Art, Drama, and Music Teachers, Postsecondary	81,050.00
Artists and Related Workers	79,530.00
Artists and Related Workers, All Other	64,630.00
Arts, Communications, and Humanities Teachers, Postsecondary	77,980.00
Arts, Design, Entertainment, Sports, and Media Occupations	58,390.00

OCCUPATION TITLE	ANNUAL MEAN WAGE
Assemblers and Fabricators	33,610.00
Assemblers and Fabricators, All Other	31,050.00
Astronomers	110,380.00
Astronomers and Physicists	120,650.00
Athletes and Sports Competitors	83,730.00
Athletes, Coaches, Umpires, and Related Workers	42,290.00
Athletic Trainers	47,880.00
Atmospheric and Space Scientists	94,840.00
Atmospheric, Earth, Marine, and Space Sciences Teachers, Postsecondary	95,900.00
Audio and Video Equipment Technicians	47,450.00
Audiologists	79,290.00
Audio-Visual and Multimedia Collections Specialists	50,130.00
Automotive and Watercraft Service Attendants	24,280.00
Automotive Body and Related Repairers	45,180.00
Automotive Glass Installers and Repairers	36,140.00
Automotive Service Technicians and Mechanics	41,400.00
Automotive Technicians and Repairers	41,950.00
Avionics Technicians	61,390.00
Baggage Porters and Bellhops	24,910.00
Baggage Porters, Bellhops, and Concierges	27,630.00
Bailiffs	45,740.00

OCCUPATION TITLE	ANNUAL MEAN WAGE
Bailiffs, Correctional Officers, and Jailers	46,710.00
Bakers	27,110.00
Barbers	29,900.00
Barbers, Hairdressers, Hairstylists and Cosmetologists	29,600.00
Bartenders	25,580.00
Bicycle Repairers	28,520.00
Bill and Account Collectors	37,620.00
Billing and Posting Clerks	37,570.00
Biochemists and Biophysicists	94,340.00
Biological Science Teachers, Postsecondary	90,420.00
Biological Scientists	80,060.00
Biological Scientists, All Other	77,830.00
Biological Technicians	46,130.00
Biomedical Engineers	89,970.00
Boilermakers	62,200.00
Bookkeeping, Accounting, and Auditing Clerks	40,220.00
Brickmasons and Blockmasons	53,440.00
Brickmasons, Blockmasons, and Stonemasons	51,770.00
Bridge and Lock Tenders	46,680.00
Broadcast and Sound Engineering Technicians and Radio Operators	49,250.00
Broadcast News Analysts	78,200.00
Broadcast Technicians	45,430.00
Brokerage Clerks	52,380.00
Budget Analysts	77,170.00
Building and Grounds Cleaning and Maintenance Occupations	28,010.00

OCCUPATION TITLE	ANNUAL MEAN WAGE
Building Cleaning and Pest Control Workers	26,300.00
Building Cleaning Workers	26,090.00
Building Cleaning Workers, All Other	30,960.00
Bus and Truck Mechanics and Diesel Engine Specialists	46,710.00
Bus Drivers	33,760.00
Bus Drivers, School or Special Client	31,110.00
Bus Drivers, Transit and Intercity	41,780.00
Business and Financial Operations Occupations	75,070.00
Business Operations Specialists	71,840.00
Business Operations Specialists, All Other	74,870.00
Business Teachers, Postsecondary	96,770.00
Butchers and Meat Cutters	31,740.00
Butchers and Other Meat, Poultry, and Fish Processing Workers	28,140.00
Buyers and Purchasing Agents	65,390.00
Buyers and Purchasing Agents, Farm Products	63,910.00
Cabinetmakers and Bench Carpenters	34,800.00
Camera and Photographic Equipment Repairers	43,920.00
Camera Operators, Television, Video, and Motion Picture	63,200.00
Captains, Mates, and Pilots of Water Vessels	81,520.00
Cardiovascular Technologists and Technicians	57,100.00
Career/Technical Education Teachers, Middle School	60,350.00

OCCUPATION TITLE	ANNUAL MEAN WAGE
Career/Technical Education Teachers, Secondary School	59,480.00
Cargo and Freight Agents	44,250.00
Carpenters	48,340.00
Carpet Installers	44,310.00
Carpet, Floor, and Tile Installers and Finishers	43,950.00
Cartographers and Photogrammetrists	66,160.00
Cashiers	21,710.00
Cashiers	21,680.00
Cement Masons and Concrete Finishers	43,720.00
Cement Masons, Concrete Finishers, and Terrazzo Workers	43,770.00
Chefs and Head Cooks	47,390.00
Chemical Engineers	105,420.00
Chemical Equipment Operators and Tenders	50,300.00
Chemical Plant and System Operators	59,430.00
Chemical Processing Machine Setters, Operators, and Tenders	46,850.00
Chemical Technicians	49,770.00
Chemistry Teachers, Postsecondary	89,320.00
Chemists	80,820.00
Chemists and Materials Scientists	82,520.00
Chief Executives	194,350.00
Child, Family, and School Social Workers	47,510.00
Childcare Workers	22,930.00
Chiropractors	81,210.00
Choreographers	53,610.00
Civil Engineering Technicians	52,120.00

OCCUPATION TITLE	ANNUAL MEAN WAGE
Civil Engineers	89,730.00
Claims Adjusters, Appraisers, Examiners, and Investigators	65,040.00
Claims Adjusters, Examiners, and Investigators	64,990.00
Cleaners of Vehicles and Equipment	24,660.00
Cleaning, Washing, and Metal Pickling Equipment Operators and Tenders	30,590.00
Clergy	49,450.00
Clinical Laboratory Technologists and Technicians	52,280.00
Clinical, Counseling, and School Psychologists	78,690.00
Coaches and Scouts	41,000.00
Coating, Painting, and Spraying Machine Setters, Operators, and Tenders	34,460.00
Coil Winders, Tapers, and Finishers	35,340.00
Coin, Vending, and Amusement Machine Servicers and Repairers	34,860.00
Combined Food Preparation and Serving Workers, Including Fast Food	20,460.00
Commercial and Industrial Designers	70,880.00
Commercial Divers	53,990.00
Commercial Pilots	86,260.00
Communications Equipment Operators	31,130.00
Communications Equipment Operators, All Other	41,910.00
Communications Teachers, Postsecondary	74,360.00
Community and Social Service Occupations	47,200.00

OCCUPATION TITLE	ANNUAL MEAN WAGE
Community and Social Service Specialists, All Other	45,540.00
Community Health Workers	41,170.00
Compensation and Benefits Managers	126,900.00
Compensation, Benefits, and Job Analysis Specialists	66,490.00
Compliance Officers	70,250.00
Computer and Information Analysts	92,260.00
Computer and Information Research Scientists	116,320.00
Computer and Information Systems Managers	145,740.00
Computer and Mathematical Occupations	87,880.00
Computer Control Programmers and Operators	41,640.00
Computer Hardware Engineers	118,700.00
Computer Network Architects	104,240.00
Computer Network Support Specialists	67,770.00
Computer Numerically Controlled Machine Tool Programmers, Metal and Plastic	53,560.00
Computer Occupations	87,870.00
Computer Occupations, All Other	88,880.00
Computer Operators	43,880.00
Computer Programmers	85,180.00
Computer Science Teachers, Postsecondary	89,670.00
Computer Support Specialists	56,600.00
Computer Systems Analysts	91,620.00

OCCUPATION TITLE	ANNUAL MEAN WAGE
Computer User Support Specialists	53,100.00
Computer, Automated Teller, and Office Machine Repairers	39,410.00
Computer-Controlled Machine Tool Operators, Metal and Plastic	39,590.00
Concierges	31,440.00
Conservation Scientists	65,130.00
Conservation Scientists and Foresters	63,720.00
Construction and Building Inspectors	61,250.00
Construction and Extraction Occupations	48,900.00
Construction and Related Workers, All Other	40,480.00
Construction Equipment Operators	49,810.00
Construction Laborers	37,890.00
Construction Managers	99,510.00
Construction Trades Workers	47,580.00
Continuous Mining Machine Operators	52,650.00
Control and Valve Installers and Repairers	51,410.00
Control and Valve Installers and Repairers, Except Mechanical Door	56,180.00
Conveyor Operators and Tenders	33,870.00
Cooks	24,370.00
Cooks and Food Preparation Workers	23,990.00
Cooks, All Other	29,210.00
Cooks, Fast Food	20,570.00
Cooks, Institution and Cafeteria	26,370.00
Cooks, Private Household	42,220.00
Cooks, Restaurant	25,430.00
Cooks, Short Order	23,130.00

OCCUPATION TITLE	ANNUAL MEAN WAGE
Cooling and Freezing Equipment Operators and Tenders	32,100.00
Correctional Officers and Jailers	46,750.00
Correspondence Clerks	37,660.00
Cost Estimators	66,620.00
Costume Attendants	50,470.00
Counselors	49,740.00
Counselors, All Other	47,640.00
Counselors, Social Workers, and Other Community and Social Service Specialists	47,220.00
Counter and Rental Clerks	29,390.00
Counter and Rental Clerks and Parts Salespersons	30,750.00
Counter Attendants, Cafeteria, Food Concession, and Coffee Shop	21,380.00
Couriers and Messengers	29,920.00
Court Reporters	56,940.00
Court, Municipal, and License Clerks	39,160.00
Craft Artists	38,900.00
Crane and Tower Operators	55,280.00
Credit Analysts	81,160.00
Credit Authorizers, Checkers, and Clerks	39,320.00
Credit Counselors	49,480.00
Credit Counselors and Loan Officers	73,570.00
Criminal Justice and Law Enforcement Teachers, Postsecondary	67,040.00
Crossing Guards	29,190.00
Crushing, Grinding, and Polishing Machine Setters, Operators, and Tenders	36,050.00

OCCUPATION TITLE	ANNUAL MEAN WAGE
Crushing, Grinding, Polishing, Mixing, and Blending Workers	36,410.00
Curators	58,910.00
Customer Service Representatives	35,170.00
Cutters and Trimmers, Hand	29,580.00
Cutting and Slicing Machine Setters, Operators, and Tenders	34,000.00
Cutting Workers	33,170.00
Cutting, Punching, and Press Machine Setters, Operators, and Tenders, Metal and Plastic	34,210.00
Dancers and Choreographers	43,320.00
Data Entry and Information Processing Workers	33,780.00
Data Entry Keyers	31,640.00
Database Administrators	87,130.00
Database and Systems Administrators and Network Architects	89,750.00
Demonstrators and Product Promoters	30,570.00
Dental Assistants	37,890.00
Dental Hygienists	73,440.00
Dental Laboratory Technicians	40,760.00
Dentists	178,670.00
Dentists, All Other Specialists	171,900.00
Dentists, General	173,860.00
Derrick Operators, Oil and Gas	51,140.00
Derrick, Rotary Drill, and Service Unit Operators, Oil, Gas, and Mining	54,010.00
Designers	47,780.00
Designers, All Other	63,270.00

OCCUPATION TITLE	ANNUAL MEAN WAGE
Desktop Publishers	44,380.00
Detectives and Criminal Investigators	81,490.00
Diagnostic Medical Sonographers	71,750.00
Diagnostic Related Technologists and Technicians	62,960.00
Dietetic Technicians	29,360.00
Dietitians and Nutritionists	59,670.00
Dining Room and Cafeteria Attendants and Bartender Helpers	22,340.00
Directors, Religious Activities and Education	44,840.00
Dishwashers	21,260.00
Dispatchers	41,150.00
Dispatchers, Except Police, Fire, and Ambulance	41,190.00
Door-to-Door Sales Workers, News and Street Vendors, and Related Workers	28,630.00
Drafters	56,500.00
Drafters, All Other	54,410.00
Drafters, Engineering Technicians, and Mapping Technicians	57,530.00
Dredge Operators	46,530.00
Dredge, Excavating, and Loading Machine Operators	45,560.00
Drilling and Boring Machine Tool Setters, Operators, and Tenders, Metal and Plastic	38,880.00
Driver/Sales Workers	28,440.00
Driver/Sales Workers and Truck Drivers	38,900.00
Drywall and Ceiling Tile Installers	47,400.00
Drywall Installers, Ceiling Tile Installers, and Tapers	48,460.00

OCCUPATION TITLE	ANNUAL MEAN WAGE
Earth Drillers, Except Oil and Gas	51,240.00
Economics Teachers, Postsecondary	111,520.00
Economists	112,860.00
Editors	66,080.00
Education Administrators	93,160.00
Education Administrators, All Other	84,400.00
Education Administrators, Elementary and Secondary School	95,390.00
Education Administrators, Postsecondary	105,770.00
Education Administrators, Preschool and Childcare Center/Program	52,150.00
Education and Library Science Teachers, Postsecondary	70,420.00
Education Teachers, Postsecondary	70,260.00
Education, Training, and Library Occupations	54,520.00
Education, Training, and Library Workers, All Other	46,970.00
Educational, Guidance, School, and Vocational Counselors	57,620.00
Electric Motor, Power Tool, and Related Repairers	44,720.00
Electrical and Electronic Equipment Assemblers	33,700.00
Electrical and Electronic Equipment Mechanics, Installers, and Repairers	50,900.00
Electrical and Electronics Drafters	63,390.00
Electrical and Electronics Engineering Technicians	62,950.00
Electrical and Electronics Engineers	100,770.00

OCCUPATION TITLE	ANNUAL MEAN WAGE
Electrical and Electronics Installers and Repairers, Transportation Equipment	59,840.00
Electrical and Electronics Repairers, Commercial and Industrial Equipment	56,990.00
Electrical and Electronics Repairers, Powerhouse, Substation, and Relay	74,540.00
Electrical Engineers	98,620.00
Electrical Power-Line Installers and Repairers	67,160.00
Electrical, Electronics, and Electromechanical Assemblers	34,060.00
Electricians	56,650.00
Electromechanical Equipment Assemblers	35,410.00
Electro-Mechanical Technicians	57,860.00
Electronic Equipment Installers and Repairers, Motor Vehicles	34,200.00
Electronic Home Entertainment Equipment Installers and Repairers	39,340.00
Electronics Engineers, Except Computer	103,760.00
Elementary and Middle School Teachers	59,270.00
Elementary School Teachers, Except Special Education	59,020.00
Elevator Installers and Repairers	76,860.00
Eligibility Interviewers, Government Programs	43,550.00
Embalmers	42,260.00
Emergency Management Directors	78,060.00

OCCUPATION TITLE	ANNUAL MEAN WAGE
Emergency Medical Technicians and Paramedics	36,110.00
Engine and Other Machine Assemblers	43,090.00
Engineering and Architecture Teachers, Postsecondary	105,120.00
Engineering Teachers, Postsecondary	107,490.00
Engineering Technicians, Except Drafters	59,510.00
Engineering Technicians, Except Drafters, All Other	64,050.00
Engineers	96,440.00
Engineers, All Other	99,250.00
English Language and Literature Teachers, Postsecondary	76,140.00
Entertainers and Performers, Sports and Related Workers	60,910.00
Entertainment Attendants and Related Workers	22,660.00
Entertainment Attendants and Related Workers, All Other	24,610.00
Environmental Engineering Technicians	52,500.00
Environmental Engineers	88,530.00
Environmental Science and Protection Technicians, Including Health	47,930.00
Environmental Science Teachers, Postsecondary	88,880.00
Environmental Scientists and Geoscientists	83,600.00
Environmental Scientists and Specialists, Including Health	75,360.00

OCCUPATION TITLE	ANNUAL MEAN WAGE
Epidemiologists	77,720.00
Etchers and Engravers	34,390.00
Excavating and Loading Machine and Dragline Operators	45,230.00
Executive Secretaries and Executive Administrative Assistants	57,910.00
Exercise Physiologists	50,310.00
Explosives Workers, Ordnance Handling Experts, and Blasters	54,580.00
Extraction Workers	48,190.00
Extraction Workers, All Other	51,170.00
Extruding and Drawing Machine Setters, Operators, and Tenders, Metal and Plastic	35,340.00
Extruding and Forming Machine Setters, Operators, and Tenders, Synthetic and Glass Fibers	35,420.00
Extruding, Forming, Pressing, and Compacting Machine Setters, Operators, and Tenders	34,370.00
Fabric and Apparel Patternmakers	48,460.00
Fabric Menders, Except Garment	27,670.00
Fallers	42,900.00
Family and General Practitioners	200,810.00
Farm and Home Management Advisors	52,150.00
Farm Equipment Mechanics and Service Technicians	39,310.00
Farm Labor Contractors	47,290.00
Farmers, Ranchers, and Other Agricultural Managers	75,790.00

OCCUPATION TITLE	ANNUAL MEAN WAGE
Farming, Fishing, and Forestry Occupations	27,810.00
Farmworkers and Laborers, Crop, Nursery, and Greenhouse	23,820.00
Farmworkers, Farm, Ranch, and Aquacultural Animals	26,840.00
Fashion Designers	76,480.00
Fast Food and Counter Workers	20,580.00
Fence Erectors	36,380.00
Fiberglass Laminators and Fabricators	33,020.00
File Clerks	31,260.00
Film and Video Editors	82,190.00
Financial Analysts	97,640.00
Financial Analysts and Advisors	103,050.00
Financial Clerks	37,790.00
Financial Clerks, All Other	41,870.00
Financial Examiners	88,940.00
Financial Managers	139,720.00
Financial Specialists	80,700.00
Financial Specialists, All Other	76,230.00
Fine Artists, Including Painters, Sculptors, and Illustrators	57,410.00
Fire Fighting and Prevention Workers	50,890.00
Fire Inspectors	59,550.00
Fire Inspectors and Investigators	61,660.00
Firefighters	50,520.00
First-Line Supervisors of Building and Grounds Cleaning and Maintenance Workers	44,190.00
First-Line Supervisors of Construction Trades and Extraction Workers	68,040.00

OCCUPATION TITLE	ANNUAL MEAN WAGE
First-Line Supervisors of Correctional Officers	65,100.00
First-Line Supervisors of Farming, Fishing, and Forestry Workers	48,820.00
First-Line Supervisors of Fire Fighting and Prevention Workers	77,050.00
First-Line Supervisors of Food Preparation and Serving Workers	34,700.00
First-Line Supervisors of Gaming Workers	47,590.00
First-Line Supervisors of Helpers, Laborers, and Material Movers, Hand	50,160.00
First-Line Supervisors of Housekeeping and Janitorial Workers	41,240.00
First-Line Supervisors of Landscaping, Lawn Service, and Groundskeeping Workers	48,790.00
First-Line Supervisors of Law Enforcement Workers	81,380.00
First-Line Supervisors of Mechanics, Installers, and Repairers	66,730.00
First-Line Supervisors of Non-Retail Sales Workers	85,830.00
First-Line Supervisors of Office and Administrative Support Workers	57,890.00
First-Line Supervisors of Personal Service Workers	39,830.00
First-Line Supervisors of Police and Detectives	88,400.00
First-Line Supervisors of Production and Operating Workers	61,450.00

OCCUPATION TITLE	ANNUAL MEAN WAGE
First-Line Supervisors of Protective Service Workers, All Other	50,690.00
First-Line Supervisors of Retail Sales Workers	43,910.00
First-Line Supervisors of Sales Workers	51,230.00
First-Line Supervisors of Transportation and Material-Moving Machine and Vehicle Operators	59,800.00
Fish and Game Wardens	54,760.00
Fishers and Related Fishing Workers	30,740.00
Fishing and Hunting Workers	31,440.00
Fitness Trainers and Aerobics Instructors	42,780.00
Flight Attendants	51,620.00
Floor Layers, Except Carpet, Wood, and Hard Tiles	42,370.00
Floor Sanders and Finishers	38,890.00
Floral Designers	27,610.00
Food and Beverage Serving Workers	22,430.00
Food and Tobacco Roasting, Baking, and Drying Machine Operators and Tenders	30,970.00
Food Batchmakers	30,130.00
Food Cooking Machine Operators and Tenders	30,330.00
Food Preparation and Serving Related Occupations	23,850.00
Food Preparation and Serving Related Workers, All Other	23,200.00
Food Preparation Workers	22,920.00
Food Processing Workers	28,320.00

OCCUPATION TITLE	ANNUAL MEAN WAGE
Food Processing Workers, All Other	25,800.00
Food Scientists and Technologists	71,270.00
Food Servers, Nonrestaurant	23,490.00
Food Service Managers	56,010.00
Foreign Language and Literature Teachers, Postsecondary	73,750.00
Forensic Science Technicians	60,690.00
Forest and Conservation Technicians	38,630.00
Forest and Conservation Workers	31,200.00
Forest Fire Inspectors and Prevention Specialists	44,300.00
Forest, Conservation, and Logging Workers	38,210.00
Foresters	60,300.00
Forestry and Conservation Science Teachers, Postsecondary	90,480.00
Forging Machine Setters, Operators, and Tenders, Metal and Plastic	38,710.00
Forming Machine Setters, Operators, and Tenders, Metal and Plastic	37,460.00
Foundry Mold and Coremakers	36,030.00
Fundraisers	57,930.00
Funeral Attendants	27,110.00
Funeral Service Managers	88,970.00
Funeral Service Workers	38,890.00
Furnace, Kiln, Oven, Drier, and Kettle Operators and Tenders	37,600.00
Furniture Finishers	32,330.00
Gaming and Sports Book Writers and Runners	25,710.00
Gaming Cage Workers	28,120.00

OCCUPATION TITLE	ANNUAL MEAN WAGE
Gaming Change Persons and Booth Cashiers	25,940.00
Gaming Dealers	21,990.00
Gaming Managers	79,690.00
Gaming Service Workers, All Other	28,300.00
Gaming Services Workers	23,000.00
Gaming Supervisors	50,810.00
Gaming Surveillance Officers and Gaming Investigators	35,280.00
Gas Compressor and Gas Pumping Station Operators	59,620.00
Gas Plant Operators	67,980.00
General and Operations Managers	122,090.00
Genetic Counselors	74,960.00
Geographers	74,090.00
Geography Teachers, Postsecondary	84,660.00
Geological and Petroleum Technicians	62,240.00
Geoscientists, Except Hydrologists and Geographers	106,390.00
Glaziers	47,260.00
Graders and Sorters, Agricultural Products	24,280.00
Graduate Teaching Assistants	35,810.00
Graphic Designers	52,290.00
Grinding and Polishing Workers, Hand	30,860.00
Grinding, Lapping, Polishing, and Buffing Machine Tool Setters, Operators, and Tenders, Metal and Plastic	34,920.00
Grounds Maintenance Workers	29,170.00

OCCUPATION TITLE	ANNUAL MEAN WAGE
Grounds Maintenance Workers, All Other	32,930.00
Hairdressers, Hairstylists, and Cosmetologists	29,590.00
Hazardous Materials Removal Workers	45,500.00
Health and Safety Engineers, Except Mining Safety Engineers and Inspectors	90,190.00
Health Diagnosing and Treating Practitioners	98,830.00
Health Diagnosing and Treating Practitioners, All Other	84,800.00
Health Educators	57,900.00
Health Practitioner Support Technologists and Technicians	35,180.00
Health Specialties Teachers, Postsecondary	125,430.00
Health Teachers, Postsecondary	113,770.00
Health Technologists and Technicians	46,460.00
Health Technologists and Technicians, All Other	46,020.00
Healthcare Practitioners and Technical Occupations	79,160.00
Healthcare Practitioners and Technical Workers, All Other	57,960.00
Healthcare Social Workers	55,510.00
Healthcare Support Occupations	30,470.00
Healthcare Support Workers, All Other	37,720.00
Hearing Aid Specialists	53,000.00

OCCUPATION TITLE	ANNUAL MEAN WAGE
Heat Treating Equipment Setters, Operators, and Tenders, Metal and Plastic	39,010.00
Heating, Air Conditioning, and Refrigeration Mechanics and Installers	48,320.00
Heavy and Tractor-Trailer Truck Drivers	43,590.00
Heavy Vehicle and Mobile Equipment Service Technicians and Mechanics	48,920.00
Helpers, Construction Trades	30,900.00
Helpers, Construction Trades, All Other	31,450.00
Helpers—Brickmasons, Blockmasons, Stonemasons, and Tile and Marble Setters	33,610.00
Helpers—Carpenters	30,200.00
Helpers—Electricians	30,980.00
Helpers—Extraction Workers	37,160.00
Helpers—Installation, Maintenance, and Repair Workers	29,370.00
Helpers—Painters, Paperhangers, Plasterers, and Stucco Masons	28,760.00
Helpers—Pipelayers, Plumbers, Pipefitters, and Steamfitters	30,640.00
Helpers—Production Workers	26,930.00
Helpers—Roofers	28,890.00
Highway Maintenance Workers	39,540.00
Historians	60,990.00
History Teachers, Postsecondary	80,880.00
Hoist and Winch Operators	50,020.00
Home Appliance Repairers	40,390.00

OCCUPATION TITLE	ANNUAL MEAN WAGE
Home Economics Teachers, Postsecondary	72,790.00
Home Health Aides	23,600.00
Hosts and Hostesses, Restaurant, Lounge, and Coffee Shop	21,410.00
Hotel, Motel, and Resort Desk Clerks	23,530.00
Human Resources Assistants, Except Payroll and Timekeeping	40,100.00
Human Resources Managers	120,210.00
Human Resources Specialists	64,890.00
Human Resources Workers	64,780.00
Hydrologists	83,740.00
Industrial Engineering Technicians	56,920.00
Industrial Engineers	88,530.00
Industrial Engineers, Including Health and Safety	88,680.00
Industrial Machinery Installation, Repair, and Maintenance Workers	50,910.00
Industrial Machinery Mechanics	51,890.00
Industrial Production Managers	107,060.00
Industrial Truck and Tractor Operators	34,260.00
Industrial-Organizational Psychologists	104,570.00
Information and Record Clerks	34,370.00
Information and Record Clerks, All Other	40,090.00
Information Security Analysts	96,040.00
Inspectors, Testers, Sorters, Samplers, and Weighers	40,340.00
Installation, Maintenance, and Repair Occupations	46,690.00

OCCUPATION TITLE	ANNUAL MEAN WAGE
Installation, Maintenance, and Repair Workers, All Other	41,810.00
Instructional Coordinators	65,500.00
Insulation Workers	45,070.00
Insulation Workers, Floor, Ceiling, and Wall	39,490.00
Insulation Workers, Mechanical	51,100.00
Insurance Appraisers, Auto Damage	65,930.00
Insurance Claims and Policy Processing Clerks	40,780.00
Insurance Sales Agents	67,760.00
Insurance Underwriters	75,480.00
Interior Designers	56,220.00
Internists, General	201,840.00
Interpreters and Translators	51,260.00
Interviewers, Except Eligibility and Loan	33,640.00
Janitors and Cleaners, Except Maids and Housekeeping Cleaners	27,030.00
Jewelers and Precious Stone and Metal Workers	42,310.00
Judges, Magistrate Judges, and Magistrates	115,460.00
Judges, Magistrates, and Other Judicial Workers	103,740.00
Judicial Law Clerks	59,840.00
Kindergarten Teachers, Except Special Education	55,460.00
Labor Relations Specialists	64,250.00
Laborers and Freight, Stock, and Material Movers, Hand	28,720.00
Laborers and Material Movers, Hand	27,570.00

OCCUPATION TITLE	ANNUAL MEAN WAGE
Landscape Architects	68,820.00
Landscaping and Groundskeeping Workers	28,560.00
Lathe and Turning Machine Tool Setters, Operators, and Tenders, Metal and Plastic	39,630.00
Laundry and Dry-Cleaning Workers	23,210.00
Law Enforcement Workers	58,310.00
Law Teachers, Postsecondary	134,530.00
Law, Criminal Justice, and Social Work Teachers, Postsecondary	94,490.00
Lawyers	139,880.00
Lawyers and Judicial Law Clerks	138,190.00
Lawyers, Judges, and Related Workers	135,760.00
Layout Workers, Metal and Plastic	47,720.00
Legal Occupations	105,980.00
Legal Secretaries	47,900.00
Legal Support Workers	54,590.00
Legal Support Workers, All Other	66,170.00
Legislators	44,820.00
Librarians	59,870.00
Librarians, Curators, and Archivists	49,700.00
Library Assistants, Clerical	27,450.00
Library Science Teachers, Postsecondary	72,340.00
Library Technicians	34,780.00
Licensed Practical and Licensed Vocational Nurses	44,840.00
Life Sciences Teachers, Postsecondary	91,440.00
Life Scientists	83,080.00
Life Scientists, All Other	83,150.00

OCCUPATION TITLE	ANNUAL MEAN WAGE
Life, Physical, and Social Science Occupations	72,930.00
Life, Physical, and Social Science Technicians	48,550.00
Life, Physical, and Social Science Technicians, All Other	49,270.00
Lifeguards, Ski Patrol, and Other Recreational Protective Service Workers	22,640.00
Light Truck or Delivery Services Drivers	34,790.00
Line Installers and Repairers	61,430.00
Loading Machine Operators, Underground Mining	51,260.00
Loan Interviewers and Clerks	40,300.00
Loan Officers	76,260.00
Locker Room, Coatroom, and Dressing Room Attendants	24,390.00
Locksmiths and Safe Repairers	42,180.00
Locomotive Engineers	61,020.00
Locomotive Engineers and Operators	60,230.00
Locomotive Firers	63,750.00
Lodging Managers	59,410.00
Log Graders and Scalers	38,150.00
Logging Equipment Operators	38,880.00
Logging Workers	39,510.00
Logging Workers, All Other	40,560.00
Logisticians	77,810.00
Machine Feeders and Offbearers	30,490.00
Machine Tool Cutting Setters, Operators, and Tenders, Metal and Plastic	35,470.00

OCCUPATION TITLE	ANNUAL MEAN WAGE
Machinists	43,220.00
Magnetic Resonance Imaging Technologists	69,240.00
Maids and Housekeeping Cleaners	23,830.00
Mail Clerks and Mail Machine Operators, Except Postal Service	30,580.00
Maintenance and Repair Workers, General	39,360.00
Maintenance Workers, Machinery	46,000.00
Makeup Artists, Theatrical and Performance	71,590.00
Management Analysts	91,910.00
Management Occupations	118,020.00
Managers, All Other	112,150.00
Manicurists and Pedicurists	24,330.00
Manufactured Building and Mobile Home Installers	31,030.00
Marine Engineers and Naval Architects	99,860.00
Market Research Analysts and Marketing Specialists	70,620.00
Marketing and Sales Managers	138,350.00
Marketing Managers	144,140.00
Marriage and Family Therapists	54,090.00
Massage Therapists	44,480.00
Material Moving Workers	29,360.00
Material Moving Workers, All Other	34,540.00
Material Recording, Scheduling, Dispatching, and Distributing Workers	34,150.00
Materials Engineers	97,050.00
Materials Scientists	101,570.00

OCCUPATION TITLE	ANNUAL MEAN WAGE
Math and Computer Teachers, Postsecondary	85,350.00
Mathematical Science Occupations	88,230.00
Mathematical Science Occupations, All Other	77,550.00
Mathematical Science Teachers, Postsecondary	82,650.00
Mathematical Technicians	58,490.00
Mathematicians	105,600.00
Meat, Poultry, and Fish Cutters and Trimmers	25,510.00
Mechanical Door Repairers	40,420.00
Mechanical Drafters	57,480.00
Mechanical Engineering Technicians	57,180.00
Mechanical Engineers	89,800.00
Media and Communication Equipment Workers	55,520.00
Media and Communication Equipment Workers, All Other	76,500.00
Media and Communication Workers	63,130.00
Media and Communication Workers, All Other	50,860.00
Medical and Clinical Laboratory Technicians	41,700.00
Medical and Clinical Laboratory Technologists	62,440.00
Medical and Health Services Managers	109,370.00
Medical Appliance Technicians	39,880.00
Medical Assistants	32,850.00
Medical Equipment Preparers	35,960.00
Medical Equipment Repairers	50,910.00

OCCUPATION TITLE	ANNUAL MEAN WAGE
Medical Records and Health Information Technicians	41,460.00
Medical Scientists	94,150.00
Medical Scientists, Except Epidemiologists	95,000.00
Medical Secretaries	35,060.00
Medical Transcriptionists	37,150.00
Medical, Dental, and Ophthalmic Laboratory Technicians	38,270.00
Meeting, Convention, and Event Planners	52,020.00
Mental Health and Substance Abuse Social Workers	47,880.00
Mental Health Counselors	46,050.00
Merchandise Displayers and Window Trimmers	30,090.00
Metal Furnace Operators, Tenders, Pourers, and Casters	40,360.00
Metal Workers and Plastic Workers	39,830.00
Metal Workers and Plastic Workers, All Other	35,780.00
Metal-Refining Furnace Operators and Tenders	41,840.00
Meter Readers, Utilities	41,890.00
Microbiologists	76,850.00
Middle School Teachers, Except Special and Career/Technical Education	59,800.00
Milling and Planing Machine Setters, Operators, and Tenders, Metal and Plastic	41,180.00
Millwrights	53,950.00

OCCUPATION TITLE	ANNUAL MEAN WAGE
Mine Cutting and Channeling Machine Operators	50,670.00
Mine Shuttle Car Operators	56,370.00
Mining and Geological Engineers, Including Mining Safety Engineers	103,010.00
Mining Machine Operators	51,800.00
Mining Machine Operators, All Other	50,220.00
Miscellaneous Agricultural Workers	24,860.00
Miscellaneous Assemblers and Fabricators	32,310.00
Miscellaneous Community and Social Service Specialists	41,270.00
Miscellaneous Construction and Related Workers	40,190.00
Miscellaneous Electrical and Electronic Equipment Mechanics, Installers, and Repairers	52,170.00
Miscellaneous Entertainment Attendants and Related Workers	22,830.00
Miscellaneous Food Processing Workers	29,470.00
Miscellaneous Health Practitioners and Technical Workers	54,830.00
Miscellaneous Health Technologists and Technicians	47,680.00
Miscellaneous Healthcare Support Occupations	34,260.00
Miscellaneous Installation, Maintenance, and Repair Workers	37,940.00
Miscellaneous Legal Support Workers	57,940.00
Miscellaneous Life, Physical, and Social Science Technicians	47,940.00

OCCUPATION TITLE	ANNUAL MEAN WAGE
Miscellaneous Mathematical Science Occupations	73,700.00
Miscellaneous Media and Communication Workers	51,130.00
Miscellaneous Metal Workers and Plastic Workers	37,090.00
Miscellaneous Personal Appearance Workers	28,210.00
Miscellaneous Plant and System Operators	63,750.00
Miscellaneous Postsecondary Teachers	58,150.00
Miscellaneous Production Workers	30,680.00
Miscellaneous Protective Service Workers	29,230.00
Miscellaneous Sales and Related Workers	42,000.00
Miscellaneous Social Scientists and Related Workers	81,570.00
Miscellaneous Teachers and Instructors	36,310.00
Miscellaneous Textile, Apparel, and Furnishings Workers	35,030.00
Miscellaneous Vehicle and Mobile Equipment Mechanics, Installers, and Repairers	28,360.00
Mixing and Blending Machine Setters, Operators, and Tenders	37,630.00
Mobile Heavy Equipment Mechanics, Except Engines	50,810.00
Model Makers and Patternmakers, Metal and Plastic	48,280.00
Model Makers and Patternmakers, Wood	47,660.00
Model Makers, Metal and Plastic	50,360.00

OCCUPATION TITLE	ANNUAL MEAN WAGE
Model Makers, Wood	47,480.00
Models	36,560.00
Models, Demonstrators, and Product Promoters	30,860.00
Molders and Molding Machine Setters, Operators, and Tenders, Metal and Plastic	32,930.00
Molders, Shapers, and Casters, Except Metal and Plastic	32,590.00
Molding, Coremaking, and Casting Machine Setters, Operators, and Tenders, Metal and Plastic	32,660.00
Morticians, Undertakers, and Funeral Directors	54,700.00
Motion Picture Projectionists	24,750.00
Motor Vehicle Operators	37,280.00
Motor Vehicle Operators, All Other	32,930.00
Motorboat Mechanics and Service Technicians	40,860.00
Motorboat Operators	43,340.00
Motorcycle Mechanics	37,040.00
Multimedia Artists and Animators	72,200.00
Multiple Machine Tool Setters, Operators, and Tenders, Metal and Plastic	36,190.00
Museum Technicians and Conservators	44,780.00
Music Directors and Composers	60,630.00
Musical Instrument Repairers and Tuners	37,690.00
Natural Sciences Managers	136,150.00
Network and Computer Systems Administrators	84,500.00

OCCUPATION TITLE	ANNUAL MEAN WAGE
New Accounts Clerks	36,480.00
News Analysts, Reporters and Correspondents	52,960.00
Nonfarm Animal Caretakers	24,420.00
Nuclear Engineers	105,950.00
Nuclear Medicine Technologists	75,960.00
Nuclear Power Reactor Operators	91,370.00
Nuclear Technicians	77,820.00
Nurse Anesthetists	164,030.00
Nurse Midwives	102,390.00
Nurse Practitioners	104,610.00
Nursing Assistants	27,650.00
Nursing Instructors and Teachers, Postsecondary	75,030.00
Nursing, Psychiatric, and Home Health Aides	26,320.00
Obstetricians and Gynecologists	234,310.00
Occupational Health and Safety Specialists	72,480.00
Occupational Health and Safety Specialists and Technicians	68,930.00
Occupational Health and Safety Technicians	52,520.00
Occupational Therapists	83,730.00
Occupational Therapy Aides	31,840.00
Occupational Therapy and Physical Therapist Assistants and Aides	48,410.00
Occupational Therapy Assistants	59,530.00
Occupational Therapy Assistants and Aides	55,130.00
Office and Administrative Support Occupations	37,260.00

OCCUPATION TITLE	ANNUAL MEAN WAGE
Office and Administrative Support Workers, All Other	36,040.00
Office Clerks, General	33,010.00
Office Machine Operators, Except Computer	32,390.00
Operating Engineers and Other Construction Equipment Operators	50,560.00
Operations Research Analysts	84,340.00
Operations Specialties Managers	125,470.00
Ophthalmic Laboratory Technicians	34,220.00
Ophthalmic Medical Technicians	37,040.00
Opticians, Dispensing	37,860.00
Optometrists	117,580.00
Oral and Maxillofacial Surgeons	232,870.00
Order Clerks	35,160.00
Orderlies	28,550.00
Orthodontists	228,780.00
Orthotists and Prosthetists	69,920.00
Other Construction and Related Workers	47,670.00
Other Education, Training, and Library Occupations	32,420.00
Other Food Preparation and Serving Related Workers	21,710.00
Other Healthcare Practitioners and Technical Occupations	63,250.00
Other Healthcare Support Occupations	34,920.00
Other Installation, Maintenance, and Repair Occupations	44,270.00
Other Management Occupations	97,480.00
Other Office and Administrative Support Workers	33,930.00

OCCUPATION TITLE	ANNUAL MEAN WAGE
Other Personal Care and Service Workers	25,410.00
Other Production Occupations	34,950.00
Other Protective Service Workers	30,130.00
Other Sales and Related Workers	49,440.00
Other Teachers and Instructors	38,560.00
Other Transportation Workers	30,230.00
Outdoor Power Equipment and Other Small Engine Mechanics	35,320.00
Packaging and Filling Machine Operators and Tenders	30,910.00
Packers and Packagers, Hand	24,430.00
Painters and Paperhangers	41,430.00
Painters, Construction and Maintenance	41,510.00
Painters, Transportation Equipment	46,270.00
Painting Workers	38,370.00
Painting, Coating, and Decorating Workers	32,040.00
Paper Goods Machine Setters, Operators, and Tenders	38,570.00
Paperhangers	36,470.00
Paralegals and Legal Assistants	53,180.00
Parking Enforcement Workers	39,650.00
Parking Lot Attendants	23,250.00
Parts Salespersons	33,220.00
Patternmakers, Metal and Plastic	44,490.00
Patternmakers, Wood	47,850.00
Paving, Surfacing, and Tamping Equipment Operators	43,800.00
Payroll and Timekeeping Clerks	43,580.00
Pediatricians, General	184,240.00

OCCUPATION TITLE	ANNUAL MEAN WAGE
Personal Appearance Workers	29,190.00
Personal Care Aides	22,710.00
Personal Care and Service Occupations	26,510.00
Personal Care and Service Workers, All Other	27,460.00
Personal Financial Advisors	123,100.00
Pest Control Workers	35,020.00
Pesticide Handlers, Sprayers, and Applicators, Vegetation	35,720.00
Petroleum Engineers	147,030.00
Petroleum Pump System Operators, Refinery Operators, and Gaugers	67,870.00
Pharmacists	120,270.00
Pharmacy Aides	28,420.00
Pharmacy Technicians	32,170.00
Philosophy and Religion Teachers, Postsecondary	77,420.00
Phlebotomists	33,750.00
Photographers	42,640.00
Photographic Process Workers and Processing Machine Operators	31,740.00
Physical Sciences Teachers, Postsecondary	92,900.00
Physical Scientists	87,310.00
Physical Scientists, All Other	98,460.00
Physical Therapist Aides	27,890.00
Physical Therapist Assistants	56,850.00
Physical Therapist Assistants and Aides	46,170.00
Physical Therapists	87,220.00
Physician Assistants	102,090.00

OCCUPATION TITLE	ANNUAL MEAN WAGE
Physicians and Surgeons	210,170.00
Physicians and Surgeons, All Other	205,560.00
Physicists	121,770.00
Physics Teachers, Postsecondary	97,520.00
Pile-Driver Operators	61,740.00
Pipelayers	42,860.00
Pipelayers, Plumbers, Pipefitters, and Steamfitters	54,870.00
Plant and System Operators	59,980.00
Plant and System Operators, All Other	55,340.00
Plasterers and Stucco Masons	44,070.00
Plating and Coating Machine Setters, Operators, and Tenders, Metal and Plastic	33,690.00
Plumbers, Pipefitters, and Steamfitters	56,030.00
Podiatrists	144,110.00
Police and Sheriff's Patrol Officers	62,760.00
Police Officers	62,790.00
Police, Fire, and Ambulance Dispatchers	41,070.00
Political Science Teachers, Postsecondary	94,090.00
Political Scientists	112,250.00
Postal Service Clerks	48,360.00
Postal Service Mail Carriers	50,610.00
Postal Service Mail Sorters, Processors, and Processing Machine Operators	49,710.00
Postal Service Workers	50,070.00
Postmasters and Mail Superintendents	71,980.00

OCCUPATION TITLE	ANNUAL MEAN WAGE
Postsecondary Teachers	81,880.00
Postsecondary Teachers, All Other	73,990.00
Pourers and Casters, Metal	37,300.00
Power Distributors and Dispatchers	81,500.00
Power Plant Operators	73,800.00
Power Plant Operators, Distributors, and Dispatchers	77,790.00
Precision Instrument and Equipment Repairers	49,680.00
Precision Instrument and Equipment Repairers, All Other	56,570.00
Prepress Technicians and Workers	40,640.00
Preschool and Kindergarten Teachers	39,550.00
Preschool Teachers, Except Special Education	33,300.00
Preschool, Primary, Secondary, and Special Education School Teachers	57,470.00
Pressers, Textile, Garment, and Related Materials	22,270.00
Print Binding and Finishing Workers	33,270.00
Printing Press Operators	37,460.00
Printing Workers	37,010.00
Private Detectives and Investigators	53,530.00
Probation Officers and Correctional Treatment Specialists	55,380.00
Procurement Clerks	41,980.00
Producers and Directors	93,840.00
Production Occupations	37,190.00
Production Workers, All Other	32,380.00
Production, Planning, and Expediting Clerks	49,050.00
Proofreaders and Copy Markers	39,640.00

OCCUPATION TITLE	ANNUAL MEAN WAGE
Property, Real Estate, and Community Association Managers	70,290.00
Prosthodontists	168,140.00
Protective Service Occupations	45,810.00
Protective Service Workers, All Other	32,880.00
Psychiatric Aides	28,770.00
Psychiatric Technicians	35,870.00
Psychiatrists	200,220.00
Psychologists	80,640.00
Psychologists, All Other	94,650.00
Psychology Teachers, Postsecondary	84,440.00
Public Address System and Other Announcers	42,740.00
Public Relations and Fundraising Managers	123,360.00
Public Relations Specialists	66,540.00
Pump Operators, Except Wellhead Pumpers	46,270.00
Pumping Station Operators	50,030.00
Purchasing Agents, Except Wholesale, Retail, and Farm Products	67,420.00
Purchasing Managers	117,720.00
Radiation Therapists	84,980.00
Radio and Telecommunications Equipment Installers and Repairers	54,460.00
Radio and Television Announcers	48,170.00
Radio Operators	46,780.00
Radio, Cellular, and Tower Equipment Installers and Repairers	53,620.00
Radiologic Technologists	59,260.00
Rail Car Repairers	53,590.00

OCCUPATION TITLE	ANNUAL MEAN WAGE
Rail Transportation Workers	58,950.00
Rail Transportation Workers, All Other	59,480.00
Rail Yard Engineers, Dinkey Operators, and Hostlers	52,320.00
Railroad Brake, Signal, and Switch Operators	55,320.00
Railroad Conductors and Yardmasters	58,220.00
Rail-Track Laying and Maintenance Equipment Operators	52,810.00
Real Estate Brokers	79,340.00
Real Estate Brokers and Sales Agents	63,590.00
Real Estate Sales Agents	59,360.00
Receptionists and Information Clerks	29,120.00
Recreation and Fitness Studies Teachers, Postsecondary	67,870.00
Recreation and Fitness Workers	33,970.00
Recreation Workers	27,230.00
Recreational Therapists	48,190.00
Recreational Vehicle Service Technicians	38,040.00
Refractory Materials Repairers, Except Brickmasons	47,000.00
Refuse and Recyclable Material Collectors	37,690.00
Registered Nurses	72,180.00
Rehabilitation Counselors	38,740.00
Reinforcing Iron and Rebar Workers	53,600.00
Religious Workers	46,630.00
Religious Workers, All Other	34,300.00
Reporters and Correspondents	49,770.00

OCCUPATION TITLE	ANNUAL MEAN WAGE
Reservation and Transportation Ticket Agents and Travel Clerks	38,050.00
Residential Advisors	27,690.00
Respiratory Therapists	60,640.00
Respiratory Therapy Technicians	50,520.00
Retail Sales Workers	25,250.00
Retail Salespersons	27,180.00
Riggers	49,030.00
Rock Splitters, Quarry	34,860.00
Rolling Machine Setters, Operators, and Tenders, Metal and Plastic	41,900.00
Roof Bolters, Mining	58,110.00
Roofers	42,080.00
Rotary Drill Operators, Oil and Gas	57,140.00
Roustabouts, Oil and Gas	40,480.00
Sailors and Marine Oilers	46,170.00
Sales and Related Occupations	40,560.00
Sales and Related Workers, All Other	43,330.00
Sales Engineers	108,880.00
Sales Managers	135,090.00
Sales Representatives, Services	70,510.00
Sales Representatives, Services, All Other	63,070.00
Sales Representatives, Wholesale and Manufacturing	73,060.00
Sales Representatives, Wholesale and Manufacturing, Except Technical and Scientific Products	68,410.00
Sales Representatives, Wholesale and Manufacturing, Technical and Scientific Products	92,910.00

OCCUPATION TITLE	ANNUAL MEAN WAGE
Sawing Machine Setters, Operators, and Tenders, Wood	29,960.00
Secondary School Teachers	61,280.00
Secondary School Teachers, Except Special and Career/Technical Education	61,420.00
Secretaries and Administrative Assistants	40,330.00
Secretaries and Administrative Assistants, Except Legal, Medical, and Executive	36,140.00
Securities, Commodities, and Financial Services Sales Agents	102,260.00
Security and Fire Alarm Systems Installers	45,660.00
Security Guards	29,730.00
Security Guards and Gaming Surveillance Officers	29,780.00
Segmental Pavers	34,160.00
Self-Enrichment Education Teachers	43,150.00
Semiconductor Processors	37,890.00
Separating, Filtering, Clarifying, Precipitating, and Still Machine Setters, Operators, and Tenders	41,450.00
Septic Tank Servicers and Sewer Pipe Cleaners	38,870.00
Service Unit Operators, Oil, Gas, and Mining	53,520.00
Set and Exhibit Designers	57,600.00
Sewers, Hand	25,630.00
Sewing Machine Operators	25,830.00
Shampooers	20,960.00
Sheet Metal Workers	51,080.00

OCCUPATION TITLE	ANNUAL MEAN WAGE
Ship and Boat Captains and Operators	78,380.00
Ship Engineers	74,120.00
Shipping, Receiving, and Traffic Clerks	33,150.00
Shoe and Leather Workers	26,190.00
Shoe and Leather Workers and Repairers	26,040.00
Shoe Machine Operators and Tenders	26,530.00
Signal and Track Switch Repairers	62,710.00
Skincare Specialists	35,160.00
Slaughterers and Meat Packers	27,040.00
Slot Supervisors	38,300.00
Small Engine Mechanics	37,340.00
Social and Community Service Managers	70,870.00
Social and Human Service Assistants	34,120.00
Social Science Research Assistants	46,820.00
Social Sciences Teachers, Postsecondary	89,150.00
Social Sciences Teachers, Postsecondary, All Other	85,950.00
Social Scientists and Related Workers	81,380.00
Social Scientists and Related Workers, All Other	80,860.00
Social Work Teachers, Postsecondary	74,280.00
Social Workers	50,710.00
Social Workers, All Other	59,410.00
Sociologists	86,840.00
Sociology Teachers, Postsecondary	81,600.00
Software Developers and Programmers	100,080.00

OCCUPATION TITLE	ANNUAL MEAN WAGE
Software Developers, Applications	104,300.00
Software Developers, Systems Software	110,590.00
Soil and Plant Scientists	69,290.00
Solar Photovoltaic Installers	42,500.00
Sound Engineering Technicians	65,240.00
Special Education Teachers	61,280.00
Special Education Teachers, All Other	59,450.00
Special Education Teachers, Kindergarten and Elementary School	60,090.00
Special Education Teachers, Middle School	61,910.00
Special Education Teachers, Preschool	56,990.00
Special Education Teachers, Secondary School	64,020.00
Speech-Language Pathologists	78,210.00
Stationary Engineers and Boiler Operators	61,410.00
Statistical Assistants	48,300.00
Statisticians	85,160.00
Stock Clerks and Order Fillers	26,670.00
Stonemasons	43,650.00
Structural Iron and Steel Workers	56,040.00
Structural Metal Fabricators and Fitters	40,000.00
Substance Abuse and Behavioral Disorder Counselors	44,160.00
Substitute Teachers	30,900.00
Subway and Streetcar Operators	62,380.00
Supervisors of Food Preparation and Serving Workers	36,340.00

OCCUPATION TITLE	ANNUAL MEAN WAGE
Supervisors of Personal Care and Service Workers	40,880.00
Supervisors of Protective Service Workers	72,300.00
Supervisors of Transportation and Material Moving Workers	55,160.00
Surgeons	252,910.00
Surgical Technologists	46,800.00
Survey Researchers	59,950.00
Surveying and Mapping Technicians	45,490.00
Surveyors	63,480.00
Surveyors, Cartographers, and Photogrammetrists	64,070.00
Switchboard Operators, Including Answering Service	29,720.00
Tailors, Dressmakers, and Custom Sewers	30,670.00
Tailors, Dressmakers, and Sewers	29,500.00
Tank Car, Truck, and Ship Loaders	39,590.00
Tapers	53,790.00
Tax Examiners and Collectors, and Revenue Agents	57,950.00
Tax Examiners, Collectors and Preparers, and Revenue Agents	51,080.00
Tax Preparers	45,340.00
Taxi Drivers and Chauffeurs	26,790.00
Teacher Assistants	27,120.00
Teachers and Instructors, All Other, Except Substitute Teachers	47,570.00
Team Assemblers	32,550.00
Technical Writers	73,160.00
Telecommunications Equipment Installers and Repairers, Except Line Installers	54,520.00

OCCUPATION TITLE	ANNUAL MEAN WAGE
Telecommunications Line Installers and Repairers	54,700.00
Telemarketers	27,170.00
Telephone Operators	43,030.00
Television, Video, and Motion Picture Camera Operators and Editors	74,200.00
Tellers	28,060.00
Terrazzo Workers and Finishers	45,990.00
Textile Bleaching and Dyeing Machine Operators and Tenders	28,480.00
Textile Cutting Machine Setters, Operators, and Tenders	27,860.00
Textile Knitting and Weaving Machine Setters, Operators, and Tenders	28,380.00
Textile Machine Setters, Operators, and Tenders	28,190.00
Textile Winding, Twisting, and Drawing Out Machine Setters, Operators, and Tenders	28,110.00
Textile, Apparel, and Furnishings Workers	26,270.00
Textile, Apparel, and Furnishings Workers, All Other	30,830.00
Therapists	77,540.00
Therapists, All Other	60,590.00
Tile and Marble Setters	44,770.00
Timing Device Assemblers and Adjusters	42,470.00
Tire Builders	42,230.00
Tire Repairers and Changers	27,150.00
Title Examiners, Abstractors, and Searchers	51,490.00

OCCUPATION TITLE	ANNUAL MEAN WAGE
Tool and Die Makers	51,610.00
Tool Grinders, Filers, and Sharpeners	38,860.00
Top Executives	126,950.00
Tour and Travel Guides	28,670.00
Tour Guides and Escorts	28,100.00
Traffic Technicians	48,650.00
Training and Development Managers	115,180.00
Training and Development Specialists	63,350.00
Transit and Railroad Police	67,850.00
Transportation and Material Moving Occupations	36,070.00
Transportation Attendants, Except Flight Attendants	31,080.00
Transportation Inspectors	72,650.00
Transportation Security Screeners	40,160.00
Transportation Workers, All Other	38,740.00
Transportation, Storage, and Distribution Managers	97,630.00
Travel Agents	39,900.00
Travel Guides	35,930.00
Tree Trimmers and Pruners	37,310.00
Umpires, Referees, and Other Sports Officials	35,540.00
Upholsterers	34,640.00
Urban and Regional Planners	73,060.00
Ushers, Lobby Attendants, and Ticket Takers	21,740.00
Vehicle and Mobile Equipment Mechanics, Installers, and Repairers	43,710.00
Veterinarians	100,560.00
Veterinary Assistants and Laboratory Animal Caretakers	26,810.00

OCCUPATION TITLE	ANNUAL MEAN WAGE
Veterinary Technologists and Technicians	33,870.00
Vocational Education Teachers, Postsecondary	55,730.00
Waiters and Waitresses	24,410.00
Watch Repairers	39,720.00
Water and Wastewater Treatment Plant and System Operators	47,930.00
Water Transportation Workers	65,140.00
Web Developers	72,150.00
Weighers, Measurers, Checkers, and Samplers, Recordkeeping	31,080.00
Welders, Cutters, Solderers, and Brazers	42,450.00
Welding, Soldering, and Brazing Machine Setters, Operators, and Tenders	38,380.00
Welding, Soldering, and Brazing Workers	42,010.00
Wellhead Pumpers	50,730.00
Wholesale and Retail Buyers, Except Farm Products	60,040.00
Wind Turbine Service Technicians	54,360.00
Woodworkers	32,170.00
Woodworkers, All Other	31,780.00
Woodworking Machine Setters, Operators, and Tenders	29,900.00
Woodworking Machine Setters, Operators, and Tenders, Except Sawing	29,850.00
Word Processors and Typists	39,970.00
Writers and Authors	71,920.00
Writers and Editors	69,280.00

OCCUPATION TITLE	ANNUAL MEAN WAGE
Zoologists and Wildlife Biologists	64,890.00

Appendix B
Jobs Most and Least Vulnerable to Robotics
(From Least to Most Computerizable)

From Benedikt Frey, Carl, and Michael A. Osborne. THE FUTURE OF EMPLOYMENT: HOW SUSCEPTIBLE ARE JOBS TO COMPUTERISATION? University of Oxford. September 17, 2013. https://www.oxfordmartin.ox.ac.uk/downloads/academic

1. Recreational Therapists
2. First-Line Supervisors of Mechanics, Installers, and Repairers
3. Emergency Management Directors
4. Mental Health and Substance Abuse Social Workers
5. Audiologists
6. Occupational Therapists
7. Orthotists and Prosthetists
8. Healthcare Social Workers
9. Oral and Maxillofacial Surgeons
10. First-Line Supervisors of Fire Fighting and Prevention Workers
11. Dietitians and Nutritionists
12. Lodging Managers
13. Choreographers
14. Sales Engineers
15. Physicians and Surgeons
16. Instructional Coordinators
17. Psychologists, All Other
18. First-Line Supervisors of Police and Detectives
19. Dentists, General
20. Elementary School Teachers, Except Special Education
21. Medical Scientists, Except Epidemiologists
22. Education Administrators, Elementary and Secondary School
23. Podiatrists

24. Clinical, Counseling, and School Psychologists
25. Mental Health Counselors
26. Fabric and Apparel Patternmakers
27. Set and Exhibit Designers
28. Human Resources Managers
29. Recreation Workers
30. Training and Development Managers
31. Speech-Language Pathologists
32. Computer Systems Analysts
33. Social and Community Service Managers
34. Curators
35. Athletic Trainers
36. Medical and Health Services Managers
37. Preschool Teachers, Except Special Education
38. Farm and Home Management Advisors
39. Anthropologists and Archeologists
40. Special Education Teachers, Secondary School
41. Secondary School Teachers, Except Special and Career/Technical Education
42. Clergy
43. Foresters
44. Educational, Guidance, School, and Vocational Counselors
45. Career/Technical Education Teachers, Secondary School
46. Registered Nurses
47. Rehabilitation Counselors
48. Teachers and Instructors, All Other
49. Forensic Science Technicians
50. Makeup Artists, Theatrical and Performance
51. Marine Engineers and Naval Architects
52. Education Administrators, Postsecondary
53. Mechanical Engineers

54. Pharmacists

55. Logisticians

56. Microbiologists

57. Industrial-Organizational Psychologists

58. Coaches and Scouts

59. Sales Managers

60. Hydrologists

61. Marketing Managers

62. Marriage and Family Therapists

63. Engineers, All Other

64. Training and Development Specialists

65. First-Line Supervisors of Office and Administrative Support Workers

66. Biological Scientists, All Other

67. Public Relations and Fundraising Managers

68. Multimedia Artists and Animators

69. Computer and Information Research Scientists

70. Chief Executives

71. Education Administrators, Preschool and Childcare Center/ Program

72. Music Directors and Composers

73. First-Line Supervisors of Production and Operating Workers

74. Securities, Commodities, and Financial Services Sales Agents

75. Conservation Scientists

76. Special Education Teachers, Middle School

77. Chemical Engineers

78. Architectural and Engineering Managers

79. Aerospace Engineers

80. Natural Sciences Managers

81. Environmental Engineers

82. Architects, Except Landscape and Naval

83. Physical Therapist Assistants

84. Civil Engineers

85. Health Diagnosing and Treating Practitioners, All Other

86. Soil and Plant Scientists

87. Materials Scientists

88. Materials Engineers

89. Fashion Designers

90. Physical Therapists

91. Photographers

92. Producers and Directors

93. Interior Designers

94. Orthodontists

95. Art Directors

96. First-Line Supervisors of Correctional Officers

97. Directors, Religious Activities and Education

98. Electronics Engineers, Except Computer

99. Biochemists and Biophysicists

100. Chiropractors

101. Occupational Therapy Assistants

102. Child, Family, and School Social Workers

103. Health and Safety Engineers, Except Mining Safety Engineers and Inspectors

104. Industrial Engineers

105. First-Line Supervisors of Transportation and Material-Moving Machine

106. Veterinary Technologists and Technicians

107. Industrial Production Managers

108. Industrial Engineering Technicians

109. Network and Computer Systems Administrators

110. Database Administrators

111. Purchasing Managers

112. Postsecondary Teachers

113. Environmental Scientists and Specialists, Including Health

114. Substance Abuse and Behavioral Disorder Counselors

115. Lawyers

116. Craft Artists

117. Operations Research Analysts

118. Computer and Information Systems Managers

119. Commercial and Industrial Designers

120. Biomedical Engineers

121. Meeting, Convention, and Event Planners

122. Veterinarians

123. Writers and Authors

124. Advertising and Promotions Managers

125. Political Scientists

126. Credit Counselors

127. Social Scientists and Related Workers, All Other

128. Astronomers

129. Ship Engineers

130. Software Developers, Applications

131. Fine Artists, Including Painters, Sculptors, and Illustrators

132. Psychiatric Technicians

133. Landscape Architects

134. Health Educators

135. Mathematicians

136. Floral Designers

137. Farmers, Ranchers, and Other Agricultural Managers

138. Forest Fire Inspectors and Prevention Specialists

139. Emergency Medical Technicians and Paramedics

140. Editors

141. Prosthodontists

142. Healthcare Practitioners and Technical Workers, All Other

143. Travel Guides

144. Licensed Practical and Licensed Vocational Nurses

145. Sociologists

146. Arbitrators, Mediators, and Conciliators

147. Animal Scientists

148. Residential Advisors

149. Aircraft Cargo Handling Supervisors

150. Respiratory Therapists

151. Broadcast News Analysts

152. Financial Managers

153. Nuclear Engineers

154. Construction Managers

155. Musicians and Singers

156. First-Line Supervisors of Non-Retail Sales Workers

157. First-Line Supervisors of Personal Service Workers

158. Food Scientists and Technologists

159. Compliance Officers

160. Fish and Game Wardens

161. Graphic Designers

162. Food Service Managers

163. Childcare Workers

164. Fitness Trainers and Aerobics Instructors

165. Gaming Managers

166. Electrical Power-Line Installers and Repairers

167. Police and Sheriff's Patrol Officers

168. Travel Agents

169. Chefs and Head Cooks

170. Animal Trainers

171. Radio and Television Announcers

172. Electrical Engineers

173. Chemists

174. Respiratory Therapy Technicians

175. Physicists

176. Hairdressers, Hairstylists, and Cosmetologists

177. Reporters and Correspondents

178. Air Traffic Controllers

179. Dancers

180. Nuclear Medicine Technologists

181. Software Developers, Systems Software

182. Management Analysts

183. Dietetic Technicians

184. Urban and Regional Planners

185. Social and Human Service Assistants

186. Self-Enrichment Education Teachers

187. Sound Engineering Technicians

188. Optometrists

189. Mining and Geological Engineers, Including Mining Safety Engineers

190. Physician Assistants

191. Kindergarten Teachers, Except Special Education

192. Electricians

193. Petroleum Engineers

194. Desktop Publishers

195. General and Operations Managers

196. Occupational Health and Safety Specialists

197. Firefighters

198. Financial Examiners

199. First-Line Supervisors of Construction Trades and Extraction Workers

200. Middle School Teachers, Except Special and Career/Technical Education

201. Public Relations Specialists

202. Commercial Divers

203. Manufactured Building and Mobile Home Installers

204. Airline Pilots, Copilots, and Flight Engineers

205. Adult Basic and Secondary Education and Literacy Teachers and Instructors

206. Epidemiologists

207. Funeral Service Managers, Directors, Morticians, and Undertakers

208. Information Security Analysts, Web Developers, and Computer Network Architects

209. Actuaries

210. Animal Control Workers

211. Concierges

212. Computer Occupations, All Other

213. Statisticians

214. Computer Hardware Engineers

215. Survey Researchers

216. Business Operations Specialists, All Other

217. Financial Analysts

218. Radiologic Technologists and Technicians

219. Cardiovascular Technologists and Technicians

220. Agents and Business Managers of Artists, Performers, and Athletes

221. Engineering Technicians, Except Drafters, All Other

222. Geographers

223. Occupational Health and Safety Technicians

224. Probation Officers and Correctional Treatment Specialists

225. Environmental Engineering Technicians

226. Managers, All Other

227. Ambulance Drivers and Attendants, Except Emergency Medical Technicians

228. Sales Representatives, Wholesale and Manufacturing, Technical and

229. Career/Technical Education Teachers, Middle School

230. Captains, Mates, and Pilots of Water Vessels

231. Occupational Therapy Aides

232. Medical Equipment Repairers

233. First-Line Supervisors of Retail Sales Workers

234. Athletes and Sports Competitors

235. Gaming Supervisors

236. Skincare Specialists

237. Wholesale and Retail Buyers, Except Farm Products

238. Biological Technicians

239. Medical Assistants

240. Zoologists and Wildlife Biologists

241. Cooks, Private Household

242. Human Resources, Training, and Labor Relations Specialists, All Other

243. Private Detectives and Investigators

244. Film and Video Editors

245. Financial Specialists, All Other

246. Detectives and Criminal Investigators

247. Surgical Technologists

248. Radiation Therapists

249. Plumbers, Pipefitters, and Steamfitters

250. Flight Attendants

251. Diagnostic Medical Sonographers

252. Bailiffs

253. Computer Numerically Controlled Machine Tool Programmers, Metal and Plastic

254. Telecommunications Equipment Installers and Repairers, Except Line Installers

255. Furnace, Kiln, Oven, Drier, and Kettle Operators and Tenders

256. Cleaners of Vehicles and Equipment

257. Funeral Attendants

258. Helpers–Extraction Workers

259. Actors

260. Mine Shuttle Car Operators

261. Electrical and Electronics Repairers, Powerhouse, Substation, and Relay

262. Surveyors

263. Mechanical Engineering Technicians

264. Packers and Packagers, Hand

265. Interpreters and Translators

266. Home Health Aides

267. Upholsterers

268. Elevator Installers and Repairers

269. Gaming Cage Workers

270. Audio-Visual and Multimedia Collections Specialists

271. Judges, Magistrate Judges, and Magistrates

272. Mobile Heavy Equipment Mechanics, Except Engines

273. Health Technologists and Technicians, All Other

274. Graders and Sorters, Agricultural Products

275. Structural Metal Fabricators and Fitters

276. Judicial Law Clerks

277. Electrical and Electronics Repairers, Commercial and Industrial Equipment

278. Forest and Conservation Technicians

279. First-Line Supervisors of Helpers, Laborers, and Material Movers, Hand

280. Locker Room, Coatroom, and Dressing Room Attendants

281. Physical Scientists, All Other

282. Economists

283. Historians

284. Medical Appliance Technicians

285. Court, Municipal, and License Clerks

286. Compensation, Benefits, and Job Analysis Specialists

287. Psychiatric Aides

288. Medical and Clinical Laboratory Technicians

289. Fire Inspectors and Investigators

290. Aerospace Engineering and Operations Technicians

291. Merchandise Displayers and Window Trimmers

292. Explosives Workers, Ordnance Handling Experts, and Blasters

293. Computer Programmers

294. Crossing Guards

295. Agricultural Engineers

296. Roof Bolters, Mining

297. Telecommunications Line Installers and Repairers

298. Police, Fire, and Ambulance Dispatchers

299. Loading Machine Operators, Underground Mining

300. Installation, Maintenance, and Repair Workers, All Other

301. Court Reporters

302. Demonstrators and Product Promoters

303. Dental Assistants

304. Shoe and Leather Workers and Repairers

305. Architectural and Civil Drafters

306. Rotary Drill Operators, Oil and Gas

307. Hazardous Materials Removal Workers

308. Embalmers

309. Continuous Mining Machine Operators

310. Slot Supervisors

311. Massage Therapists

312. Advertising Sales Agents

313. Automotive Glass Installers and Repairers

314. Commercial Pilots

315. Customer Service Representatives

316. Audio and Video Equipment Technicians

317. Teacher Assistants

318. First-Line Supervisors of Farming, Fishing, and Forestry Workers

319. Chemical Technicians

320. Helpers–Pipelayers, Plumbers, Pipefitters, and Steamfitters

321. Cost Estimators

322. Transit and Railroad Police

323. First-Line Supervisors of Landscaping, Lawn Service, and Groundskeeping Workers

324. Personal Financial Advisors

325. Millwrights

326. Museum Technicians and Conservators

327. Mine Cutting and Channeling Machine Operators

328. Transportation, Storage, and Distribution Managers

329. Recreational Vehicle Service Technicians

330. Automotive Service Technicians and Mechanics

331. Correctional Officers and Jailers

332. Camera Operators, Television, Video, and Motion Picture

333. Slaughterers and Meat Packers

334. Electronic Equipment Installers and Repairers, Motor Vehicles

335. Physical Therapist Aides

336. Costume Attendants

337. Market Research Analysts and Marketing Specialists

338. Reservation and Transportation Ticket Agents and Travel Clerks

339. Water and Wastewater Treatment Plant and System Operators

340. Life, Physical, and Social Science Technicians, All Other

341. Food Cooking Machine Operators and Tenders

342. Welding, Soldering, and Brazing Machine Setters, Operators, and Tenders

343. Motorboat Operators

344. Tapers

345. Pipelayers

346. Geoscientists, Except Hydrologists and Geographers

347. Control and Valve Installers and Repairers, Except Mechanical Door

348. Healthcare Support Workers, All Other

349. First-Line Supervisors of Food Preparation and Serving Workers

350. Construction and Building Inspectors

351. Cutters and Trimmers, Hand

352. Maintenance and Repair Workers, General

353. Administrative Law Judges, Adjudicators, and Hearing Officers

354. Stock Clerks and Order Fillers

355. Power Distributors and Dispatchers

356. Insulation Workers, Mechanical

357. Social Science Research Assistants

358. Machinists

359. Computer Support Specialists

360. Librarians

361. Electronic Home Entertainment Equipment Installers and Repairers

362. Heating, Air Conditioning, and Refrigeration Mechanics and Installers

363. Hoist and Winch Operators

364. Pest Control Workers

365. Helpers—Production Workers

366. Statistical Assistants

367. Janitors and Cleaners, Except Maids and Housekeeping Cleaners

368. Motorboat Mechanics and Service Technicians

369. Paper Goods Machine Setters, Operators, and Tenders

370. Foundry Mold and Coremakers

371. Atmospheric and Space Scientists

372. Bus Drivers, Transit and Intercity

373. Lifeguards, Ski Patrol, and Other Recreational Protective Service Workers

374. Industrial Machinery Mechanics

375. Postal Service Mail Carriers

376. Roustabouts, Oil and Gas

377. Boilermakers

378. Mechanical Drafters

379. Dental Hygienists

380. Light Truck or Delivery Services Drivers

381. Maids and Housekeeping Cleaners

382. Painters, Transportation Equipment

383. Eligibility Interviewers, Government Programs

384. Tire Repairers and Changers

385. Food Batchmakers

386. Avionics Technicians

387. Aircraft Mechanics and Service Technicians

388. Airfield Operations Specialists

389. Petroleum Pump System Operators, Refinery Operators, and Gaugers

390. Construction and Related Workers, All Other

391. Opticians, Dispensing

392. Laundry and Dry-Cleaning Workers

393. Amusement and Recreation Attendants

394. Pharmacy Aides

395. Helpers—Roofers

396. Tank Car, Truck, and Ship Loaders

397. Home Appliance Repairers

398. Carpenters

399. Public Address System and Other Announcers

400. Textile Knitting and Weaving Machine Setters, Operators, and Tenders

401. Administrative Services Managers

402. Glaziers

403. Coil Winders, Tapers, and Finishers

404. Bus and Truck Mechanics and Diesel Engine Specialists

405. Computer, Automated Teller, and Office Machine Repairers

406. Personal Care Aides

407. Broadcast Technicians

408. Helpers–Electricians

409. Postmasters and Mail Superintendents

410. Tile and Marble Setters

411. Painters, Construction and Maintenance

412. Transportation Attendants, Except Flight Attendants

413. Civil Engineering Technicians

414. Farm Equipment Mechanics and Service Technicians

415. Archivists

416. Chemical Equipment Operators and Tenders

417. Electric Motor, Power Tool, and Related Repairers

418. Fallers

419. Environmental Science and Protection Technicians, Including Health

420. Locksmiths and Safe Repairers

421. Tree Trimmers and Pruners

422. Bartenders

423. Purchasing Agents, Except Wholesale, Retail, and Farm Products

424. Dishwashers

425. Hunters and Trappers

426. Medical Equipment Preparers

427. Cutting, Punching, and Press Machine Setters, Operators, and Tenders

428. Computer Operators

429. Gas Plant Operators

430. Postal Service Mail Sorters, Processors, and Processing Machine Operators

431. Heavy and Tractor-Trailer Truck Drivers

432. Shampooers

433. Drywall and Ceiling Tile Installers

434. Helpers–Installation, Maintenance, and Repair Workers

435. Motorcycle Mechanics

436. Aircraft Structure, Surfaces, Rigging, and Systems Assemblers

437. Logging Equipment Operators

438. Floor Layers, Except Carpet, Wood, and Hard Tiles

439. Barbers

440. Derrick Operators, Oil and Gas

441. Cooks, Fast Food

442. Word Processors and Typists

443. Electrical and Electronics Drafters

444. Electro-Mechanical Technicians

445. Cleaning, Washing, and Metal Pickling Equipment Operators and Tenders

446. Property, Real Estate, and Community Association Managers

447. Medical Secretaries

448. Pressers, Textile, Garment, and Related Materials

449. Engine and Other Machine Assemblers

450. Security and Fire Alarm Systems Installers

451. Refractory Materials Repairers, Except Brickmasons

452. Nonfarm Animal Caretakers

453. Sheet Metal Workers

454. Pile-Driver Operators

455. Brickmasons and Blockmasons

456. Fishers and Related Fishing Workers

457. Structural Iron and Steel Workers

458. Railroad Brake, Signal, and Switch Operators

459. Railroad Conductors and Yardmasters

460. Cooks, Institution and Cafeteria

461. Sailors and Marine Oilers

462. Mixing and Blending Machine Setters, Operators, and Tenders

463. Helpers—Brickmasons, Blockmasons, Stonemasons, and Tile and Marble Setters

464. Segmental Pavers

465. Insulation Workers, Floor, Ceiling, and Wall

466. Printing Press Operators

467. Automotive and Watercraft Service Attendants

468. Septic Tank Servicers and Sewer Pipe Cleaners

469. Baggage Porters and Bellhops

470. Gaming Change Persons and Booth Cashiers

471. Rolling Machine Setters, Operators, and Tenders, Metal and Plastic

472. Paving, Surfacing, and Tamping Equipment Operators

473. Tool and Die Makers

474. Electrical and Electronics Engineering Technicians

475. Plasterers and Stucco Masons

476. Layout Workers, Metal and Plastic

477. Lathe and Turning Machine Tool Setters, Operators, and Tenders, Metal and Plastic

478. Security Guards

479. Tailors, Dressmakers, and Custom Sewers

480. Wellhead Pumpers

481. Proofreaders and Copy Markers

482. Parking Enforcement Workers

483. Laborers and Freight, Stock, and Material Movers, Hand

484. Sales Representatives, Wholesale and Manufacturing, Except Technical and Scientific Products

485. Meter Readers, Utilities

486. Power Plant Operators

487. Chemical Plant and System Operators

488. Earth Drillers, Except Oil and Gas

489. Nuclear Technicians

490. Executive Secretaries and Executive Administrative Assistants

491. Plant and System Operators, All Other

492. Food Servers, Nonrestaurant

493. Sawing Machine Setters, Operators, and Tenders, Wood

494. Subway and Streetcar Operators

495. Veterinary Assistants and Laboratory Animal Caretakers

496. Cutting and Slicing Machine Setters, Operators, and Tenders

497. Real Estate Sales Agents

498. Computer-Controlled Machine Tool Operators, Metal and Plastic

499. Maintenance Workers, Machinery

500. Correspondence Clerks

501. Miscellaneous Agricultural Workers

502. Forest and Conservation Workers

503. Pourers and Casters, Metal

504. Carpet Installers

505. Paperhangers

506. Buyers and Purchasing Agents, Farm Products

507. Furniture Finishers

508. Food Preparation Workers

509. Floor Sanders and Finishers

510. Parking Lot Attendants

511. Highway Maintenance Workers

512. Construction Laborers

513. Production, Planning, and Expediting Clerks

514. Semiconductor Processors

515. Cartographers and Photogrammetrists

516. Metal-Refining Furnace Operators and Tenders

517. Separating, Filtering, Clarifying, Precipitating, and Still Machine Setters, Operators, and Tenders

518. Extruding and Forming Machine Setters, Operators, and Tenders, Synthetic and Glass Fibers

519. Terrazzo Workers and Finishers

520. Tool Grinders, Filers, and Sharpeners

521. Rail Car Repairers

522. Bakers

523. Medical Transcriptionists

524. Stonemasons

525. Bus Drivers, School or Special Client

526. Technical Writers

527. Riggers

528. Rail-Track Laying and Maintenance Equipment Operators

529. Stationary Engineers and Boiler Operators

530. Sewing Machine Operators

531. Taxi Drivers and Chauffeurs

532. Human Resources Assistants, Except Payroll and Timekeeping

533. Medical and Clinical Laboratory Technologists

534. Reinforcing Iron and Rebar Workers

535. Roofers

536. Crane and Tower Operators

537. Traffic Technicians

538. Transportation Inspectors

539. Patternmakers, Metal and Plastic

540. Molders, Shapers, and Casters, Except Metal and Plastic

541. Appraisers and Assessors of Real Estate

542. Pump Operators, Except Wellhead Pumpers

543. Signal and Track Switch Repairers

544. Gaming and Sports Book Writers and Runners

545. Musical Instrument Repairers and Tuners

546. Tour Guides and Escorts

547. Mechanical Door Repairers

548. Food and Tobacco Roasting, Baking, and Drying Machine Operators and Tenders

549. Gas Compressor and Gas Pumping Station Operators

550. Medical Records and Health Information Technicians

551. Coating, Painting, and Spraying Machine Setters, Operators, and Tenders

552. Multiple Machine Tool Setters, Operators, and Tenders, Metal and Plastic

553. Rail Yard Engineers, Dinkey Operators, and Hostlers

554. Electrical and Electronics Installers and Repairers, Transportation Equipment

555. Dining Room and Cafeteria Attendants and Bartender Helpers

556. Heat Treating Equipment Setters, Operators, and Tenders, Metal and Plastic

557. Geological and Petroleum Technicians

558. Automotive Body and Related Repairers

559. Patternmakers, Wood

560. Extruding and Drawing Machine Setters, Operators, and Tenders, Metal and Plastic

561. Office Machine Operators, Except Computer

562. Pharmacy Technicians

563. Loan Interviewers and Clerks

564. Dredge Operators

565. Insurance Sales Agents

566. Cabinetmakers and Bench Carpenters

567. Painting, Coating, and Decorating Workers

568. Fence Erectors

569. Plating and Coating Machine Setters, Operators, and Tenders, Metal and Plastic

570. Retail Salespersons

571. Combined Food Preparation and Serving Workers, Including Fast Food

572. Production Workers, All Other

573. Helpers–Carpenters

574. Cooling and Freezing Equipment Operators and Tenders

575. Fiberglass Laminators and Fabricators

576. Service Unit Operators, Oil, Gas, and Mining

577. Conveyor Operators and Tenders

578. Outdoor Power Equipment and Other Small Engine Mechanics

579. Locomotive Firers

580. Machine Feeders and Offbearers

581. Model Makers, Metal and Plastic

582. Radio, Cellular, and Tower Equipment Installers and Repairs

583. Butchers and Meat Cutters

584. Extruding, Forming, Pressing, and Compacting Machine Setters, Operators, and Tenders

585. Refuse and Recyclable Material Collectors

586. Tax Examiners and Collectors, and Revenue Agents

587. Forging Machine Setters, Operators, and Tenders, Metal and Plastic

588. Industrial Truck and Tractor Operators

589. Accountants and Auditors

590. Drilling and Boring Machine Tool Setters, Operators, and Tenders, Metal and Plastic

591. Mail Clerks and Mail Machine Operators, Except Postal Service

592. Waiters and Waitresses

593. Meat, Poultry, and Fish Cutters and Trimmers

594. Budget Analysts

595. Cement Masons and Concrete Finishers

596. Bicycle Repairers

597. Coin, Vending, and Amusement Machine Servicers and Repairers

598. Welders, Cutters, Solderers, and Brazers

599. Couriers and Messengers

600. Interviewers, Except Eligibility and Loan

601. Cooks, Short Order

602. Excavating and Loading Machine and Dragline Operators

603. Helpers–Painters, Paperhangers, Plasterers, and Stucco Masons

604. Hotel, Motel, and Resort Desk Clerks

605. Tire Builders

606. Door-to-Door Sales Workers, News and Street Vendors, and Related Workers

607. First-Line Supervisors of Housekeeping and Janitorial Workers

608. Agricultural Inspectors

609. Paralegals and Legal Assistants

610. Manicurists and Pedicurists

611. Weighers, Measurers, Checkers, and Samplers, Recordkeeping

612. Textile Cutting Machine Setters, Operators, and Tenders

613. Bill and Account Collectors

614. Nuclear Power Reactor Operators

615. Gaming Surveillance Officers and Gaming Investigators

616. Library Assistants, Clerical

617. Operating Engineers and Other Construction Equipment Operators

618. Print Binding and Finishing Workers

619. Animal Breeders

620. Molding, Coremaking, and Casting Machine Setters, Operators, and Tenders, Metal and Plastic

621. Electrical and Electronic Equipment Assemblers

622. Adhesive Bonding Machine Operators and Tenders

623. Landscaping and Groundskeeping Workers

624. Grinding, Lapping, Polishing, and Buffing Machine Tool Setters, Operators, and Tenders, Metal and Plastic

625. Postal Service Clerks

626. Jewelers and Precious Stone and Metal Workers

627. Dispatchers, Except Police, Fire, and Ambulance

628. Receptionists and Information Clerks

629. Office Clerks, General

630. Compensation and Benefits Managers

631. Switchboard Operators, Including Answering Service

632. Counter Attendants, Cafeteria, Food Concession, and Coffee Shop

633. Rock Splitters, Quarry

634. Secretaries and Administrative Assistants, Except Legal, Medical, and Executive

635. Surveying and Mapping Technicians

636. Model Makers, Wood

637. Textile Winding, Twisting, and Drawing Out Machine Setters, Operators, and Tenders

638. Locomotive Engineers

639. Gaming Dealers

640. Fabric Menders, Except Garment

641. Cooks, Restaurant

642. Ushers, Lobby Attendants, and Ticket Takers

643. Billing and Posting Clerks

644. Bridge and Lock Tenders

645. Woodworking Machine Setters, Operators, and Tenders, Except Sawing

646. Team Assemblers

647. Shoe Machine Operators and Tenders

648. Electromechanical Equipment Assemblers

649. Farm Labor Contractors

650. Textile Bleaching and Dyeing Machine Operators and Tenders

651. Dental Laboratory Technicians

652. Crushing, Grinding, and Polishing Machine Setters, Operators, and Tenders

653. Grinding and Polishing Workers, Hand

654. Pesticide Handlers, Sprayers, and Applicators, Vegetation

655. Log Graders and Scalers

656. Ophthalmic Laboratory Technicians

657. Cashiers

658. Camera and Photographic Equipment Repairers

659. Motion Picture Projectionists

660. Prepress Technicians and Workers

661. Counter and Rental Clerks

662. File Clerks

663. Real Estate Brokers

664. Telephone Operators

665. Agricultural and Food Science Technicians

666. Payroll and Timekeeping Clerks

667. Credit Authorizers, Checkers, and Clerks

668. Hosts and Hostesses, Restaurant, Lounge, and Coffee Shop

669. Models

670. Inspectors, Testers, Sorters, Samplers, and Weighers

671. Bookkeeping, Accounting, and Auditing Clerks

672. Legal Secretaries

673. Radio Operators

674. Driver/Sales Workers

675. Claims Adjusters, Examiners, and Investigators

676. Parts Salespersons

677. Credit Analysts

678. Milling and Planing Machine Setters, Operators, and Tenders, Metal and Plastic

679. Shipping, Receiving, and Traffic Clerks

680. Procurement Clerks

681. Packaging and Filling Machine Operators and Tenders

682. Etchers and Engravers

683. Tellers

684. Umpires, Referees, and Other Sports Officials

685. Insurance Appraisers, Auto Damage

686. Loan Officers

687. Order Clerks

688. Brokerage Clerks

689. Insurance Claims and Policy Processing Clerks

690. Timing Device Assemblers and Adjusters

691. Data Entry Keyers

692. Library Technicians

693. New Accounts Clerks

694. Photographic Process Workers and Processing Machine Operators

695. Tax Preparers

696. Cargo and Freight Agents

697. Watch Repairers

698. Insurance Underwriters

699. Mathematical Technicians

700. Sewers, Hand

701. Title Examiners, Abstractors, and Searchers

702. Telemarketers

1. Torres, Craig. "Fault Lines Exposed in Fed Survey Showing Wide Prosperity Divide." *Bloomberg News*, May 19, 2017.

2. Woolley, Suzanne. "Who Says You Need Tax Breaks for Retirement Savings?" Bloomberg.com. May 11, 2017. Accessed February 01, 2019. https://www.bloomberg.com/news/articles/2017-05-11/tax-breaks-aren-t-the-only-way-to-get-people-to-save.

3. "Digest of Education Statistics, 2017." National Center for Education Statistics (NCES) Home Page, a Part of the U.S. Department of Education. January 2018. Accessed February 02, 2019. https://nces.ed.gov/programs/digest/d17/. Table 322.10

4. Grant, Kelli B. "Employers Are Hiring Grads with These In-Demand Majors." CNBC. April 27, 2017. Accessed February 02, 2019. https://www.cnbc.com/2017/04/27/employers-want-to-hire-grads-with-these-in-demand-majors.html.

5. Moody, Kathryn, and Valerie Bolden-Barrett. "Why Blue-Collar Industries Are Facing Such a Massive Skills Shortage." HR Dive. April 11, 2017. Accessed February 02, 2019. https://www.hrdive.com/news/why-blue-collar-industries-are-facing-such-a-massive-skills-shortage/439756/.

6. Wright, Joshua. "America's Skilled Trades Dilemma: Shortages Loom As Most-In-Demand Group Of Workers Ages." *Forbes*. March 23, 2013. Accessed February 02, 2019. https://www.forbes.com/sites/emsi/2013/03/07/americas-skilled-trades-dilemma-shortages-loom-as-most-in-demand-group-of-workers-ages/#3decb2de6397.

7. U.S. Bureau of Labor Statistics. "Unemployment Rates and Earnings by Educational Attainment, 2017." March 27, 2018. Accessed February 17, 2019. https://www.bls.gov/emp/chart-unemployment-earnings-education.htm.

8. Kaplan, Rob. "America Has to Close the Workforce Skills Gap: Rob Kaplan." Bloomberg.com. April 12, 2017. Accessed February 02, 2019. https://www.bloomberg.com/opinion/articles/2017-04-12/america-has-to-close-the-workforce-skills-gap.

9. Hymowitz, Carol. "Millions of Manufacturing Jobs Could Go Unfilled." Bloomberg.com. March 16, 2017. Accessed February 02, 2019. https://www.bloomberg.com/news/articles/2017-03-16/millions-of-manufacturing-jobs-could-go-unfilled.

10. "Farm Population Lowest Since 1850's." *The New York Times.* July 20, 1988. Accessed February 02, 2019. https://www.nytimes.com/1988/07/20/us/farm-population-lowest-since-1850-s.html.

11. Spielmaker, Debra. "Historical Timeline: Farmers & the Land." National Agriculture in the Classroom. Accessed February 02, 2019. https://www.agclassroom.org/gan/timeline/farmers_land.htm.

12. Martin, Jim. "Fewer Farmers in US, Erie Region Grow More Food than Ever." GoErie.com. April 06, 2017. Accessed February 02, 2019. https://www.goerie.com/news/20170409/fewer-farmers-in-us-erie-region-grow-more-food-than-ever.

13. Scully, Matt. "Trump's America Is Facing a $13 Trillion Consumer Debt Hangover." Bloomberg.com. June 06, 2017. Accessed February 02, 2019. https://www.bloomberg.com/news/articles/2017-06-06/trump-s-america-is-facing-a-13-trillion-consumer-debt-hangover.

14. "The Bad News--and Some Good News--About Depreciation" *Edmunds.* September 24, 2010. Accessed February 6, 2019. https://www.edmunds.com/car-buying/how-fast-does-my-new-car-lose-value-infographic.html

15. Kusisto, Laura. "Millennials Want to Buy Homes but Aren't Saving for Down Payments." *The Wall Street Journal.* May 25, 2017. Accessed February 03, 2019. https://www.wsj.com/articles/millennials-want-to-buy-homes-but-arent-saving-for-down-payments-1495731583.

16. Golle, Vince. "In Debt We Trust for U.S. Consumers With $12.7 Trillion Burden." Bloomberg.com. August 10, 2017. Accessed February 03, 2019. https://www.bloomberg.com/news/articles/2017-08-10/in-debt-we-trust-for-u-s-consumers-with-12-7-trillion-burden.

17. Reproduced with permission from Federal Reserve Bank of New York, "Press Briefing on Household Debt, with Focus on Student Debt," April 2017. Available at https://www.newyorkfed.org/medialibrary/media/press/pressbriefing-household-student-debt-april32017.pdf.

18. Jackson, Abby. "This Chart Shows How Quickly College Tuition Has Skyrocketed since 1980." *Business Insider.* July 20, 2015. Accessed February 03, 2019. https://www.businessinsider.com/this-chart-shows-how-quickly-college-tuition-has-skyrocketed-since-1980-2015-7.

19. Tergesen, Anne. "Why Retirees Cut Back on Spending: A Growing Pessimism, It Seems." *The Wall Street Journal.* May 16, 2017. Accessed February 07, 2019. https://www.wsj.com/articles/why-retirees-cut-back-on-spending-a-growing-pessimism-it-seems-1494900001.

20. Yadoo, Jordan. "Americans Are Cutting a Shorter and Cheaper Path to Decent Pay." Bloomberg.com. July 26, 2017. Accessed February 07, 2019. https://www.bloomberg.com/news/articles/2017-07-26/americans-are-cutting-a-shorter-and-cheaper-path-to-decent-pay.

21. Anderson, Tom. "Public Colleges Will Be an Even Better Deal in 2025." CNBC. July 06, 2015. Accessed February 10, 2019. https://www.cnbc.com/2015/07/03/do-public-colleges-offer-the-best-return-on-investment.html.

22. Petrie, Shannon. "Annual Expenses of Homeownership." HGTV. September 17, 2018. Accessed February 11, 2019. https://www.hgtv.com/design/real-estate/annual-expenses-of-homeownership.

23. J.P. Morgan Asset Management, "Guide to the Markets U.S. Q1." As of December 31, 2018. Slide 64. Available at https://am.jpmorgan.com/blob-gim/1383407651970/83456/MI-GTM_1Q19_Linked.pdf

24. Anderson, Tom. "Active Fund Managers Rarely Beat Their Benchmarks Year after Year." CNBC. February 27, 2017. Accessed February 13, 2019. https://www.cnbc.com/2017/02/27/active-fund-managers-rarely-beat-their-benchmarks-year-after-year.html.

25. Hulbert, Mark. "This Is How Many Fund Managers Actually Beat Index Funds." MarketWatch. May 13, 2017. Accessed February 13, 2019. https://www.marketwatch.com/story/why-way-fewer-actively-managed-funds-beat-the-sp-than-we-thought-2017-04-24.

26. French, Kenneth R. "The Cost of Active Investing." April 9, 2008. Accessed February 12, 2019. https://papers.ssrn.com/sol3/papers.cfm?abstract_id=1105775.

27. ICI Research Perspective, "Trends in the Expenses and Fees of Funds, 2016." May 2017. Volume 23, No. 3. Available at https://www.ici.org/pdf/per23-03.pdf

28. Reproduced with permission from Trading Economics, "US GDP Growth Rate," December 2017. Available at https https://tradingeconomics.com/united-states/gdp-growth

29. "Board of Governors of the Federal Reserve System." State and Local Government Pension Funding Ratios, 2002 - 2016. October 4, 2018. Accessed February 17, 2019. https://www. federalreserve.gov/releases/z1/dataviz/pension/funding_ratio/ table/

30. Copyright © 2019 The Pew Charitable Trusts. All Rights Reserved. Reproduced with permission. Any use without the express written consent of The Pew Charitable Trusts is prohibited.

31. "Fertility Rate, Total (births per Woman)." The World Bank. Accessed February 17, 2019. https://data.worldbank.org/ indicator/SP.DYN.TFRT.IN?locations=US.

32. US Census Bureau. "2017 National Population Projections Tables." September 06, 2018. Accessed February 17, 2019. https://www.census.gov/data/tables/2017/demo/ popproj/2017-summary-tables.html.

33. Osterland, Andrew. "Elders and Equities: How Much Stock Should Retirees Own?" CNBC. August 10, 2016. Accessed February 18, 2019. https://www.cnbc.com/2016/08/10/elders- and-equities-how-much-stock-should-retirees-own.html.

34. Frankel, Matthew. "9 Baby-Boomer Statistics That Will Blow You Away." The Motley Fool. July 29, 2017. Accessed February 18, 2019. https://www.fool.com/retirement/2017/07/29/9- baby-boomer-statistics-that-will-blow-you-away.aspx.

35. Krause, Reinhardt. "Here's One More Thing Amazon May Be Killing." Investor's Business Daily. May 15, 2017. Accessed February 18, 2019. https://www.investors.com/news/ technology/why-yellen-co-should-pay-attention-to-amazon- com/.

About the Author

Corey developed a passion for finance and investing when he first learned how banks and savings accounts work. The idea of parking money at the bank while it "magically" grew was astonishing to Corey. Around the time that he achieved becoming an Eagle Scout in his late teens, he opened his first IRA, or Individual Retirement Account. He also went on to earn a bachelor of science from the University of Maine with a concentration in Finance and a member of the University's SPIFFY student investment club.

Now having over a dozen years in the financial services industry, Corey currently works at one of the best capitalized banks in New Hampshire, Piscataqua Savings Bank. Corey is a Portfolio Manager in the trust and investment department, where he has co-managed the investments since 2014, currently over 300 million dollars. Corey creates investment solutions for trust funds, retirement accounts, charitable endowments, and managed client investment accounts. Prior to this, Corey worked for Fidelity Investments for about 7 years in various roles supporting the investment process.

In addition to all that, he received the chartered financial analyst, or CFA, designation. The CFA is considered a graduate level of difficulty that is designed specifically for asset management. Corey is occasionally a guest speaker to local high schools where he talks about investing and the financial services industry. He currently lives in Portsmouth, New Hampshire.